SOCRATIC EDUCATION IN PLATO'S EARLY DIALOGUES

Socratic Education
in Plato's Early Dialogues

HENRY TELOH

WITHDRAWN

University of Notre Dame Press
Notre Dame, Indiana 46556

Library of Congress Cataloging in Publication Data

Teloh, Henry, 1944-
    Socratic education in Plato's early dialogues.

    Bibliography: p.
    Includes index.
    1. Plato. Dialogues.   2. Socrates.   3. Education,
Greek—Philosophy.   4. Questioning.   I. Title.
LB85.P7T45   1986   370'.1   86-40245
ISBN 0-268-01724-7

Manufactured in the United States of America

Contents

Preface

I want to address two audiences with these essays: those who at any level read or teach Plato's early dialogues, and scholars in diverse fields who are interested in the more specialized topic of Socratic education. Because of these audiences I keep technical language to a minimum, and I transliterate all Greek words. I intend for these essays to be general introductions to the early dialogues, although I cannot discuss all possible topics without a loss of focus. My theme is what the dramatic character Socrates tries to accomplish educationally by his different verbal maneuvers. Hence I am less interested in the logical soundness of his arguments than in their intended effects on his hearers. To develop my theme I focus on the characters of the interlocutors and the dramatic features of the dialogues.

My Socrates is not all that much like a modern philosopher. But then one purpose for studying the history of anything is to see alternatives to present practices, especially when those practices seem so inevitable and correct. The amount of recent secondary literature on the early dialogues is immense, and my bibliography reflects only a small portion of this literature. My reason for this is that I learned over time that an emphasis on secondary sources tends to dull the joy of discovering one's own questions and answers about the dialogues, even if they are not original.

The chapters on the *Gorgias* and *Euthyphro* were read in earlier versions before the Society for Ancient Greek Philosophy. I read a summary of my major theme at the Boston Area Colloquium for Ancient Philosophy. I thank these audiences for their help. I also want to thank my colleagues and seminar participants at Vanderbilt University, especially Alasdair MacIntyre and William Race, for their help. And I am also grateful to Chris Bastian for typing the manuscript.

1. Introduction

The purpose of this study is to give an interpretation of Socratic education in Plato's early dialogues. There are a number of interrelated theses
I will argue for in this work; among them are: (1) Socrates invariably
fits his *logoi* (words, statements, or arguments) to the conditions of
the *psychai* (souls) of the persons with whom he talks, (2) Socratic dialectic frequently is *ad hominem* in the way in which it tests the beliefs
of an interlocutor, (3) One must look at the specific character of each
interlocutor both to appreciate what each says and to understand how
Socrates attempts to educate them, and (4) Socratic dialectic (question and answer) has two major aspects: *elenchus* (refutation) and
psychagogia (*psychē*-leading); how Socrates uses these aspects depends
upon the specific character — psychic condition — of a particular interlocutor. The principle that different conditions of *psychai* educationally require different types of *logoi* I will call the "*Phaedrus* principle," in order that we may have a name to refer to this concept. Plato
states such a principle in the late dialogue *Phaedrus* (270b-d), but
Socrates, I will show, employs this principle in the early dialogues.

This study opposes the following claims: (A) Socratic dialectic
should be judged primarily by the excellence of its logic.[1] Some commentators believe that what is most important about the dialogues
is whether or not Socrates' arguments are sound. In contrast I will show
that we must also attend to what Socrates attempts to achieve by his
arguments, e.g. confusion, shame, and/or *aporia* (perplexity). Sound
arguments do not always achieve these effects, and hence they do not
always benefit the *psychē*. For example Socrates sometimes uses arguments with premises he rejects in order to produce *aporia*. An interlocutor, however, must agree to these premises. In the *Laches*, as I
will show, he uses the premise that courage is a part of virtue to reject
the apparent result of the dialogue that courage is the knowledge of
good and evil. This rejection stimulates us to rethink the argument,
and when we do this we see that Socrates provides no reason to believe

1

that virtue has parts. (B) Socrates searches for "universally valid truth";[2] he seeks for a truth which is independent of beliefs, conceptual schemes and historicity. The notion of "universally valid truth" is anachronistic. Socrates has no such technical notion. Moreover, such a claim is misleading. Much of what Socrates does is *ad hominem*; that is, he investigates the belief structure of an interlocutor. When Socrates does this, the arguments start from premises assented to by an interlocutor, and hence we cannot attribute these arguments to Socrates. When Socrates states that he is justified in claiming to know something, he admits that his claim is open to revision.[3] Truth is the aim, but justified belief—belief which satisfies a dialectic test—is the means, and our grasp of truth is dependent upon our best dialectical effort at any time. (C) Socratic dialectic is negative;[4] Socrates refutes the positions of others, but he neither offers nor suggests alternatives because he does not hold positions. I will show that Socratic dialectic is not entirely negative. Indeed, much of what Socrates does is *psychagogia*. Socrates usually does not state positions;[5] rather he draws the *psychē* to them by innuendo, suggestion, and paradox. Socrates can draw the *psychē* indirectly to beliefs because he, himself, has beliefs which have survived previous dialectical testing. Socrates usually does not state positions because he does not believe that one should teach by telling. But how Socrates refutes a position often insinuates to the reader, as it should to the interlocutor, what the Socratic position on an issue is. Socrates usually does not state his view because he does not want to become the new authority; he does not want to produce people like Nicias in the *Laches*, people who repeat without understanding what he says.

This essay has an introduction, and a chapter on each of the major, early dialogues.[6] I hope in this essay to engage both the expert and the generally informed reader. On the one hand these essays are introductions to each of the early dialogues, on the other they all focus on a particular topic—education—which is both of general interest and of special interest to scholars. In this introduction I will outline my major claims and discuss certain subsidiary matters pertaining to interpretation and organization.

Why do I limit my discussion of Socratic education to the early dialogues? What unifies these dialogues, and makes them distinct from the rest of the Platonic corpus? Some scholars believe in a chronological unity for the so-called early dialogues—they were all written before the midddle and late ones—based upon stylistic considerations sup-

plemented by theories about the unity or development of Plato's views.[7]
I believe that the early dialogues were indeed written before the rest,
but the evidence for this is far from conclusive. Since Plato is a great
stylist it is even possible that he wrote the "early" dialogues at any
time in his life, and consciously used the same style in all of them.
We cannot, then, safely use stylistic features to group dialogues chron-
ologically into periods. But what does hold together these dialogues
is a picture of Socrates the educator. In these dialogues Socrates employs
the "*Phaedrus* principle" while in the others he does not, or does so
to a very limited extent. Socratic education is person centered, it focuses
on the characters and beliefs of an interlocutor; in the middle and late
dialogues the center of gravity is the *logos*. Both Socrates and the interlocutors follow in these later dialogues an account which is to a great
extent independent of the interlocutors. There is, then, a *metabasis
eis allo genus* between the foci of the early and that of the middle
and late dialogues.

The introduction of music and gymnastics in the *Republic*, to
some extent, explains this change. The interlocutors in the early dialogues do not have the benefit of such an education. They are, as
a result, spoiled in some way or another, or else they are mere youths
with great potential, which potential can be actualized for either good
or evil. But in the middle and late dialogues the interlocutors are more
amenable to Socrates; they are either philosophers or those who are
sympathetic to philosophy. Most important of all, in the middle and
late dialogues—except for the *Theaetetus*—Plato teaches by stating
his views. He rejects the Socratic strictures against teaching by telling,
and now has a need to state his positions. We see these statements
at great length in dialogues like the *Phaedo* and *Timaeus*.

Among the early dialogues the *Apology, Crito, Euthyphro,
Laches, Charmides, Lysis,* and *Republic* I appear to be earlier than the
Meno, Gorgias, Hippias Major, Euthydemus, and *Protagoras*. The latter
employ both more sophisticated argumentation, and concepts not
found in the former dialogues. For example the *Meno* introduces recollection, the *Gorgias* the *psyche* as a *cosmos*, and the *Euthydemus*
an interest in Eleatic techniques of argument. We also see in these
"later" dialogues more sophisticated educational techniques. In the
Gorgias Socrates uses a vast repertoire of methods, including threatening
speeches, and he even diagnoses his own inability to educate Callicles;
it is due to Callicles' love of demos. But we do not have strong evidence

about which early dialogues are more mature than others. For Socrates may not need to introduce some notion into a particular dialogue; the *Euthyphro*, for example, does not require a doctrine of recollection. No thesis in this essay depends upon an order for the early dialogues, or on whether the early dialogues form a chronological unity.

It is not my purpose to add to debate on the question about whether or to what extent the early dialogues are an accurate portrait of Socrates. I agree with Gregory Vlastos that they depict Socrates, and that they need not be accurate in many details.[8] In this essay "Socrates" refers to the dramatic figure of the dialogues, and "Plato" to their author. My main interest is in what Socrates educationally does with his interlocutors, but at times I will speculate about what Plato intends to convey to the reader by how he depicts Socrates. My evidence, for both sorts of tasks, is the texts, and my claims about Plato's intent are more speculative because we cannot identify totally his intent with that of the dramatic character Socrates. Socrates we can argue about from the texts, but Plato's intent depends upon not only the texts but also his background beliefs which we must speculate about from the texts. What does Plato intend, for example, when he shows us a Socrates who fails to educate interlocutors? Why does Plato depict Socrates as he does?

I approach each dialogue as a dramatic and philosophical whole, and I devote a single chapter to each dialogue. But this sort of exposition is more repetitive than one divided by topics; moreover, to discuss a whole dialogue requires some exposition of its general positions. Thus my method of procedure needs justification. The early dialogues should be treated as dramatic and philosophical wholes. First, the behaviors and statements of the interlocutors display to us their characters. Their characters, in turn, give us an enriched understanding of their beliefs. These characters, moreover, influence how Socrates employs dialectic with them, and, as I will show, even how the dialogues end. By the "*Phaedrus* principle" the type of refutation Socrates employs, as well as the type of *aporia* he engenders, depends upon the types of *psychai* he faces. Second, we only understand a dialogue when we see it as a whole. Take the *Laches* as an example. The first half of the dialogue displays to us the generals' purported strengths; Laches is a man of deeds who subordinates *logoi*, and Nicias is the opposite. The second half of the dialogue shows us how each general fails in respect of his apparent strength. Laches will not endure in the discussion, and Nicias does not understand the *logoi* he appropriates from others. The defects of the generals, in turn, suggest to us what a true man of words and deeds is like. But this insight derives from seeing the dialogue as a whole. Since the early dialogues are dramatic and philosophical wholes, they should be discussed as wholes, and key moves in these dialogues are open to misunderstanding when abstracted from the whole dialogue context.

I do not, then, isolate topics apart from my discussions of each dialogue. But in some dialogues I will emphasize a topic; for example, I focus on irony in the *Euthyphro*, and the background to Socratic education in the *Apology*. The reader should consult the index to locate these more extensive discussions. Also at the end of this introduction I will describe the two phases of Socratic dialectic, *elenchus* and *psychagogia* to avoid repetition in my discussion of each dialogue.

Why does Plato present Socrates through dialogue, and not a treatise? There are a number of answers to this question, but I will focus on two which are related to Socrates' educational mission. First dialogue, unlike treatise, not only allows us to see the "*Phaedrus* principle" in action, but itself imitates different conversations with the *psychai* of different interlocutors in a way that is impossible for a treatise. Second most Socratic dialogues end in *aporia*, and hence they should affect the reader in the same way that Socrates hopes to affect his interlocutors. A Socratic dialogue should stimulate the reader to desire to break the *aporia*, and solve the problem; it should make the readers want to engage in dialectic.

Background Assumptions

I will now turn to my positions about some key notions in the early dialogues, positions defended in detail in chapter 1 of my *The Development of Plato's Metaphysics*.[9] I want to emphasize that a reader who disagrees with the following views need not reject entirely my claims about Socratic education, which are largely independent of them.

The *psychē* in the early dialogues is both an agent's source of motion, and a web of beliefs. Soul brings life, and outside the probably spurious *Alcibiades* I where "Socrates" views the body as a tool of the *psychē*, there is little evidence that Socrates sees the *psychē* as a substance which is distinct from the living body. Socrates' view is akin to Aristotle's where the *psychē* actualizes the body, vivifies it, and yet may somehow after death survive the body. In the *Charmides* (156b-157a) Socrates says that all good and evil springs from the *psychē*, and in the same dialogue the psychic powers are said to do things as agents do them (167c-e). Sight sees things, love loves its objects, and the like. But Socrates also views the *psychē* as a web of beliefs.[10] For Socrates there is an isomorphic relationship between beliefs and motives for action. The stronger the belief, the greater the motive force for action, and every motive force has a correlative belief. To know oneself is to observe the condition of one's *psychē* which means both to test one's beliefs to see if they are justified or not, and *a fortiori* to see how one's desires—motive forces for action—are arranged. *Logoi* emerge from the *psychē*, and they are the means by which one can test the condition of a *psychē*. What one honestly says and does is a manifestation of the order and arrangement of desires in a *psychē*. Hence we should look both at how interlocutors act and at what they say. We learn, for example, what Thrasymachus is like—a wild beast— from his behavior, and from what he says.

Socrates treats virtues just like the *psychē* because the virtues are motive forces of the *psychē*.[11] Socratic dialectic, then, tests both an interlocutor's intellectual condition, and his virtue. A Socratic test involves, as Nicias realizes (*Laches* 187e-188a), "giving an account of one's life and one's ways." If one cannot state, clarify, and defend an account of an excellence, then this is both an intellectual and a moral failure just because one acts on one's beliefs.

Socrates holds the psychological assumption that all persons seek what they take to be their own well-being. The gap between what is our own well-being and what we take to be so is the gap between the knowledge of good and evil and our false beliefs about what is good. Since one will act on one's conception of what is good for oneself, one will also act on the knowledge of good and evil. Hence this is the sort of wisdom which is the source of human well-being. Each virtue, I believe, is this wisdom, and thus the virtues are identical.[12] The behavioral and contextual criteria for distinguishing one virtue from another only are accidental features of them.[13] Courage is the knowledge of good and evil exhibited in such and such contexts, and temperance is the same knowledge exhibited in other contexts, but each virtue is the psychic motive force—the knowledge of good and evil. This knowledge is a condition of the *psychē* which also manifests itself as an ability to state, clarify, and defend one's beliefs. Hence a virtue is manifest both in words and in deeds. Socrates, in all the early dialogues, and especially in the *Crito*, shows a harmony between his words and his deeds. In the *Crito* he not only argues that he would stay in prison and drink the hemlock, but he does it; he acts as his conception of the good says that he should.

Socratic Education: Outline of the Argument

First I will outline the defects Socrates sees in the education of his time. Then I will discuss the major educational themes of the early dialogues. Finally I will show why Socrates is both an educational failure, and an educational hero.

Socrates rejects three educational authorities: poets, sophists, and typical Athenian gentlemen. Each of these purported educators inculcates behavior and transmits (cf. *Meno* 93b) *logoi* to the passive pupil. Poetic material is sung, memorized, remembered, and recited by the learners. Sophists display their wisdom most frequently through speeches which the passive young men learn.[14] The learner is not invited to analyze the sung poem, or to dissect the numerous claims in a heard speech. Moreover, poets like Homer, Hesiod, and Simonides, and later on some sophists, represent the collective wisdom, and they disseminate this wisdom in an authoritarian manner. Also the good and noble gentlemen, as Anytus and Protagoras would have it, educate other citizens into the tongue and values of the city state. Such gentlemen are models, and the young men imitate their behavior. Such imitation starts early in life, and is for the most part unconscious; it does not foster critical intelligence. Hence all three sources act as authorities who produce passive recipients. Socrates, in contrast, does not state views because he does not want to be one more new authority who stifles dialectic; thus he ends his discussions in *aporia*. Moreover, Socrates by his behavior and words attempts to develop a respect for dialectic.

Socrates' attacks on poetic education take a number of forms. In the *Lysis* (214a-215e) he rejects the inconsistent poetic views about friendship. Since Homer and Hesiod hold contrary views they cannot both be authorities; nor do we know how to settle a dispute, within the poetic educational model, when the poets disagree. In the *Apology*

(22b-c) and *Republic* I (332bff.) Socrates states his position about poets: they are inspired but do not know what they, themselves, say. Poetic inspiration must be interpreted by dialectical scrutiny.

The early dialogues give us an extensive picture of Socrates' charges against the sophists. The brothers of the *Euthydemus* last year taught fighting in armor; but this year they teach *aretē* (excellence) because it pays better. These brothers are not serious; they really are not concerned for the *psychē* of the young Cleinias, or for their own *psychai*. The theme of the *Euthydemus* is who is and who is not a serious person. Socrates emphasizes in the *Apology* (19e-20c) that sophists take fees for their teaching. This is not as trivial a complaint as it may appear. To do something primarily for a fee is to mislocate the purpose of an art. An art is for the sake of its subject matter (*Rep.* I 341c-d, *Gorgias* 464c-465a), and education, which is an art, is for the sake of a person's *psychē*.[15] Sophists, who teach primarily for a fee, are not serious about their task; they do not care for the *psychai* of their students.

Gorgias and Polus are enamoured of rhetoric as a mere technology. A mere technology is a repertoire of techniques to accomplish some end without any consideration of the value of that end. Gorgias praises the power of rhetoricians to persuade even when the relevant experts cannot. Gorgias, the rhetoric teacher, says that if the learners of rhetoric misuse this powerful tool, then the teachers should not be blamed for such misuse (*Gorgias* 456d-457e). Gorgias shows a lack of concern not only for individual *psychai*, but also for the whole city. Socrates eventually shames Gorgias into the admission that if one of his students does not know what *aretē* is then he, Gorgias, will teach that to him. This admission is ironical in that Gorgias does not think that *aretē* can be taught (cf. *Meno* 95c). The noble and beautiful Hippias in the *Hippias Major* is going to address young men about what pursuits are noble and good. But Hippias cannot give an account of the noble, which is a defect he shares with other sophists. Hippias, moreover, is a polymath. He remembers a lot about a lot, and most of it is trivia. For Socrates broad knowledge, like that of Hippias, is shallow knowledge. Finally Meno and Socrates in the *Meno* (95b) agree that neither sophists nor Athenian gentlemen transmit *aretē*, and hence *aretē* is not a sort of knowledge. These admissions are ironical especially since Meno claims to be a student of Gorgias. But the sophists cannot transmit what they mistakenly think is *aretē* because it is an appearance in which luck plays a large role, and they cannot transmit real *aretē* because it is the sort of knowledge which cannot be transmitted.

Furthermore, neither Pericles nor the other Athenian gentlemen can make their sons virtuous, although they desire to do so. They cannot transmit virtue by example since being at the right place, at the right time, and with the right speech cannot be transmitted. The grandfathers in the *Laches*, though men of distinction, have sons who are not even up to the standards of demotic virtue. Frequently in the early dialogues we see Socrates press the point that important fathers have bad sons, but this also shows that the fathers are not as good as one might think.

These three educational authorities fail to educate properly the youth, and they fail to meet the needs of their time. The strains of the Peloponnesian War caused a breakdown in the shared values of the *polis* (city state). The old poetic education does not hold the minds of men, and the new sophistic one preaches a false *aretē*. Socrates suggests the dialectic of question and answer as the rational alternative; we ought to accept as true whatever survives a proper dialectical test.

The number and order of interlocutors in a dialogue are of educational importance. The *Gorgias* and *Republic* I are the only dialogues where Socrates speaks with three interlocutors one after the other. The sequences Gorgias, Polus, Callicles, and Cephalus, Polemarchus, Thrasymachus are not, I maintain, accidental. Each interlocutor sets the educational and intellectual conditions for his successors. Gorgias, for example, the teacher of a mere technology of rhetoric, sets the educational agenda for Polus who writes a text book on rhetorical technique, and Gorgias' praise for the power of rhetoric becomes in Polus a praise for tyrants. In turn Polus spawns Callicles who uses rhetoric to behave as a tyrant. The order of interlocutors, I will argue, shows us much about how Socrates sees the causes and effects of certain social and educational phenomena, including different types of characters.

The *Charmides, Lysis,* and *Euthydemus* have as their foci some young men who are full of potential, and very much in need of education. These dialogues display Socrates as only one of the influences on these young men; there are others, and they sometimes win in the contest for the *psychai* of these young men. All of these dialogues show Socrates in such a contest. In the *Charmides* Socrates must compete with Critias; in the *Lysis* with Ctesippus, Hippothales, and even Menexenus; and in the *Euthydemus* with Euthydemus, Dionysodorus, Ctesippus, and an unnamed writer of rhetorical speeches. These interlocutors represent forces which persuade the young men to one type of life or another, and these dialogues show Socrates in agonistic competition for the *psychai* of the young. All three of these dialogues leave us in suspense in the end about who wins, although history may unravel the mystery. Charmides wants to be charmed by Socrates every day for the rest of his life, but at the very end (*Charmides* 176c-d) he joins Critias in threatening force, and later they both became members of the Thirty Tyrants. Lysis is most friendly to Socrates, but Lysis' *paidagogoi* fetch him home at the end which symbolizes the victory of the family influence over that of Socrates.

The *Laches* has a different and no less interesting educational structure. The generals, Laches and Nicias, cannot both be authorities on how to educate young men because they disagree with one another, and they disagree about what any good military man should know: what is courage. The two generals, moreover, display opposite defects; Laches is all deeds and few words, and Nicias is all words and few deeds. But we also come to see that each general is defective in his purported strength; Laches does not endure in the discussion, and Nicias, whose *logoi* are all heard from others, can neither explain nor defend his words. In contrast with the two generals, Socrates' words and deeds are in harmony, and neither of them proves defective. The whole structure of the *Laches* must be understood in order to identify its educational thesis. Words and deeds must be harmonized, but they must be words and deeds of a certain sort.

The *Protagoras, Euthyphro, Meno*, and *Hippias Major* juxtapose Socrates with a single interlocutor, in order to show the differences between Socrates and his protagonists. The *Euthyphro*, for example, has numerous contrasts between Socrates and Euthyphro:[16] Euthyphro brings an accusation, Socrates is accused; Euthyphro is certain about what piety is, Socrates is not; Euthyphro is certain about the future, Socrates is not; Socrates wants to continue the discussion, but Euthyphro leaves; and there are many more contrasts. In the *Hippias Major* Socrates' single-minded pursuit of the noble is in contrast to Hippias' polymathic knowledge; Socrates is serious about the pursuit of the noble, but Hippias only wants to silence the unidentified persistent questioner. Hippias is an eristic who does not care about the *psychai* of the young men even though he is about to give a speech to them. I will argue that in all the early dialogues Socrates exemplifies what it is to be an educated person; he has both the intellectual skills and the character traits of a good dialectician. By contrast his interlocutors exhibit a variety of intellectual and character defects.

Character Types and Educational Techniques

Certain character traits are important for a good dialectical partner. One is shame. Shame is the condition of an interlocutor who admits that his real moral beliefs are at odds with his words or actions. Shame is a major motif of the *Gorgias*. Polus says that he will not be as easily shamed as Gorgias, and Callicles declares that he cannot be shamed at all. Gorgias shows shame when he admits that he would teach virtue to a student who does not possess it, and Polus is shamed when he admits that it is uglier to do rather than suffer an injustice. Callicles avoids shame, but to do so he must be dishonest in the conversation.

Socrates ironically praises Callicles for his knowledge, frankness, and good will (487a). The praise is ironical because we immediately see that Callicles is defective in these characteristics, and thus is not a fit partner in a good dialectical discussion. By knowledge Socrates means what an interlocutor would possess who had thought about his position enough to state, clarify, and defend it against objections. Callicles cannot do these things. He cannot identify who the naturally stronger are, nor can he defend his own nature/convention distinction.

If an interlocutor is not frank, then he will not say what he really believes. He is, then, not committed to his statements nor to their refutation, in which case beneficial *aporia* cannot occur. Callicles is not frank; he dissimulates about what his real position is, and eventually refuses to answer at all. Callicles sees the discussion with Socrates as an *agon* (contest), and for this reason he is not frank. Dissimulation, Callicles believes, might win him the contest, or at least it will keep him from losing it. Callicles, moreover, thinks that Socrates is contentious, and he becomes contentious himself. Callicles' good will completely vanishes when he exchanges insults with Socrates.

Republic I emphasizes in its opening paragraphs the theme of listening/not listening. Socrates wants to persuade Polemarchus to let him go, but Polemarchus will not listen. Later on Thrasymachus will not listen either, although he claims that Socrates does not listen to him. Socrates does not listen in that he does not accept Thrasymachus' false views; Thrasymachus does not listen because he continues to hold refuted positions, and finally he literally ceases to listen. The leitmotif of the *Euthydemus* is the serious man. The eristic brothers and Ctesippus, who readily learns their tricks, are not serious; they do not care for the *psyche* of Cleinias. Socrates, by his dialectical exhortation of the boy, shows that he cares; he sincerely urges Cleinias to seek wisdom. The two brothers and Ctesippus mimic dialectic, but their eristic tricks do not have a serious educational intent. They do not employ the "*Phaedrus* principle" but aim their verbal arrows at anyone anytime. A good dialectical partner must listen, and he must be serious.

A good dialectical partner should not be set in his ways. Cephalus in *Republic* I is not open to dialectical conversation even though he is good at chit chat. Cephalus lives at the level of ritual praying and sacrificing, and when he must defend an account, he passes on the responsibility for this to his son. Socrates lets the old man go without a dialectical test, for such a test with a man of Cephalus' age and dogmatic belief system would have no effect.

Besides character traits a good dialectical partner also needs certain intellectual traits. Lysimachus, for example, in the *Laches* (189c) has such a poor memory that he cannot participate in a conversation. Callicles and Nicias lack sufficient knowledge, and Chaerephon is intellectually very slow.

Plato makes these traits subject matter for the discussions. On one level we have the behavior and actual conversations, and on the other we have their significance. When Thrasymachus refuses to listen to Socrates, his action symbolizes something important about education. One must be willing to listen, in order to be educated. When Callicles declares that he will not be shamed, we see that shame is an essential step in education, and hence that Callicles cannot be educated. A very large part of the dialogue action, I will show, is of educational significance.

Socrates employs the "*Phaedrus* principle" with a number of different characters. He has his most complete and successful discussion with Meno's slave; the slave first comes to see his error about a geometrical problem, and then what the solution to the problem is. The slave has no vested interest in the topic, and no prior education to spoil him as an answerer, but since he speaks Greek he has enough intelligence and background to answer. Socrates displays a paradigm of question and answer dialectic in this friction free environment. He uses an unconcealed *elenchus* to refute the slave's false view, and then *psychagogia* to lead him to the correct answer. Lysis and Cleinias are also young men who have not come under the influence of a bad education. They are full of potential, and this potential can be actualized as either good or evil. Socrates employs with these youths a form of discussion in which he directly urges them to seek wisdom. His discussions with the youths only have the appearance of *elenchus* because Socrates does not so much refute what they say as benignly exhort them to search for wisdom. Socrates' educational method is suited to the *psychai* of these youths.

Polus enters the *Gorgias* discussion by denouncing the small inconsistency in which Socrates has trapped Gorgias and by asserting that he will not be easily shamed. We soon see that Polus is young and fresh, and that he does not listen very well. How will Socrates approach this type of character? He opposes Polus' freshness with sarcasm, and his inability to listen with a coercive speech which makes Polus listen. Socrates then uses a coercive *elenchus*, composed of many short questions and answers, which compels Polus to be consistent. At the very end of their discussion Polus admits that what Socrates has just said — that one should use rhetoric to insure the punishment for wrongdoing of one's friends and escape from punishment for wrongdoing of one's enemies — follows from what went before, but he still cannot quite believe it (480e). Socrates forces Polus to be consistent even if he does not convert him.

Other psychic *topoi* (types) require different medicines. Euthyphro is dogmatic; he always looks to the Homeric gods for the standard of piety. I will show that Socrates intentionally tries to confuse Euthyphro though a series of irrelevant analogies. Confusion is just what a dogmatic character like Euthyphro needs, and Socrates momentarily succeeds in getting Euthyphro to change his position (10d). With Meno Socrates uses *ad hominem* arguments which drive Meno to conclude that he cannot teach virtue. Meno's virtue is demotic virtue and Socrates gets Meno to concede that neither gentlemen, poets, nor sophists transmit this virtue. Since these are for Meno the only possible teachers of it, it cannot be taught, and thus is not knowledge. Politicians with demotic virtue must, then, have acquired it by chance. Socrates designs these moves to paralyze a dogmatic, intellectually sluggish, and pedagogically dangerous Meno who does not see the difference between real and demotic virtue. Real virtue is knowledge of good and evil which is acquired through the practice of dialectic; demotic virtue is a knack which requires luck.

Cephalus and Callicles are contrasting *topoi*. Cephalus has no views about justice, and Socrates must work to distill an account from some comments Cephalus makes (Rep. I 331a-c). Cephalus has not seen Socrates for a long time, which shows that Cephalus is not much of a man of *logoi*. Socrates leaves Cephalus alone. Callicles, in contrast, is a vibrant man of distinct views; he believes that justice is the interest of the naturally stronger, and that the stronger man makes his desires grow as strong as possible and satisfies them. Callicles and Socrates are polar opposites; when Callicles enters the discussion he boldly states that if what Socrates has been saying to Polus is true, then all of life must be turned upside down (*Gorgias* 481c). Callicles, as we have seen, lacks the character traits for a good dialectical partner. How is Socrates to educate Callicles? He uses two techniques: unmitigated ironical opposition, and true rhetoric. His rhetoric includes persuasive images, monologue completions of arguments, and the great speech at the end of the *Gorgias* where he threatens Callicles with a just judgment in the afterlife. Socrates, in the discussion with Callicles, states what a true rhetoric would be like (cf. *Gorgias* 503a-b), and then he practices it on Callicles. True rhetoric must aim at making the *psychē* better, but only dialectic, as I will argue, can produce knowledge. True rhetoric persuades the *psychē* to hold true beliefs and attitudes, and thus it is a correct educational method, but only as a propaedeutic to dialectic. True rhetoric, for example, might persuade someone to care for their *psychē*. In the *Gorgias* Socrates uses true rhetoric to attempt to make Callicles amenable to dialectic. Whether or not Socrates succeeds, he uses a method fitted to Callicles' *psychē*.

The above examples illustrate how Socrates instantiates the "*Phaedrus* principle." One reason Socrates is a true teacher is because he attempts to fit his *logoi* to the *psychai* of his answerers. Socrates practices a true pedagogical art which: (1) looks at the nature of its subject, (2) discerns how that nature can be made excellent, and (3) looks for means to engender this improvement (cf. *Gorgias* 501e, 503a-b). Sometimes Socrates intentionally confuses an interlocutor, and sometimes as with Callicles he is antagonistic, but he always intends the improvement of the interlocutors' *psychai*. We may, of course, disagree with Socrates' methods, but this is, to some extent, an empirical matter. We must experiment to see how different *logoi* affect different *psychai*.

Opening Scenes of Dialogues

A dialogue's opening scenes frequently are of great importance to its educational themes. The opening of the *Laches* provides a panoramic view of the state of Athenian education. The prominent grandfathers did not educate their sons; these sons do not know how to educate their sons; and the expert generals are called to their aid. The *Gorgias* opens with Gorgias just having completed a display, a display of rhetorical power. Everyone in the *Gorgias* gives a display, and the sort of display one gives depends upon one's education. Polus and Callicles are inept at dialectic; Callicles threatens that Socrates will be inept if he is hauled into court; Socrates threatens Callicles with an inept display before just judges in the afterlife.

Meno opens the *Meno* by asking Socrates whether *aretē* comes through teaching, or practice, or nature, or in some other way. Meno invites us, by the disjunctive nature of his question, to select one and only one alternative. But Socrates, I will argue, not only distinguishes two interpretations for each of these notions, but also he shows that in the right way teaching, practice, *and* nature are necessary for the acquisition of *aretē*. The opening lines of the *Meno* establish the statement whose denial allows us to see the correct educational theory. *Republic* I opens with the themes of persuasion/coercion and listening/not listening. Thrasymachus uses force, and he will not listen. Since he will not listen, Socrates' persuasion becomes more forceful. The delicate interplay of coercion and persuasion is central to the educational moves of *Republic* I. Thus the openings of some dialogues are important for understanding the educational themes of those dialogues.

Socratic Dialectic

Socrates questions each interlocutor about what I will call his "core beliefs." Socrates does not ask about the weather or how one's children are; rather he asks about those beliefs which form the core of one's self-image. For example, he wants to know from Gorgias, who sees himself as a rhetorician, what rhetoric is; he questions the generals, Laches and Nicias, about courage; and he interrogates the self-proclaimed religious seer, Euthyphro, about piety. With young men like Lysis, who do not yet have a mature self-image, Socrates inquires about friendship; for Lysis' friendship with Menexenus is the most important facet of his life.

The questions Socrates asks and the counterclaims he makes often aim at the beliefs of an interlocutor. His paradoxes in the *Gorgias* — for example, that the rhetorician is powerless in his own state — directly confront Polus' conventional beliefs. Socratic dialectic is in these senses *ad hominem*; it starts with core beliefs, works with other beliefs of an interlocutor, and often confronts these beliefs.

Socrates requires an interlocutor to give an account of his life, that is, of his core beliefs which direct that life (cf. *Laches* 187e-188a). But an answerer is not always willing to state his core beliefs; in fact to do so is sometimes painful, and certainly dangerous when one converses with Socrates. The danger is that one could be made to look a fool. It is here that Socratic irony enters. Socrates is ironical when he claims ignorance or when he states a desire to become Euthyphro's student, and the like. Socrates' irony has a distinct educational function. It opens a space where an interlocutor believes he is free to state his core beliefs in a nonthreatening environment. Irony overcomes the resistance which Socrates' reputation, a crowd of onlookers, and natural reticence to state core beliefs, produces. Irony permits the interlocutor to think that he is an expert, and is in control of the conversation. In such a context an answerer is often willing to say what he really thinks. But does not Socrates use irony excessively? Need he be ironical with someone like Thrasymachus who seems anxious to state his positions (*Rep.* I 336b-337a)? I am not clear about how to answer these questions. The written dialogue does not capture every aspect of a live conversation, and perhaps in live conversation irony is more essential to break down a reluctance to state one's core beliefs.

Socrates' irony appears to some as arrogance, since it does not conceal the fact that he knows how to refute people. Partially hidden excellence can appear to be arrogance. Socrates' irony is, I will argue, ambiguous. The ambiguity is in how one interprets Socrates' denial that he has knowledge. If by "knowledge" one means the sort of dogmatic certainty which comes from the gods, then Socrates does not know. If one means by "knowledge" the up till now defended, successfully but still revisable results of prior dialectical argument, then Socrates knows many things.[17] Socratic irony is ambiguous, and because of its ambiguity it is misleading. Answerers sometimes take Socrates to be acknowledging without qualification that he does not know anything and they are then surprised, if not outraged, to find that he has some very strong beliefs indeed.

What sort of reply does Socrates want from an interlocutor? He will not accept reports of the common usage of terms, or analyses of concepts. Nor will he accept examples. Socrates believes that these sorts of answers do not reveal the real nature of virtue, and it is important to discover the real nature of virtue in order to settle intractable ethical disputes.

Elsewhere I argue that Socrates neither seeks accounts of characteristics of acts nor of transcendent Forms.[18] Interlocutors often start by picking out features of acts, but Socrates rejects them as either too broad or too narrow. He wants to locate a condition of the *psychē*, and the Socratic turn in ethics is away from behavior and towards the psychic motive force which explains behavior. Socrates wants to discover the motive force in the *psychē* which makes one virtuous.

To find this motive force Socrates gains agreement with his interlocutors about what a virtue must be like. He employs, with the answerers' assent, what I will call "regulatory premises." For example, he and Laches agree that whatever courage is, it is a noble and good thing (*Laches* 192c), and he and Charmides also agree that temperance is a good thing (*Charmides* 159b-c). These apparently innocuous agreements have far reaching and, to the answerers, unexpected results. Socrates uses these simple premises to refute one account after another, and to suggest his own position:

A virtue φ is necessarily beneficial.
Only the knowledge of good and evil is necessarily beneficial.
$\therefore$ φ is the knowledge of good and evil.

Elsewhere I argue that Socrates accepts the above argument, and since φ can have as its values any virtue, Socrates believes that the virtues are identical.[19]

After an interlocutor gives an account, Socrates begins question and answer dialectic. The *Gorgias* is an important source of information about dialectic because it is self-reflexive. Within the *Gorgias* there are numerous comments about conversation which are themselves parts of the conversation. Socrates gives many rules for how to conduct question and answer; for example, one should ask a question and not give a speech (as Gorgias and Polus do), one should ask a single question and not two or more questions, and the like. In my essay on the *Gorgias*

I will enumerate such rules. But the *Gorgias*, I will show, goes beyond an analysis of dialectic; it also announces a true form of rhetoric, one whose proper educational function is that of a propaedeutic to dialectic.

Richard Robinson thoroughly discusses the logic of *elenchus*, and so I immediately may focus on some educational features of *elenchus*, and describe some examples of *psychagogia*.[20] The latter is important because commentators either ignore *psychē*-leading or deny that Socrates implies positions usually because they believe that he does not have any positions to imply.[21]

Elenchus is essentially *ad hominem* in that its aim is to refute the beliefs of the answerer. Socrates ironically says to Gorgias that he is not aiming at him, but that Gorgias should complete his own statement in his own way (*Gorgias* 454c). Gorgias must complete his own statement in his own way so that he is committed to it, and eventually to its refutation. Gorgias is refuted only if *his* beliefs fall, and only this sort of refutation can produce the beneficial awareness of self-ignorance.

It is not essential to *elenchus* that Socrates use sound arguments. It is essential that an interlocutor assent to each premise whether or not Socrates believes them to be true. If an interlocutor assents to a false premise, and is refuted, the refutation is *fair* given the rules of dialectic. For *elenchus* tests whether an interlocutor can defend a position, and part of this defense is to detect bad arguments against the original thesis. An answerer who accepts a refutation based on a bad argument shows that he does not have knowledge. If a refutation by an unsound argument produces an awareness of one's own ignorance, then such a refutation is a benefit to the *psychē*. Socrates is not so concerned with sound arguments as is often supposed because he argues from the beliefs of an answerer, and sometimes does not question whether these beliefs are true or false.

Socrates varies the tone of *elenchus* depending upon the type of *psychē* he encounters. With young men like Lysis and Cleinias the refutation is so mild that one hardly can distinguish it from *psychagogia*. With Polus and Polemarchus the refutations are more forceful, and with Callicles they are harsh. Socrates exemplifies the "*Phaedrus* principle" with respect to the coercive character of his refutations.

Socrates uses *psychagogia* to suggest indirectly what he takes the correct position to be. *Psychagogia* frequently operates in the following way: Socrates rejects an account in such a paradoxical manner that the refutation should stimulate the answerer to *wonder* what went wrong. Furthermore, Socrates frequently uses *psychagogia* to suggest that a virtue is the knowledge of good and evil. It seems likely, then, that Socrates endorses this position. Let us look at some instances of *psychagogia*.

Socrates constrains Laches to concede the absurd conclusion that courage is foolish endurance (193d). But foolish endurance surely is not a good thing. What has gone wrong here? Laches' original account is that courage is wise endurance, and the only sort of knowledge Laches seems to be familiar with is technical expertise. But with this conception of knowledge Socrates is able to offer a counterexample to Laches' account: he who dives into a well to save someone, and who has the knowledge of diving, is not as brave as he who does the same thing but without this knowledge. It now seems that the man who endures foolishly is braver than he who endures wisely. This conclusion is counterintuitive and shocking. It motivates one to investigate the presupposition of the argument. The most relevant presupposition is that the courageous man has only technical knowledge, but this is false. The courageous man should have that other sort of knowledge, the knowledge of what on the whole it is best to do. When we substitute this sort of knowledge for technical expertise, Socrates' counterexamples fail.

In *Republic* I (334a) Polemarchus is forced to concede that the just man is the skilled thief. This shocking conclusion should motivate both us and Polemarchus to *wonder* what went wrong. Throughout the conversation Polemarchus sees justice as some sort of technical knowledge like cobbling, farming, doctoring, and the like (332eff.). But these arts, Socrates argues, admit what I call the "bivalence principle."[22] He who is good at the art of φ-ing is also good at the opposite of φ-ing. The doctor, for example, is good at killing a patient. When Polemarchus claims that the just man is good at guarding money, Socrates plugs in the bivalence principle to show that the just man is also the expert thief. Again we must seek for the presuppositions of this refutation; the main one is that justice is some sort of technical knowledge. But is there any sort of knowledge not susceptible to the bivalence principle? The knowledge of good and evil is not because a person with this knowledge would not act badly, given Socrates' psychological assumption that all men act on their conception of what is best. The *psychagogia* again suggests that a virtue is the knowledge of good and evil.

I will argue that the second half of the *Meno* and the conclusions of the *Laches* and *Charmides* also lead us to the same conclusion. The arguments in these dialogues are complex examples of *psychē*-leading. There are also more direct examples of *psychagogia*. Gorgias cannot help but see that rhetoric, in some way, requires *aretē*, and Socrates directly leads Lysis and Cleinias to see that they should seek wisdom. The type of *psychagogia* Socrates uses is fitted to the condition of an interlocutor's *psychē*. But even with Meno's slave Socrates does not teach if by "teach" is meant "transmit or hand over knowledge." Socrates' direct *psychagogia* elicits the *logoi* from within the slave; no matter how leading the question it is still the slave who answers. Socrates does not become a new authority by transmitting his beliefs to others. *Psychagogia* is a pervasive, but to a great extent unrecognized, phenomenon in the early dialogues.

Socrates' refutations are intended to end in *aporia*. *Aporia* is the puzzlement and lack of passage one feels when one's beliefs suffer a Socratic refutation. *Aporia* is closely associated with the awareness of one's own ignorance, and such ignorance should motivate a person to seek knowledge. Since Socrates believes that dialectic is the only way to acquire the knowledge of *aretē*, Socrates desires that his interlocutors do dialectic.

Answerers often agree with Socrates that if one knows that φ, then one can say that φ, where Socrates means by "say that φ" that one can state, clarify, and defend an account. But what do interlocutors actually admit when their accounts fail? Meno's slave, Lysis, and Cleinias admit their ignorance, but they are too young and inexperienced to be wedded to their accounts. Many interlocutors attempt to avoid *aporia* by the ploy that they cannot quite express what they, nevertheless, know. Laches does this even though he earlier admits that if one knows that φ, then one can say that φ (*Laches* 190c, 194b). Callicles and Thrasymachus simply will not have their mouths shut by Socrates; they will not be pushed into *aporia*. In the essays which follow I pay close attention to how interlocutors do or do not avoid *aporia*, and the diverse methods of avoidance are integrated closely with the types of character.

Socrates: The Tragic Educational Hero

The Socrates of the early dialogues is a pedagogical failure. Few interlocutors admit their ignorance, and none of them, so far as we know, become true dialecticians. But why does Socrates fail? His failure primarily is due to the conditions of his culture, conditions which produce the prior educations of his interlocutors. An agonistic culture turns Socrates' search for truth into a contest, and in a contest it is difficult for interlocutors to admit their ignorance, especially in front of an audience. Moreover, most interlocutors already have their beliefs and patterns of desires firmly fastened in their *psychai*, and dialectical argument is not the source of that fastening. In the *Gorgias* Socrates diagnoses his failure to educate Callicles as due to Callicles' love of demos (513c-d). Socrates is a pedagogical failure because he uses a method which does not work in the prevailing conditions.

But Socrates is also, I maintain, the educational hero of the early dialogues. A hero can, and often does, fail. A hero even can fail often, and Socrates does. Socrates practices the only method which could achieve his purpose. If he were to transmit beliefs, then the subject matter of education would not be the beliefs of the answerer but a subject matter independent of the answerer. Furthermore, if Socrates were to transmit beliefs, then he would face the "Nicias problem." Everything Nicias believes is appropriated thoughtlessly from what he has heard authorities say. Greek culture, as much as our own, favored teaching by transmission, but Socrates rejects transmission. Socrates uses the only method which he believes could motivate people to engage in dialectic.

The Socrates of the early dialogues is a decent person who cares for the *psychai* of his interlocutors. Socrates is the model of the good man, whether or not he is copied. The beginning of the *Charmides* shows us that Socrates is temperate. He relinquishes his greatest desire which is for conversation to go to war; he is modest about his bravery in battle; and he controls his physical desires. In the *Laches* we see that Socrates is courageous; he endures both in battle and in the conversation. The *Euthydemus* shows us a Socrates who is a serious man; he cares about the *psyche* of Cleinias. In the *Gorgias* we learn that Socrates is the man who knows. His beliefs are tied down in his *psyche* by reasons of iron (509a); in other words, Socrates' views have survived previous dialectical inquiry. In an uncharacteristically frank statement Socrates says that he is the only one in Athens to practice the true political art (*Gorgias* 521d-e). This practice consists both in having justified beliefs and in using correct pedagogical methods.

Dialectic and Knowledge

How can dialectic produce knowledge? If by "knowledge" is meant a final certainty with guaranteed truth, then it cannot. But dialectic can produce justified claims to knowledge. In the *Meno* we learn that the difference between knowledge and belief is that the former is tied down in the *psychē* by reason (85c-d, 98a), while the latter is not. Belief can come through just about any means, and can just as easily depart from the *psychē*. Knowledge, on the other hand, only comes through dialectic. But how does dialectic produce knowledge, and what sort of knowledge does it produce? One possesses a justified claim to knowledge when one can state, clarify, and defend that claim against Socratic interrogation and objection. Since there are greater and lesser degrees of clarification and defense, there will be stronger and weaker justified claims to knowledge. Also the dialectical test is only as good as the tester, and the stated objections to a claim need not have included all of the plausible objections. For this reason Socrates treats his own knowledge claims as revisable (cf. *Crito* 49d-e). Knowledge in itself is for Socrates a regulatory ideal, the ideal of a completely defended and defensible account. We never in fact achieve this ideal. Complete virtue would be this ideal knowledge, but no one ever achieves this. Human virtue admits of degrees, and these degrees are proportioned to the degree of justified belief. Socrates achieves this virtue in a degree higher than any other person of his time.

A Brief Description of *Elenchus and Psychagogia*

Dialectic includes both *elenchus* and *psychagogia*, and they are types of dialectical discussion. Both types of discussion can be done separately, although *psychagogia* is usually done with *elenchus*. Frequently Socrates starts with elenchus and moves to a mixture of both forms. In some conversations with uncorrupted young men *psychagogia* is dominant, but in most conversations the *psychagogia* is subordinate to Socrates' aporetic aim.

My categories for describing Socrates' behavior, however, are too crude. Both types of discussion take on many different forms as we should expect since there are many different psychic conditions. Neither type of discussion is a single monolithic tactic, and when commentators make the mistake of attributing to Socrates a single elenctic method, then they erroneously attribute to Socrates a single goal—refutation, the search for universally valid truth, and the like. Although *elenchus* and *psychagogia* are best explained through examples, in general we may describe them as follows:

> *Elenchus* is both refutation and the attempt to refute. Socratic refutations aim at the core beliefs of an answerer. Refutations proceed by making use of other beliefs of an answerer, and hence we cannot infer that Socrates endorses the premises used in refutation. *Elenchus* is *ad hominem* because it starts from and focuses on the interlocutor's own beliefs. If an answerer has shame, then a completed *elenchus* should end in *aporia*.

> *Psychagogia* occurs when Socrates indirectly tries to lead a *psychē* to some position. There are many types of indirect leading. Sometimes Socrates' refutation of a position is so startling that it should produce wonder at what went wrong. The refutation invites us to investigate its assumptions, and usually there are suggestions about which assumptions are wrong. Sometimes the *psychagogia* is more direct. With uncorrupted young men like Lysis Socrates gently, through questions, leads them to see that, for example, wisdom is the only intrinsic good.

2. Irony and Confusion
in the *Euthyphro*

The *Euthyphro* is a short, apparently simple, and yet enigmatic dialogue which raises serious questions for its readers. Why is the *Euthyphro* so aporetic, and why do Socrates and Euthyphro make so little progress in the search for piety? Moreover why does the *Euthyphro* tell us so little about the nature of piety? Or are we simply missing the point of the dialogue? I think that we can answer these questions when we focus on the character of Euthyphro, and on how Socrates attempts to educate him.

The Contrast Between Socrates and Euthyphro

The introductory paragraph of the *Euthyphro* is very important. We are told that it is something new or perhaps even strange that Socrates who usually passes his time in the Lyceum is now spending it before the bench of the king archon (2a). The suggested contrast here is between the free, unfettered discussions after truth in the Lyceum, and the regulated, sophistic discourses or set speeches of the law courts. Socrates' *logoi* (words) excel in the one on one, dialectic conversation in the Lyceum, but do not persuade the multitude in the court. Euthyphro, on the other hand, speaks, if ineffectively, before the assembly (3b-c), and is more than willing to find Meletus' weak spot, and make use of it in court (4c). Socrates is new at the legal game, and will appear in the eyes of the many laughable; Euthyphro is untried in socratic *elenchus* (refutation), and will prove to be inadequate to the test. Socrates' failure in court will not be a moral one, Euthyphro's failure at discussion will. Euthyphro corrupts his father and the citizens by his misguided attempts at teaching, Socrates does not. All of this is hinted at in the opening lines of the *Euthyphro* by the distinction between the Lyceum and the bench of the king archon, and Socrates' familiarity to the former but strangeness to the latter.[1]

Socrates' first words at 2a sharpen the contrast between him and Euthyphro. Socrates is involved in a *graphē*, a public suit or indictment; Euthyphro in a *dikē*, a private suit. We have, then, the juxtaposition between public and private. Socrates does not indict, but is the passive recipient of the charge; Euthyphro charges his father. Hence we have the juxtaposition of active and passive, indictor and indicted.

Socrates is under a public indictment partly because of his private *daimon* (3b). He purportedly corrupts the youth because of his educational mission of testing, and the *daimon* never forbids such a mission. Apollo, in fact, requires it. Thus Socrates is under a public indictment because of his private divinity, and his personal mission of *elenchus*. The divinity does not forbid the publicly outrageous behavior of questioning; hence the divinity is an assault on the city, its laws and gods.[2] Socrates' private divinity is at odds with the *polis*. Socrates the private man with private conversations and a private divinity is under public attack.

Euthyphro, although he pursues a private suit against his father, fancies himself a public personage. He is proud of the very fine speeches which he makes to the assembly (3b-c). Ironically Euthyphro's private suit does not receive public support; the many are even hostile to Euthyphro (4b-c). Moreover, they laugh at Euthyphro's speeches about the gods in the assembly (3c). Euthyphro tries very hard to be a public figure, but he fails. There is ample reason, as we shall see, to believe that Euthyphro does not achieve even the level of public opinion or conventional wisdom. Euthyphro will prove to be a conservative anachronism.[3]

The *Euthyphro* is unusual among early dialogues because there are only two characters, Euthyphro and Socrates. Plato can thus draw a stark contrast between them, and we already have seen some of these contrasts. These contrasts help us to see the divergent characters and values of Socrates and Euthyphro. When we see what Euthyphro is like, then we will be in a better position to understand how Socrates attempts to educate him.

There are, moreover, other important contrasts.[4] Euthyphro thinks himself an expert about piety and impiety; he has exact knowledge about all such matters (4e-5a). Socrates disclaims any such knowledge

(2c). Euthyphro believes himself to be a public official about religious matters, but Socrates is only thought to teach privately about such things (3d). Euthyphro literally and whole-heartedly believes the stories about the Homeric gods, but Socrates disbelieves such stories (6a-b), and is disinterested in them (6c-d). Euthyphro is confident both about religious matters and the outcome of his case; Socrates is not confident at all. Euthyphro boldly predicts a successful outcome for Socrates against his accusers (3e); Socrates does not predict the future because, as he says in the *Laches*, a seer's knowledge is not wisdom (cf. *Laches* 195e-196a).

Socrates is thought by the Athenians to be a teacher (3c-e), but he disclaims the title in the *Meno*.[5] The Athenians are mistaken about this because what they mean by "teacher" is a giver of speeches which are impressed upon passive recipients. We learn from the *Gorgias* that false rhetorical speeches use persuasion merely to gratify, rather than aim at the real benefit of a *psychē*. Socratic *elenchus* does not gratify the answerer, nor can it be done with the masses. The Athenians, oddly enough, do not think that Euthyphro is a teacher, although he satisfies their criteria for the title. Euthyphro's speeches before the assembly probably so gratify the citizens that they transgress the boundary between the serious and the comic. In any case, Euthyphro is laughed at in the assembly (3d-e). The irony is that Socrates the real teacher through *elenchus* is thought conventionally to teach, and by this means corrupt the youth, while Euthyphro, the speechmaker, is not thought to teach at all. A second irony is that the Athenians, by laughing at Euthyphro's speeches about the gods of the city, show that they have the impiety which they believe that Socrates has.

Socrates is charged with corrupting the youth, and he says about his accuser Meletus (2c-d):

> And he seems to me to be the only one of the public men who begins in the right way; for the right way is to take care of the young men first, to make them as good as possible, just as a good husbandman will naturally take care of the young plants first and afterwards of the rest.

The irony here is that while education should begin with the young, Meletus indicts, and hence hopes to correct, old Socrates. As Socrates makes clear by his discussion with Meletus in the *Apology*, Meletus has no educational intent or theory at all. Socrates, on the other hand, begins with the young—all of the young men who observe him asking questions and seeking answers from their elders. The contrast between Socrates and Euthyphro is even stronger. Euthyphro attacks a father who is as far advanced in age as he probably is fixed in opinion. Socrates is charged with corrupting the youth, but Euthyphro charges an elderly man.

The final irony is when Socrates offers to become Euthyphro's pupil in order to receive instruction about religious matters (5a-c). Euthyphro eagerly undertakes to instruct Socrates in correct religion. The real teacher, however, will not place himself into the hands of a religious anachronism, but Socrates' irony prepares Euthyphro to speak his mind about piety.

We learn the following about Euthyphro's character. Euthyphro is confident and brash. He is confident about his grasp of piety, and hence he boldly pursues his father and offers to instruct Socrates. Euthyphro's suit against his father is all the more remarkable given the dubious nature of the case against the old man. Euthyphro also is confident that his accounts of piety will stand the test of discussion, and when they fail he charges Socrates with their failure. He brashly predicts the outcome of Socrates' case, and he assumes that the gods will support his suit. Euthyphro is hubristic when he claims that his behavior is no different than Zeus' to Cronos, and Cronos' to Heaven. Socrates, as we shall see, wants men to be godlike, but how one conceives of divinity and the activity of divinity makes all the difference.[6]

Euthyphro is dogmatic, and he is not very bright. His dogmatism is best displayed by his return to—circling back to—his earlier account of piety at the end of the *Euthyphro*. Ending where one begins, or always saying the same thing about the same thing, is not in itself bad, but Euthyphro reasserts the very same position which Socrates soundly refuted earlier (cf. 15af.). A key to understanding the lack of philosophical development in the *Euthyphro*—its aporetic structure and sparse hints of Socrates' own position—is Euthyphro's dogmatism. Since Euthyphro is always looking to the Homeric/Hesiodic gods for "knowledge" of piety and impiety, Socrates cannot get Euthyphro to look inward at the condition of his own *psychē*. Thus the *Euthyphro* remains at the superficial level where piety is the Olympian god-loved.

Euthyphro's dogmatism is an aspect of his lack of knowledge. Euthyphro also is unschooled and inept at dialectic. At 10d, for example, he contradicts his own position. Out of confusion and not through rational persuasion, as I will show, Euthyphro concedes that the gods love piety for what it is, not that piety is what it is because the gods love it. Socrates confuses Euthyphro with a series of irrelevant analogies to make him, at least momentarily, embrace the correct position. We will look at Socrates' educational intent when I analyze this passage in detail below. Suffice to say that Euthyphro is not suited intellectually to the rigors of Socratic debate.

Euthyphroian Religion

A close look at Euthyphro's theology reveals that he is an incoherent mixture of several different strands of religious thought. The dominant strand is Olympian. Euthyphro prides himself on his knowledge of and literal adherence to the tales about the gods (6a-c). He justifies his suit against his father by an unreflective appeal to what is told about what Zeus and Cronos did to their fathers (6a). Euthyphro's appeal to such stories commits him to the further claim that the gods quarrel with one another, and Socrates uses this admission to attack Euthyphro's view that piety is the god-loved (6d-7a). But Euthyphro's main reason for prosecuting his father is not Olympian; it is older and more earth oriented. Euthyphro fears blood pollution (*miasma*) from not proceeding against his father and hence purifying the household (4c).[8] Blood pollution is connected with the worship of life and death forces as seen in the Dionysian rites. But there is yet a third dimension to Euthyphro's thought: it is law (*nomos*), and the city. The traditional gods were closely allied with the city, and Euthyphro sees himself as a protector of civic right and law. Euthyphro appeals to democratic *nomos* in prosecuting his father; he says that it is irrelevant who it is, stranger or relative, who died through his father's carelessness (4b). Whoever it is, he is obligated to prosecute his father. Thus Euthyphro has several different and unrelated reasons for prosecuting his father. Euthyphro does not have a coherent set of beliefs in the very area where he prides himself as an expert.

Euthyphro is laughed at in the assembly when he propounds divine things (3b-c). He is laughed at because his religious beliefs are antiquated. Few Athenian intellectuals, at that time, believed in strict interpretations of Homer and Hesiod. But the *Euthyphro* is not an outmoded attack on antiquated religious beliefs. Euthyphro is a conservative anachronism; his religion went out with the stresses and strains of the Peloponnesian War. Nevertheless, no viable religious alternatives have yet emerged. Plato will develop such an alternative, but first he must critique the tradition. One task of the *Euthyphro* is to put the Homeric divinities to rest, and to clear the religious ground to make possible a purified religion. The *Euthyphro* does for religion what Socratic *elenchus* should do for the individual: demolish the old dogmatic beliefs to make room for the acquisition of knowledge.

Euthyphro's Suit against his Father

Euthyphro's charge against his father has three different types of purported justification: law, pollution, and Homeric example. Many essays have been written about the following topics:[8] (1) the legal standing of Euthyphro's suit, that is whether any court would hear such a case, (2) the probable outcome of Euthyphro's suit if it were heard, and (3) Euthyphro's actual intentions toward his father, that is, does he really want him convicted or what? Under (3) some commentators speculate that it is sufficient for Euthyphro simply to bring the suit, even if the court refuses to hear it, to believe himself exonerated from the blood pollution. Euthyphro would then have done all that he could. From a moral perspective Euthyphro seems, to our modern ears, to have his strongest case when he appeals to the democratic *nomos* that kinship and status are irrelevant in such a case. But from a religious perspective Euthyphro's father is quite scrupulous. Since the hired man probably was caught in the act of murder, and at an estate possibly outside the jurisdiction of Athens, the father under Greek convention could dispatch the hired man on the spot. Instead he sends to the religious exegete for instruction. Now we might believe that the father was negligent toward his prisoner, and Euthyphro appeals to this very un-Homeric notion (4d), but the father may reasonably expect the exegete to permit him to dispatch the murderer.

What should we conclude from the description of Euthyphro's suit? The vehemence with which modern commentators argue about it, and the extent to which their positions go beyond our explicit evidence, suggest that the suit is morally, legally, and religiously murky, and Plato intends it that way.[9] The ambiguous nature of Euthyphro's suit motivates the need to understand what piety really is; a clear case would have no such power. Only an intimate knowledge of piety as a paradigm could help us see whether Euthyphro's action is pious. Below I will explain what sort of paradigm piety is, and how a knowledge of this paradigm will help us solve difficult questions.

Socratic Irony

Socrates' irony occurs in several ways: (1) Socrates self-effaces himself through repeated claims of ignorance; (2) Socrates suggests that Meletus starts at the right place, with the supposed corruptor of the youth; (3) Socrates offers to become Euthyphro's pupil; and (4) Socrates ironically praises Euthyphro's knowledge and wisdom, or at least suggests that Euthyphro must have such knowledge (4e).

Readers of Plato, and contemporaries of Socrates, discern a certain arrogance behind Socrates' ironic mask. This arrogance comes, in part, from the deceptive nature of the irony. Socrates may praise Meletus for starting at the right place, but in the *Apology* we learn that Meletus is just stupid about educational matters (24c-26b). Socrates praises Euthyphro's knowledge, but the *Euthyphro* displays Euthyphro's ignorance. Socrates' self-effacement, on the other hand, does not successfully hide his dialectical ability. Socrates' expertise is not hidden by his irony, and partially hidden excellence can appear as arrogance.

Is such irony pedagogically justifiable? A case can be made against Socratic irony. First some answerers are aware that Socrates is ironical. In *Rep*. I (337a), Thrasymachus makes Socrates' irony an issue, and complains bitterly about it. In the *Laches* (187e-188c) Nicias claims to know that the coversation will be about him, and how he leads his life. Nicias "knows" the intended effect of Socratic irony; he understands that Socrates is wise enough to test the lives of others, and hence that his irony is a mask. But that Socrates is found out is not the center of the charge against him. Rather Socrates' irony is said to produce hostility against him by introducing an element of dishonesty into a conversation. Since Socrates admits that honesty, good-will, and frankness are prerequisites for a good conversation (see *Gorgias* 187a), his irony could interfere with the dialectical search for truth. Socrates' irony produces hard feelings against him, and dialectical conversation only can occur if the discussants are of frank, good-will.

We partially can defend Socrates against this charge by appeal to the educational purpose of his irony. Socrates' questions are *ad hominem*; he does not engage, except in rare circumstances, in abusive or circumstantial *ad hominem* arguments; rather he aims at the core beliefs of his interlocutors.[10] The generals, Laches and Nicias, are to state what courage is, and courage is central to the life of a general. Socrates asks *Gorgias*, the rhetorician, to define his art; Euthyphro, the religious seer, is to tell what piety is. Socrates aims at core beliefs— those beliefs which define and defend the center of one's personality. The men mentioned above live and act by the beliefs which Socrates questions.

Socratic education is great because of its *ad hominem* nature; this educational method has as its subject matter the core beliefs of an interlocutor. But Socrates usually cannot elicit an honest statement of a core belief without resistance, dissimulation, and/or escape behavior. It is painful to articulate and justify one's life and one's ways. Thus Socrates engages in irony, and his irony produces an opening, a space, where the answerer can put forth his beliefs in a seemingly nonthreatening and accepting environment. The pedagogical function of Socratic irony is, then, to overcome an answerer's resistance and to provide an opening where the answerer can display his beliefs. It is essential to Socratic dialectic that an answerer honestly state his beliefs so that he is committed to them, and ultimately to their refutation. But the irony appears very sneaky when Socrates proceeds to refute what one says, if an interlocutor does not realize the benefits of refutation.

Would Euthyphro state his beliefs honestly without Socratic irony, and is the irony necessary to Socrates' method? I do not know the answer to those questions. Euthyphro seems anxious to state his views on piety, but Socrates' irony has been at work from the beginning of the dialogue. It is hard to say whether Euthyphro would have been so willing to display his "knowledge" in the absence of irony.

Socrates' irony is thought to have a deceptive element. Socrates is not as ignorant as he seems. This charge has a number of different levels. First Socrates does know how to refute people; he has the technique of refutation. Second Socrates is more knowledgeable than others because he knows that he does not know anything of importance (*Apology* 23a-b). Third Socrates claims to believe some things very firmly, and even to know some other things. In the *Meno* (98b) he knows that true belief and knowledge are different, and that Meno's paradox will make people indolent. In the *Crito* (49d) he expresses strong belief in the claim that one should never do wrong, or return wrong with wrong. In the *Gorgias* (508e-509a) he says that his positions in that dialogue are "firm and fastened — if I may put it rather bluntly — with reasons of iron and adamant . . ." The second and third claims, above, appear on the surface contradictory. A simple but important distinction resolves this problem. Socrates does not know anything in the sense of irrevisable knowledge; all knowledge claims are revisable, that is open to further inquiry and revision.[11] Socrates is willing to reopen any claim even if it is tied down with reasons of "iron and adamant" (*Gorgias* 509a). But Socrates does know some things in the sense that some of his accounts have again and again survived *elenchus.* Thus the tension between the last two claims is removed by distinguishing two sorts of knowledge. Socrates is ignorant only in the sense of irrevisable, divine knowledge.

The distinction between irrevisable knowledge, and revisable, defended claims helps us to see the purported deception in Socrates' irony. When Socrates claims ignorance he does not deceive in one sense; but he does deceive if by "knowledge" is meant "revisable, defended claims." Interlocutors may believe that Socrates denies that he has any sort of knowledge. Hence Socratic irony does and does not involve deception, but it is ambiguous. Part of the danger of Socratic irony, to Socrates and to a good discussion, is the ambiguity which lies behind the mask.

The Paradigm of Piety

Socrates gives the following hints about the ontological status of piety: (1) piety is *in* all and only pious acts (5c-d); (2) piety is an *eidos* common to all pious things (5c-d, 6d-e); (3) piety is a *paradigm* which one may look upon and use to see what is and is not pious (6d-e); and (4) piety is that *by which* all pious acts are pious.

There are at least three plausible interpretations about what Socrates seeks. W. K. C. Guthrie implies that piety is a characteristic of acts.[12] Some feature of acts correctly delineates the pious from the impious ones. Being god-loved, staying steadfast at one's post, and quiet behavior are all characteristics of acts. Interlocutors do give, at least initially, accounts which specify characteristics of acts. For Euthyphro piety is prosecuting wrongdoers, or what is god-loved. Guthrie can also explain (1)-(4) above; the pious making characteristic metaphorically is in all and only pious acts, and it is that feature of an act by which the act is pious. Moreover, we can through dialectic metaphorically come to see this characteristic, and hence the characteristic can be a paradigm by which to judge whether or not an act is pious.[13]

R. E. Allen argues that the virtues in the early dialogues are separate essences or Forms, although they are not more real than their instances.[14] This last qualification is all that distinguishes a virtue from a middle period Form. Piety, according to Allen, is an aspatial, atemporal paradigm which we may look upon and use to adjudicate ethical and religious disputes. Piety is also like an Aristotelian formal cause, and hence it is that by which all pious things are pious. Piety is also in all pious acts in the sense that it is a universal common to but not more real than those acts.

T. Penner argues that the virtues are motive forces or states of the *psychē*.[15] The virtues are not dispositions which we individuate by behavior; rather they are identical with a single state—the knowledge of good and evil—which explains all the virtuous dispositions for behavior. Thus the virtues are really identical because they are all a single state. Socrates is asking the substantial psychological question about what it is in a person's *psychē* which makes him pious. Piety is in all pious actions in that it is manifest or displayed in all pious acts. Piety is that by which all pious acts are pious because it is like an Aristotelian efficient cause; the *psychē* is the source of motion, and particular psychic states motivate us in specific ways.

Each of the above interpretations is plausible, and each has its ardent supporters. The text of the *Euthyphro* itself does not help us decide between these mutually inconsistent theories; the text evidentially underdetermines these interpretations, and is compatible with each of them. But why is the status of the paradigm of piety so unclear in the *Euthyphro*? The level of a Socratic dialogue must dovetail with the educational attainment of its interlocutors. Euthyphro is very dogmatic; he always looks to the Homeric divinities for piety. Socrates is unable to break through this dogmatism, and hence he does not have the opportunity to lead Euthyphro to the type of entity which he seeks.

Nevertheless, I recommend the following theory, based on evidence in other early dialogues and hints at the end of the *Euthyphro*, about what Socrates seeks.[16] Piety is the psychic state, the knowledge of good and evil. All of the other virtues are also this psychic state, and hence all of the virtues are identical. Socrates believes, as a psychological assumption, that all persons will do what, on the whole, seems best to them, and since the knowledge of good and evil embraces an estimation of what is best on the whole, we act in accordance with such knowledge, or in accordance with beliefs which may pretend to the status of such knowledge. If we act from a knowledge of good and evil, then that knowledge is that by which—an efficient motivating cause—our act occurs. But what, at least in outline, does such knowledge look like, and how will it help solve a case like Euthyphro's? First we should remember that Socrates never claims to have such knowledge. The knowledge of good and evil is a regulatory ideal; it is the true account which survives all possible dialectical attacks. In practice we must be satisfied with approximations of such knowledge. The best example of the application of such knowledge to a problem occurs, I believe, in the *Crito*. There Socrates uses some dialectically defended principles—e.g. one ought not commit an injustice—and he applies them to the complex question of whether or not he should escape from prison. Socrates also attempts to rebut Crito's objections to his staying in prison. The knowledge of good and evil is not some mysterious metaphysical entity, but rather it is hard thinking about difficult and complex cases.

Euthyphro's Accounts

Euthyphro first says that piety is doing what he is now doing, prosecuting a wrongdoer who commits murder, or steals from temples, or the like (5d-e). First Euthyphro's answer is vacuous. Nobody denies that murder or theft is wrong; but as Socrates later points out (8b-d) the question is whether some event is murder or justified killing. Second, Socrates explicitly rejects Euthyphro's account because it only gives examples. Euthyphro's account is not in terms of examples since it does pick out classes of actions, but Socrates is correct to imply that the account is too narrow. There are some pious acts that are not acts of prosecuting others; Euthyphro himself mentions praying and sacrificing (14b). Third, Euthyphro's justification for the account is strictly Hesiodic: Zeus chastized his father, and Cronos his, so Euthyphro is perfectly correct, he claims, in attacking his father.

Euthyphro's second definition is that piety is what is loved by the gods (6e-7a). Several Stephanus pages earlier Socrates had gained Euthyphro's assent that there are wars and enmities between the gods. It is not hard for Socrates to show that if the gods disagree, then they disagree about important matters such as justice and piety. Thus some gods may love and some hate the very same thing, and hence on Euthyphro's view it is pious and impious, but Socrates does not want to be told what is both pious and impious (8a).

At 9c Socrates offers to help Euthyphro amend his account. Let us say that what all the gods love is pious, what they all hate is impious, and what is inbetween is inbetween. Right at this point a shift occurs in the dialogue.[17] Before 9c Euthyphro without help simply states his positions, and Socrates refutes them; after 9c Socrates leads Euthyphro to positions, and as I will show, some of these positions contain correct Socratic beliefs. The shift is between pure *elenchus* (refutation) and *elenchus* mixed with *psychagogia* (*psychē*-leading).[18] In the former Socrates tries to refute Euthyphro, to turn him away from the Homeric gods. In the latter Socrates also tries to lead Euthyphro to correct positions, and the reader can see something correct hinted at in the discussion even if Euthyphro does not see it. Socrates suggests, implies, and presupposes correct beliefs that lie, frequently, just under the surface. For example, we will see Socrates imply the following: (1) piety is valuable in its own right, (2) the gods cherish what is really valuable, and (3) the gods cherish what is really valuable because they are good.

That the gods are good and are free from human wants and desires is not part of the Homeric/Hesiodic view Euthyphro starts with. The mythical gods notoriously are capricious in their alliances, favors, and needs. Socrates tries indirectly to lead Euthyphro to a more elevated view of divinity. But *psychagogia* is psychologically a very complex occurrence. Euthyphro's explicit theology would not include the gods' goodness. On the other hand, Euthyphro easily assents to the premise that the gods cannot be made better by our attention to them (13c-d). Euthyphro is confused, and Socrates attempts to lead him to that part of his implicit belief structure which is defensible. Euthyphro, like many of us, probably believes that the better something is the more worthy of divinity it is. By playing on this "comon sense" belief Socrates leads Euthyphro into an admission which is inconsistent with his explicit views. We must remember that considerable theological revision of Homeric thought already has occurred by the dramatic date of the *Euthyphro*, and this makes possible Euthyphro's assent.

Educational Confusion

At 9e-10a Socrates poses a crucial question: "Is the pious loved by the gods because it is pious, or is it pious because it is loved by the gods?" Euthyphro does not understand the question, and so Socrates "instructs" him with a flock of analogies to "clarify" matters (10b-c):

(1) Is the seen thing seen because someone (or something) sees it, or does someone see it because it is a seen thing?
(2) Is the led thing led because someone leads it, or does someone lead it because it is a led thing?
(3) Is the beloved thing beloved because someone loves it, or does someone love it because it is a beloved thing?

The former alternative is correct in each case. For example, a beloved thing is beloved because someone loves it. Commentators spend much effort on the logical structure and rational import of these analogies, and there is considerable disagreement about these issues. But the educational purpose of these analogies is to produce confusion.[19] Socrates is trying simply to confuse Euthyphro. Immediately after the analogies he asks Euthyphro what he now thinks about piety, and Euthyphro flatly contradicts his previous position (10d). He now says that piety is loved because it is pious, not pious because it is loved. But Euthyphro is not argued into this admission; he is confused into it. The analogies have the logical force of a cloud of dust in his face. Euthyphro comes in saying one thing, and leaves saying the opposite. As far as the analogies are concerned, Euthyphro simply could continue to maintain his position. It is consistent to claim that a seen thing is seen because someone sees it, a beloved thing is beloved because someone loves it, and piety is pious because the gods love it. The multiplicity of analogies Socrates throws at Euthyphro, as well as their lack of logical and persuasive force, suggest that Socrates does not intend a straightforward refutation of Euthyphro.

Does not my interpretation impute to Socrates an immoral use of rhetoric? In the *Gorgias* Socrates distinguishes between bad and good rhetoric; the former is mere persuasion of belief, while the latter is persuasion for the real good of the *psychē*.[20] Socrates does not practice bad rhetoric because confusion is a good educational remedy for a dogmatic character like Euthyphro.

At 11b Euthyphro says that he merely does not know how to state what he knows. The irony is that Socrates believes that if you know that *p*, then you can state and defend that *p*. Euthyphro cannot state what he thinks because he does not think anything clearly and correctly. But Euthyphro is still not in touch with his own ignorance. Euthyphro and Socrates then banter about who makes the *logoi* move about, and not stay fixed (11c-e). Euthyphro is unwilling to accept responsibility for the movement—that is failure—of his own *logoi*; Socrates, he thinks, makes them move, not him. Socrates also disclaims responsibility; he does not make the *logoi* move. Socrates' disclaimer is literally false since his questions produce the refutations. But Euthyphro is responsible for putting forth thoughtless accounts which betray a thoughtless life. Euthyphro never sees the failure as his own, and thus he never sees his own ignorance. Hence the Socratic *elenchus* fails to improve Euthyphro.

Socrates continues the *elenchus* and *psychagogia* at 11e-f by suggesting that the pious is a part of the right. Euthyphro again fails to follow Socrates, and so Socrates instructs him with some analogies. Finally he leads Euthyphro to say that piety is that part of the right which deals with our attention (*therapeia*) to the gods; the rest of the right deals with men (12e). Socrates will want to know what this attention is.

Socrates first interprets "attention" on the model of what a groom or trainer does for a horse. Such attention aims at the benefit of its subject (13b). But this is not correct because Euthyphro concedes that the gods are not improved by our attention to them (13c). Socrates attempts to draw Euthyphro to a more worthy conception of divinity, one where the divine cannot be improved by human actions.

A Hint at the Nature of Piety

Socrates then prods Euthyphro to say that attention is a service to the gods like what servants pay to their masters (13d). He pushes Euthyphro to say what our service to the gods helps them to accomplish (13e). Euthyphro can only claim that the gods do many fine things, but he does not know what we should do in order to serve them. He lamely suggests that we gratify them by praying and sacrificing to them

(14b), which position Socrates easily turns into Euthyphro's earlier account that piety is what is loved by the gods.

At 14b-c Socrates asserts that Euthyphro is *very close to answering his question, and instructing him, but he turns aside at the last moment (from the correct answer)*. This is an important clue to Socrates' position.[21] The gods do only fine things. How are we to be the servants of the gods, and make ourselves godlike? The obvious inference is that we become godlike by also doing fine and noble things. Euthyphro does not see this inference, and so the *psychagogia* fails. If Euthyphro had seen the inference, then Socrates could ask about what is necessary and sufficient for us to do good and noble things. The Socratic answer to this is the knowledge of good and evil. There is a slight hint at the importance of knowledge when Socrates twice describes Euthyphro's bastard knack of sacrificing and praying as knowledge (*epistēmē*). But Socrates must follow the answerer wherever he leads, and Euthyphro leads away from the truth, and back to his original position.

Plato, the author of our dialogue, at 14b-c attempts to get us, the readers, to pick up the threads of the discussion. The gods do only fine things; they are responsible for the *cosmos* within the *Cosmos*. If we are to be godlike, then we too should do fine things, but such doings require the knowledge of good and evil. But if piety is the knowledge of good and evil, then it is identical with the other virtues, and hence it is not a part of justice, the part dealing with our relations to the gods.[22] How are we to untie this *aporia* which is the same *mutatis mutandis* as the *aporia* about courage at the end of the *Laches*? I suggest that we untie the knot as follows: Socrates does not give any good reason why piety is a part of justice anymore than he gives a reason why courage is a part of virtue in the *Laches*. Both moves have as their sole justification the facilitation of the discussion, and nothing more. It is of heuristic value to investigate piety as a part of justice, but if the investigation reveals that piety, the knowledge of good and evil, embraces all of virtue, then we must reject the earlier hypothesis. The conventional demarcations of the virtues, I suggest, are accidental to their real nature. All virtuous actions are the manifestation of the knowledge of good and evil in different contexts. These contexts provide the conventional demarcations of the virtues.

Part of Plato's great dramatic art is to take an interlocutor's claim and infuse it with deeper meaning and significance. Socrates often agrees with the verbal formulations of his answerers' positions, but not with their understanding of them. In *Republic* I, for example, Thrasymachus claims that justice is the interest of the stronger; Socrates would agree with this, but he does not mean by "interest" and "stronger" what Thrasymachus does. The physical strength of Thrasymachus' just man is transmuted into psychic harmony and resistance against desire; the conventional goods of Thrasymachus are converted into the psychic well-being of Socrates. In the *Laches*, Laches' claim that courage is wise endurance is true, but Laches thinks that wisdom is mere technical art. In the *Euthyphro* piety is a service to the gods, but Euthyphro does not understand what this means and requires—wisdom. Thus Euthyphro has the correct verbal formulation in front of him, but he does not know how to understand it. Socrates hints at how we are to understand this account, but then he must follow Euthyphro back to his dogmatic position.

Socrates suggests that we are to become godlike. We are to become godlike by doing on a smaller scale what the gods do in the macrocosm. We are to do good and noble things just as the gods do. It is no longer wrong to be godlike. Piety is not distinct from the general requirement to do good things, and this is why in later dialogues piety recedes from the picture as a distinct virtue.[23]

Euthyphro's last attempt to define piety is that it is a giving to and an asking from the gods; piety is barter between gods and men (14e). Socrates refutes the claim that piety is a mercantile transaction by pointing out that while the gods give us all good things, they do not benefit from any of our gifts (14e-15a). Again Socrates attempts to have Euthyphro see the correct view of divinity, but Euthyphro circles back to the claim that piety is what is loved by the gods. Euthyphro dogmatically embraces his original position, and is unshaken by Socrates' efforts.

Socrates in the end reminds Euthyphro that he, among all men, must have clear knowledge about piety, or he would not dare to prosecute his own father (15d). Socrates requests more information, but he cannot detain Euthyphro who hurries from the scene (15e). Socrates remains steadfast, and ready to continue the conversation. The symbolism is obvious: Socrates displays his piety and courage by enduring in the search for piety (cf. *Laches* 194a), while Euthyphro exhibits his impiety and cowardice by leaving; Euthyphro is no more steadfast than his accounts.

Conclusion

Socrates uses a number of different techniques to attempt to educate Euthyphro. He uses refutation, *psychē*-leading, and confusion among others. But we learn from the character sketch of Euthyphro that there is little chance of Socrates' success. For Euthyphro's beliefs are rigid and dogmatic, and the end of the *Euthyphro* reconfirms their unbreakable nature. Socrates' arsenal of educational techniques, as large as it is, is not adequate to the task at hand. Euthyphro displays adequate goodwill and frankness with Socrates, but his dogmatism and lack of desire for the truth make him an unsuitable dialectical partner.

3. Character and Education in the *Laches*

The *Laches* is a magnificent example of how Plato integrates character, *logoi* (statements), and education.[1] The characters of the *Laches'* interlocutors dovetail with the words they speak, and both reveal the educational conditions of the interlocutors. The educational condition of an interlocutor will, in turn, determine how Socrates will attempt to educate that person. Hence we will study the whole of the *Laches* — character sketches, accounts, and Socrates' refutations of these accounts.

The explicit theme of the *Laches* becomes, in the second half of the dialogue, courage, but we must not lose sight of the fact that Lysimachus and Melesias call upon the generals, Laches and Nicias, to help them in training their sons.[2] Education is, to a great extent, the most important topic of the dialogue. Socrates emerges as the real educator, and he supplants the authority of the generals. Dialectic, replaces the sophistic education of Nicias and the unanalyzed experience of Laches. Through an analysis of the generals' characters and *logoi* we will see how their educations fail them.

Interlocutors

The two fathers, Lysimachus and Melesias, ask the two generals, Nicias and Laches, for their advice about whether fighting in armor will help make something out of their sons. The generals, if anyone, should be experts about the value of such an activity as they too have sons who need to be educated. First let us see what the two fathers are like.

Lysimachus and Melesias, especially the former, tell us much about themselves. Their fathers had many noble deeds both in war and peace, both in managing the city and the affairs of the allies (179c). But it

41

is "practically the rule" that such public men treat their private concerns, in this case the education of their own children, in a "slighting, careless spirit" (180b-c). Thus neither Lysimachus nor Melesias have any important deeds of their own to report to their children. Lysimachus and Melesias are failures, but late in life—Lysimachus was a close friend of Socrates' father (180e)—they desire to find expert help for their children so that they will turn out better.

The renowned grandfathers failed to educate their children. We are alerted to the Socratic view that men of conventional fame have only opinion which is a pale shade of real virtue, and that such a counterfeit excellence is not teachable (*Meno* 99e-100b). Socrates later introduces into the *Laches* the notion that a teacher of demotic virtue could either point to his teachers (he suggests sophists), or to those whom he makes better (185bff.). Socrates eventually shelves these criteria in favor of a direct Socratic test, but they introduce the interesting theme of education and specifically why fathers fail to educate their sons, given that they would strongly desire to do so. The grandfathers, Aristeides and Thucydides, are examples of prominent men who fail at education; their failure reflects a defect in them. Our generals will display a similar defect.

The fathers have no deeds to report because they have not obtained even the level of conventional wisdom and action.[3] The fathers are stay-at-homes; Lysimachus depicts himself as a former close friend of Socrates' father Sophroniscus (180d-e), in fact as his constant close companion, but he does not know if Socrates is Sophroniscus' son (180d-e). Socrates and Lysimachus are of the same deme, the same political unit (180c), and the fathers' children have frequently talked about Socrates (180e), but Lysimachus knows nothing about Socrates. Lysimachus provides a plausible explanation for his ignorance in old age; old age makes him spend his time at home (180d). The fathers even need the generals to escort them to the exhibition of fighting in armor. One may well wonder what the problem was with these fathers before the onset of old age.

Lysimachus is no better off at *logoi*. He requests that Socrates questions the generals (189c):

> . . . be our adviser by discussing it with them. For I find that owing to my age I forget the question I intend to put, and also the answers I receive; and if the discussion changes in the middle my memory goes altogether.

The fathers' words and deeds chime in harmony together — in the mode of absence! Lysimachus is totally unskilled at dialectic, and does not even have a sufficient memory to engage in it. Nor does he have the conventional ability to make speeches. Melesias, we may presume, is no better off; for he does not even speak for the two fathers. In terms of the line and cave in the *Republic*, the fathers are at the bottom level of image thinking. They are looking at the shadows on the wall, and have not even turned towards the "real" objects in the cave. But are not the fathers better off than most because they acknowledge their ignorance? They only desire for their sons to become men of public affairs like their grandfathers. The image men desire the arena of conventional opinion, and have no understanding of anything beyond that.

How do the generals Laches and Nicias stand as educators of their children? Nicias brags that Socrates introduces to him a music teacher, Damon, pupil of Agathocles, for his son, "who is not only the most exquisitely skilled of musicians, but in every other way as profitable a companion as you could wish for young men of that age" (180c-d). We should doubt that Socrates would send a boy of any potential to a sophist. Later Nicias recounts how he entreats Socrates to care for his son, Niceratus, but that Socrates always refuses and sends him to other men (200c-d). Slowly Nicias reveals that he, himself, is a student of Damon, and Damon gaines his wisdom from the word chopper Prodicus (197c). Like father, like son. Nicias cannot educate his son, but asks Socrates to do it; when Socrates refuses, any sophist will fill the void. Niceratus must be a washout, and this throws an ironical light on the fathers' seeking expert advice from the generals about how to educate children. The generals have not made anyone better, and Nicias' teachers are sophists. Nicias' enthusiasm for sophists shows him to be a man of words, but as we shall see, in a very defective sense. Laches, we will learn, is not even a man of words; thus we do not hear how he educates his son, but we may assume that he did not do very well. I will discuss the generals at greater length below.

What do we learn about Socrates in the opening pages of the *Laches*? The most striking information comes from the purported man of deeds, Laches, who praises Socrates for his bravery in the retreat from Delium (181a-b):

> He [Socrates] accompanied me in the retreat from Delium, and I assure you that if the rest had chosen to be like him, our city would be holding up her head and would not then have had such a terrible fall.

Socrates is praised for his bravery in retreat. Laches testifies that Socrates is a proven man of deeds. Laches also shows his ineptness at dialectic, and his poor memory, when he later defines courage as staying steadfast at one's post. But what is most important about Laches' praise is that we see Socrates as a man of *erga*; Socrates is brave when he ought to be brave.

We also find out that Socrates, unlike all the others, is "always spending his time wherever there is any such excellent study or pursuit for young men as you are seeking" (180c). This is a strong hint that Socrates endures in the search for understanding, and the remainder of the dialogue will confirm this. Socrates is the hero of the dialogue; his words and deeds chime in harmony together.[4]

At 181d Socrates takes his usual ironic posture:

> It seems to me, however, most proper that I being so much younger and less experienced than you and your friends, should first hear what they have to say, and learn of them; and then, if I have anything else to suggest as against their remarks, I might try to explain it and persuade you and them to take my view.

Socrates, the man who is always investigating the value of such pursuits, declines to give a speech about fighting in heavy armor. The two generals, who are deemed by the many to be experts, become anxious to give their opinions. The Socratic irony provides an environment in which the purported experts feel comfortable and even obliged to commit themselves on some subject.

The Great Speeches of Nicias and Laches

Nicias is very enthusiastic about fighting in armor. It improves the bodily health, and is particularly fitting for a free citizen (182a). It is also advantageous in war when the ranks are broken and you must fight man to man. Nicias then makes vastly inflated claims: Whoever possesses this accomplishment will desire to learn other military matters such as the management of troops, and even the "whole art of generalship" (182b-c). Nicias' speech is full of epistemic terms to describe fighting in armor.[5] At 182c he boldly declares that it is an *epistēmē* (a knowledge).

A clear picture of Nicias' character emerges from his speech. Nicias loves any new sophistic display whether of words or fighting. Fighting in armor has just come into vogue, and Nicias uncritically embraces it. Nicias is infatuated with fighting in armor just as he is infatuated with Damon. Nicias, the man of words, the intellectual, embraces the new "arts" but he does not use discernment. Nicias will show himself to be a very defective intellectual.[6] Finally Nicias does not mention deeds at all in his speech, nor is he concerned with the background of the man who gives the exhibition.

Laches is not at all sure that the display before him is a real art, and even if it is an art, Laches is not sure that it is a good thing to learn (182d-e). Laches emphasizes that the teachers of these new fighting techniques are deficient in *erga*. These teachers avoid Lacedaimon as if it were holy ground, but there, if anywhere, they could judge the value of some military art. Moreover, none of the sophistic teachers distinguishes himself in war (183b-c). Stesilaus, who is giving the display, makes a fool of himself in actual combat with the new-fangled scyth-spear. Since Stesilaus is miserably deficient in *erga*, we should strongly suspect this new art which he purports to teach.

Laches conservatively analyzes what is new. Only if a new art or speech is supported by deeds will he see any value in it. A teacher, who is without deeds, is not to be trusted. Laches views himself as a man of deeds not words. He counterbalances Nicias who sees himself as a man of words. Nicias is so caught-up in his own rhetoric that he hardly sees Stesilaus when he claims that fighting in armor leads to the whole art of generalship. We will want to watch the generals to see if they fulfill their own opinions of themselves.[7]

The experts disagree with one another. The clear implication is that at least one of the generals must be wrong. The unbalanced nature of the speeches — between word and deed — indicates that both experts lack balance and harmony. We may strongly suspect at this point that a really courageous person would have to harmonize both words and deeds.[8]

Socrates is asked to decide the tie between the generals. He refuses and leads Melesias to agree that they need expert advice (184e-185a). Experts in such matters would either have good teachers, or could point to some young men whom they have improved. But, Socrates asks, what are these experts experts about? What is the real subject of their discourse? The generals and fathers think that the subject is fighting in armor. But Socrates through a series of analogies forces them to agree that the "present subject is an accomplishment studied for the sake of young men's *psychai*" (185d-e). Socrates, through a refinement of the question at issue, transmutes the search into a search for an expert in the "treatment of the *psychē*" (185e).[9]

Why is Socrates concerned with *psychē*? For Socrates, as well as in general Greek culture, the *psychē* is what explains why something acts or moves as it does. The *psychē* is the source of motion or the motive energy within a person. The *Laches*, unlike the *Euthyphro*, displays the Socratic turn in ethics; Socrates turns away from behavioral accounts of the virtues and into the *psychē* which causes virtuous behavior.[10] In other words Socrates is interested in what it is about a person which produces and causally explains his courageous behavior. The center of gravity for the *Laches* is the *psychē*, not the transcendent Forms,[11] nor characteristics of classes of acts. Therefore Socrates' question is the generals' question about what makes someone brave, and not the philosophical question about the meaning of the word "courage," or an analysis of the concept of courage.[12] An expert in the care of the *psychē* is needed to answer the substantial psychological question. Since neither general knows the real subject at issue, we should not be surprised to see that they are not the experts.

Socrates ironically pursues the question of who has good teachers, or who can display the young men he improves by his teaching. Nicias could, of course, display his sophist teachers, and Laches his deeds. Socrates, however, does not have any teachers, since he does not have money to pay them, but he longs for such wisdom from his youth up (186b-c). Socrates, moreover, declares that he is powerless to discover the art for himself (186c). But he would not be surprised if the generals have learnt or discovered such wisdom, for they are: (1) more wealthy, (2) older and thus have had more time to learn or discover it, and (3) confidently declare themselves about what pursuits are harmful or beneficial for a youth, and they would not do this unless they had the requisite knowledge (186c-d). Socrates is ironical in these claims; he denigrates his own wisdom, while praising on conventional grounds the "wisdom" of the generals. If Socrates is more ignorant than the generals, then they need not fear his refutations. It is essential to Socratic dialectic that an answerer's natural resistance to stating his most central beliefs be overcome. It is central to the military personality that it views itself as an expert on bravery; a challenge to this expertise would produce resistance against answering. Socratic irony overcomes the resistance, and the generals are prepared to answer.[13]

Lysimachus is quite taken with Socrates' humility, and he asks the generals to help them by answering Socrates' questions. At this point dialectic replaces the authority of the generals.[14] Both generals agree to answer, and each proceeds to pontificate about his attitude to discussion. These little speeches again set each general's character.

Nicias proclaims a firsthand acquaintance with Socrates' method of question and answer (187e-188c), and he appears to understand that Socrates' discussion will be about him and Laches and how they lead their lives. Nicias appears to see that he and Laches will have to give an account of their lives (*logon didonai*), and will have to defend their accounts against Socrates' questions. But as the dialogue progresses there is considerable reason to doubt whether Nicias has any more than the most superficial acquaintance with Socratic dialectic. At best Nicias has observed Socrates at work and can repeat what he saw, but without understanding or self-application. For Nicias' answers will reveal that he has not really thought much about the question at issue, although it is a question any general should have thought much about. Nicias consults with sophists and he consults with Socrates as another sophist; Nicias has a taste for *logoi*, but it is at the most superficial level.[15]

Nevertheless, Nicias' words alert us that Socratic education is about the learner and not some foreign subject matter. Socrates forces an interlocutor to state and to defend those beliefs which are most central to the interlocutor's self-image. Socrates does compel one to render an account of one's life, even though Nicias, as we will see, never understands fully what this means.

Laches reveals much about his character when he describes his attitude toward dicussions (188c-d):

> For you might think me a lover, and yet also a hater, of discussions: for when I hear a man discussing virtue or any kind of wisdom, one who is truly a man and worthy of his argument, I am exceedingly delighted; I take the speaker and his speech together, and observe how they sort and harmonize with each other. Such a man is exactly what I understand by "musical" – he has tuned himself with the fairest harmony . . . has made a true concord of his own life between his words and deeds. . . .

From this quote one might suppose that Laches believes in a harmony between words and deeds, but such is not the case. For Laches, when he praises Socrates—for the second time—for his courage in retreat, emphasizes that he will listen to *logoi* only when they are made by a real man (189a-b). The deeds must come first, and then one may dabble in words as an enjoyable pastime.

Laches' little speech reminds us that deeds without a proper understanding of whether and how they should be done are useless. If we do not know what courage is, then we do not know whether any particular deed is courageous. *Erga* require *logoi*, but, as we will see, they must be *logoi* of a special sort.

Nicias has at best a superficial acquaintance with Socratic dialectic, and he has no deeds to report. Nicias has never even engaged seriously in Socratic dialectic. Laches is all deeds and no words; his life also is disharmonious and full of disaster.[16] We should not be surprised if both generals, due to the lopsided nature of their lives, prove defective on all fronts.[17] They will fail as dialecticians, educators, and generals.

Socrates sets the stage for the *elenchus* (refutation). He introduces an analogy which reveals that they are searching for the virtue or excellence of a *psychē* (189e-190b). Just as sight is the proper power of the eye, so too virtue is the excellence of a *psychē*; and just as an eyedoctor attempts to produce sight in the eyes, so too a real teacher attempts to produce virtue in the *psychē* (190b). The notion of crafting or producing virtue in the *psychē* is not compatible with the transcendent theory of Forms. These Forms are ungenerated and indestructible; they are not produced in anything. Moreover, Forms are not in *psychai* because they do not depend upon them or anything else for their existence. Thus the courage which Socrates seeks is not a Form, nor is it a pale image of a Form. For nowhere in the *Laches* does Socrates talk about courage or virtue as an image or ikon of some separate Form. The center of gravity for the *Laches* is the *psychē* and not the Forms.

Socrates gains two important admissions from Laches even before Laches' first definition. These admissions will be important later in the dialogue. First, Laches assents to the claim that if you know something, then you can say what it is (190c). By "say" Socrates means "clearly state and defend against a Socratic attack." The educational attainment of an answerer can be judged by how he reacts to this claim after refutation. If an interlocutor still claims to know something even when he cannot defend it, then he does not accept his own ignorance. Second, Laches agrees that the inquiry will be easier if they discuss

only a part of virtue, the part that fighting in armor is meant to produce — courage (190c-d). No justification is given for the claim that
courage is a part of virtue, or even that virtue has parts. Nevertheless,
these claims are of great importance at the end of the dialogue where
they form the key premises in a paradox.

Laches on Courage

Laches' first account is that courage is staying at one's post, fac-
ing the enemy, and not running away (190e). Laches' account displays
his character; one can almost see Laches at Mantinea perish at his post.
Laches' words and deeds are consistent, but each is wrong. Laches has
already admitted that Socrates was brave in retreat, and so it is easy
for Socrates to refute him. Laches' memory appears to be no better
than Lysimachus'.

Socrates attempts to broaden Laches' concept of courage by stating
that he is after that courage which not only is shown in military activities of all sorts, but also in pain, fear, and the fight against desires
and pleasures (191d). Socrates so broadens the concept of courage that
it now includes what would normally be called temperance.[18] For to
fight against desire is temperance. This conflation of the behavioral
contexts for different virtues is, I will show, part of Socrates' attempt
to unite all the virtues in an identity.

Laches does not understand what Socrates seeks, and so Socrates
gives him another analogy: just as swiftness is the psychic *dynamis*
(power) to get a great deal done in a little time in many different activities, so too courage is the same psychic *dynamis* in all the different
courageous actions (192b). Socrates is after the psychic power which
produces courageous actions.

Laches understands the sort of thing Socrates seeks, and his second account is that courage is an endurance of the *psyche* (192b). The
Laches now moves to a deeper level than the *Euthyphro*; the definitions progress from a characteristic of a class of actions to the internal
psychic cause of courageous actions.

Socrates and Laches agree that whatever courage is, it is a noble
quality (192c). This premise is of crucial regulatory value for the discussion which follows.[19] Socrates uses it both to refute an interlocutor's
account, and to indirectly suggest the following Socratic argument:

(1) A virtue φ is necessarily noble and beneficial.

(2) Only knowledge of good and evil is necessarily beneficial.

∴ (3) A virtue φ is the knowledge of good and evil.

Simple endurance, Socrates points out, is not always noble; one might endure in a stupid or immoral cause. Socrates then suggests that Laches revise his account so that wise endurance is courage (192c-e). At first Laches gives his own account, but now Socrates offers to Laches a revised, better account, and this shift marks a transition in Socratic dialectic.[20] First Socrates practices pure *elenchus*, and then he moves to *elenchus* conjoined with *psychagogia*. In the former Socrates refutes Laches' attempts and seeks clarification; in the second he also suggests indirectly his own view. Socrates, as I will show, believes that, if properly interpreted, courage is wise endurance. The educational problem is to get Laches to see, for himself, how to understand this account.[21]

Socrates lodges a series of counterexamples (192e-193c) against the claim that courage is wise endurance, and all the counterexamples take knowledge to be some sort of technical ability.[22] But when technical knowledge is added to endurance, it may well be the case that the person who lacks such knowledge is more courageous than he who has it. For example, he who endures diving into a well with the technical art of such diving is less courageous than he who dives in without the art. Socrates paradoxically concludes that foolish endurance must be courage, since the man who endures without the art is more courageous than he who endures with it (193d). But foolish endurance is not always noble, so it cannot be courage. Socrates and Laches are, then, "refuted," and Socrates points out to Laches that neither of them has attuned his words with his deeds (193e). By their deeds they would be judged courageous, but not by their words.

What are we to see in this refutation? Certainly that endurance conjoined with technical expertise is not courage. But there are other types of knowledge — the knowledge of good and evil — which Laches does not consider. Socrates does not tell Laches what they are because Socrates does not want to teach by telling, since this could not produce the requisite wisdom. Since Laches does not see what sort of wisdom is required, Socrates permits the account to fail, and he presents that failure in the most paradoxical light possible. The claim that foolish endurance is courage is meant to shock and stimulate Laches and us to investigate for ourselves what courage is, and what sort of knowledge other than technical expertise it requires. But Laches does not have the appropriate dialectical skill to pick up the hints and search for the required knowledge. The refutation appropriately is also aimed at Laches who sees himself as a courageous man of endurance with little interest in words.

At the end of this disscussion Socrates admonishes Laches with what is almost a riddle (194a):

> . . . let us too be steadfast and enduring in our inquiry, so as not to be ridiculed by courage herself for failing to be courageous in our search for her when we might perchance find after all that this very endurance is courage.

This is a strong hint that endurance in the end will prove to be an aspect of courage. Endurance also seems to have two important manifestations: persistence in action in general, and persistence in the dialectical search for truth. As we shall see, *Laches fails even as a man of action because he does not endure in the search for courage*. At 196c Laches refuses to ask Nicias any more questions, and at 197e Laches refuses to attend to what Nicias says even though Socrates (ironically) claims that Nicias is worthy of further attention. Laches' failure in action results from his failure with words; he does not understand the importance of enduring in some types of actions.

194b indicates Laches' educational condition. Laches claims that he knows what courage is, but is just not quite able to state it correctly. Laches fails to remember that he agreed earlier with Socrates that if you know something, then you can state it. Laches' lapse of memory betrays a lack of that basic wisdom which is the admission of one's own ignorance. And yet Socrates' efforts with Laches are not an unambiguous failure. Even though unaccustomed to discussion, Laches desires more at least for a while, and he is puzzled that he cannot say what courage is (194a).

Nicias on Courage

As with Laches, the discussion with Nicias is divided into two sections. In the first Laches questions Nicias, and Nicias displays his verbal dexterity by confounding Laches. In the second Socrates takes hold of the conversation, and drives Nicias into a paradox. Nicias does not see how to resolve the paradox, and hence he shows that he is deficient in *logoi*.

Nicias' first account is something which he has often heard Socrates say: that a man is good in that wherein he is wise, and bad in that wherein he is unlearned (194c-d). Socrates clarifies this for Laches by claiming that Nicias means that courage is a kind of wisdom (194d). Nicias learns his account from Socrates, but as we shall see, he cannot explain it at all. Moreover, at the end of the discussion when he is refuted, Nicias says that he will consult again with the sophist Damon to remedy the defects in his account (200b). Nicias is basically a sop; he uncritically soaks up what he hears from others, and he thinks that intellectual problems can be solved simply by consulting the sophistic experts. Nicias is as defective at theory as Laches is at deeds. A real man of theory could state, clarify, and defend his account against a Socratic attack.[23]

Nicias reformulates his position by saying that courage is the knowledge of what is to be dreaded or dared either in war or in anything else (194e-195a). Laches rushes to the attack; do not doctors know what is to be dreaded and dared in disease and sickness? Are they not then courageous? Nicias replies that doctors only know what is healthy and diseased, but not whether it is better for some sick person to be healed or not (195c-d). Laches suggests that the seers must have the prerequisite knowledge, but Nicias cleverly replies that the seers only predict facts, not whether it is better or not for something to occur.[24] Nicias then distinguishes, following the sophist Prodicus, between mere fearlessness and boldness on the one hand and courage on the other, in order to rule out the Crommyonian sow and other animals as courageous. Animals have at best mere boldness. Laches becomes increasingly restive with the conversation, and finally after correctly accusing Nicias of decking himself out with fine words, he loses his endurance for it (197c-e). But Nicias, for all his fine maneuvers, does not seem to know what he is really talking about; he just keeps denying that this or that type of person has the real knowledge of what is to be dreaded and dared. Nicias is only facilely a man of *logoi*, and thus he would not know that the dialectician has the knowledge he seeks.

Socrates picks-up the questioning of Nicias, and the conversation begins to progress. First Socrates reminds Nicias that they earlier agreed that courage is only a part of virtue, there being also other parts (198a). They then agree to the following claims:

(1) Those things that are dreaded are anticipated evils, and those that are dared are anticipated goods (198b-c).

(2) There is a single knowledge of past, present, and future goods and evils (198d-199b).

∴ (3) Courage is the knowledge of all goods and evils (199b-c).

(4) But someone who knows all goods and evils would have the whole of virtue (199d-e).

∴ (5) The wisdom of good and evil is the whole of virtue.

(6) We previously agreed that courage is a part of virtue (199e).

∴ (7) We have not discovered what courage is (199e).

Nicias and Socrates have only discovered the whole of virtue, not courage, and thus they are worsted every way in their search. But the above argument is very peculiar; we are led to either agree that courage is only a part of virtue, and to find something wrong with (1) through (5), or to believe that courage is identical with the other virtues (is the whole of virtue), and to reject (6). Commentators have not been reticent to find purported logical fallacies in (1) through (5),[25] but I see no evidence in the text that Socrates wishes to relinquish these claims. For example, if there is a master art of good and evil, then it makes perfectly good sense to see this art as dealing with goods and evils at all times. (6) on the other hand was simply agreed to in order to make their conversation more convenient. If we reject (6), then courage is the whole of virtue. This conclusion would also fit with our analysis of Nicias' character. Nicias is a man of defective words; he does not understand what he hears and then repeats. In particular Nicias would not understand the "unity of the virtues," especially that courage is the whole of virtue. Nicias would then see the conversation as aporetic (perplexing), and Socrates would achieve two goals: (1) he would not be directly telling Nicias anything which Nicias could uncritically repeat, and (2) he would be using *psychagogia* (*psychē*-leading) by challenging each person to unravel the paradox. I believe that Socrates pushes Nicias to the position which he, Socrates, embraces, and then at the last moment turns it over with a contrived paradox the pedagogical purpose of which is to stun Nicias, leave him in *aporia*, and hopefully activate any potentialities for Socratic dialectic which Nicias might have.

Nicias, however, is very unpromising material. Plato gives us ample hints that his words and deeds are completely disharmonious with one another. At 198e-199a Nicias agrees that the general should give orders to the seer, not the converse; but we know from Thucydides that in the Sicilian campaign Nicias, the general, listened to the seer, and the result was disaster for Athenian arms. Nicias' words and deeds do not chime together because Nicias is not committed to what he says or hears. He simply mimics the most recent expert. Thus Nicias goes away to consult Damon, and is not stung by the Socratic *elenchus*.

The Unity of Word and Deed

Let us summarize how the various characters of the *Laches* shape up with respect to word and deed. The fathers Lysimachus and Melesias have neither words nor deeds; they live in images of conventional reality. Laches claims to be a man of deeds, but he shows himself deficient in his purported strength when he refuses to continue the conversation with Nicias. Laches' failure in deeds is also an inability to understand the importance of the search for wisdom. Nicias prides himself on his verbal dexterity; but his superficial ability at words does not help him survive a Socratic discussion. Hence Nicias does not have the intellectual resources to escape from Socrates' paradox. Nicias' military failure in the Sicilian expedition results, in part, from listening to a seer; Nicias listens to seers because he does not know how to acquire real knowledge. Socrates is the hero of the dialogue. He is courageous on the battlefield, and he endures in the discussion. Hence we see that dialectic is the real teacher, and Socrates is the real pupil. Moreover, Socrates, as his hints indicate, knows what courage is. Socrates' words and deeds chime in harmony together, and thus he is a complete person.

But what really is courage? From the discussion with Laches it would seem to be endurance, and from the discussion with Nicias the knowledge of good and evil. Courage, then, would appear to have two components. If this were so, then courage could not be simply identical with the knowledge of good and evil, since endurance would also be a necessary component of it.[26] However, just as we should unite the real strengths of wisdom and endurance in a single person, so too wisdom and endurance are not really distinct. For Socrates epistemic states are psychic motive forces.[27] The more one's beliefs are tied down in the *psychē* by reasons, the stronger is the motive force for action. In the *Meno* the difference between true belief and knowledge is twofold (98a-b): (1) knowledge is tied down in the *psychē* by reasons while mere true beliefs are not (cf. *Meno* 85cf.), and (2) knowledge unlike belief is an abiding and stable state. An abiding and stable state would, I believe, produce a strong disposition for action, one which could not be overthrown. Thus in the *Protagoras* Socrates says about knowledge (352c):

> . . . do you consider that knowledge is something noble and able to govern man, and that whoever learns what is good and what is bad will never be swayed by anything to act otherwise than as knowledge bids.

The use of force and strength terminology in this passage vividly displays the extent to which the epistemic condition of knowledge is also a motive force. Elsewhere I have argued that Socrates treats knowledge this way because he conflates two models for the *psychē*: It is like a web of belief, and Socrates tests the coherence of the web, and it is the source of motion for an agent.[28]

Why does Socrates emphasize at the end of the discussion with Laches that they should endure in the search for knowledge of courage? There are a number of reasons. The more one clarifies and defends one's beliefs the closer one comes to knowledge. The slave boy in the *Meno* (85c-d) would change true opinion into knowledge if he went over the geometrical problems in many different ways. As Gregory Vlastos emphasizes, Socratic "knowledge" is revisable; it is always possible that one is wrong, and so one must entertain new objections as they emerge.[29] Socrates does not tell us exactly when true opinion becomes knowledge.

Should Socrates identify courage with the knowledge of good and evil? What if someone practiced Socratic dialectic quite diligently and successfully but for unforeseen reasons was simply wrong? This counter-example implies that Socrates should identify courage with warranted belief, not knowledge or true belief. Courage is not knowledge because knowledge must be about what is true. Courage is not true belief because true belief can come in just about any way, and need not be warranted at all.[30] I think that it would be best to view the knowledge of good and evil as a regulative ideal. It would be the completely clear, consistent, and complete account; one which is defensible against all possible objections. Socrates identifies courage with this ideal because it is the ultimate goal we should strive for; the virtues would be identical because each virtue is a striving for the same goal. In any case, the more one's accounts are defended with reasons, the greater the motive force for action. This is the theory behind the phrase "words and deeds chiming in harmony together," and only Socrates displays such symphony.

Robert Hoerber argues that the structure of the *Laches* points to two aspects or two definitions of courage, since most things in the *Laches* occur in dyads.[31] There are two fathers, two generals, Socrates and his father, Stesilaus and whoever recommended him, and two pairs of sophists—Damon and Agathocles (180c-d), Damon and Prodicus (197d)—mentioned twice. The dialogue itself is divided into two major sections: (A) the introductory material, and (B) the discussions with the generals. (A) can be divided into (A1) the discussion of fighting in armor, and (A2) the search for excellence of the *psychē*. (B) can be divided into (B1) the discussion with Laches, and (B2) the discussion with Nicias. Both (B1) and (B2) can be divided into the *elenchus* and *psychagogia* phases discussed earlier.

The number of dyads in the *Laches* is far beyond chance, and must be intentional. This dramatic, literary structure suggests that courage is endurance and wisdom. But the greatest harmony of all is an identity. Clearly we are to unite endurance and wisdom and thus produce a complete account of courage. Socrates, the complete person, has this unity.

4. Natural Virtue and Education in the *Charmides*

Charmides and Critas are the interlocutors in the *Charmides*, and they become prominent members of the thirty tyrants, and gain renown for their intemperate, bloodthirsty behavior.[1] Charmides has a natural sort of virtue and temperance,[2] and for this reason the conversation begins with him, and the dialogue focuses on him as the center of interest.[3] At the end of the dialogue Charmides does what few interlocutors do, he admits his ignorance and says that he wants to be charmed by Socrates for the rest of his life. The *Charmides* is the arena where Socrates struggles for Charmides' *psychē* and, at least for a time, wins.[4] But what effect does Socrates have on Charmides, and is Socrates responsible for Charmides' later tyranny? Does Socrates' refusal to teach by telling promote bad behavior?

Another puzzle is that the real nature of temperance is not at all clear in the dialogue, and that the classical view of temperance as *cosmos* or harmony is not mentioned. Only a close look both at the arguments and at the drama in the *Charmides* can unravel these perplexities.[5]

Socrates' Temperance

Socrates has just returned from the terrible Athenian defeat at Potidaea, and he immediately resumes his real love: philosophical conversation. We immediately see that Socrates manifests one aspect of temperance; he postpones the gratification of conversation to do what is right, i.e. to serve in the army. We know from Alcibiades in the *Symposium* that Socrates is very brave in this battle. The men and boys in the wrestling school eagerly ask Socrates about the battle, and Socrates answers their questions, but he never mentions his own bravery

(153b-c). Thus we see Socrates manifest a second aspect of temperance — modesty. At 155d Socrates is inflamed by what he sees when Charmides' cloak accidentally falls open, but he controls himself, and proceeds to converse about temperance with Charmides. Socrates' bravery at Potidaea also is his self-control in retreat from the enemy. Hence we see Socrates practice self-control in a number of different contexts.

Socrates instantiates many of the characteristic dimensions of temperance, but most important he is single-minded about the pursuit of wisdom (153a, d). Chaerephon excessively praises Charmides' physical beauty (154c-d), as do the other numerous lovers of Charmides, but Socrates only is concerned with the boy's *psychē*. Socrates will strip Charmides' *psychē*, not his body (154e). Hence we have an important clue that wisdom, the knowledge of good and evil, grounds all true manifestations of temperance.[6]

The character sketch of Socrates immediately contrasts Socrates with Protagoras in the *Protagoras*. Protagoras denies that courage and temperance are found together, for he believes that they are antithetical virtues.[7] To have the one renders one unable to have the other. But Socrates embodies both virtues because he approximates the knowledge of good and evil, which is each virtue. The *Charmides* concludes that only the knowledge of good and evil is necessarily beneficial, but since each virtue is, according to Socrates, necessarily beneficial, we must conclude that each virtue is this knowledge.

The major regulatory premise of the *Charmides* is that temperance must be noble and beneficial (cf. 159b-c).[8] A regulatory premise is a condition which the participants agree must be satisfied by any adequate answer. If an account is to survive *elenchus* (refutation), then it must satisfy this regulatory premise. A satisfactory answer to the question "What is temperance?" must show that temperance is beneficial. All of Charmides' and Critias' attempts to define temperance fail to satisfy this regulatory premise. The same regulatory premise, but about courage, governs the conversation in the *Laches*, and courage is there also shown to be the knowledge of good and evil.

The search for temperance is the overt topic of the *Charmides*. We have already seen that Socrates illustrates several senses of "temperance." But "temperance" is a vague word with a broad range of applications.[9] On the one hand it means the "control over desires," but it also means simply "good sense." Socrates embodies all of the dimensions of temperance, and this is because he possesses their cause—the knowledge of good and evil. Socrates seeks what it is in a person which makes him be temperate and do temperate actions. Such a ground for temperance would unify and explain many of the diverse applications of the word.

Charmides and Critias

All eyes are on Charmides; even the other young boys cannot resist him (154c). Charmides has extraordinary bodily beauty (154d), as well as an excellent demeanor; he is modest in both speech and bodily comportment (158c-d, 176a-b).[10] Critias boasts that Charmides is also most temperate (157d). Socrates indicates that Charmides' temperance is natural, not acquired, since he has a noble lineage. He praises Charmides' ancestors as the cause of his renowned beauty and temperance (157e-158a). His ancestors are conventionally famous Athenians. Charmides has the right birth, at least by received standards. But his natural modesty and gracefulness is still only potentiality; his education will determine whether he becomes good or evil. But what we immediately see in the opening passages is that many compete to influence Charmides precisely because of his natural gifts.

Critias, in the *Charmides*, does not behave like the notorious tyrant he will become. He praises Charmides' natural temperance, recommends that temperance is "doing one's own business," and urges Charmides to associate with Socrates. But there are subtle hints that Critias is not what he seems to be. At 162c Critias is not able to restrain his desire to speak (Thrasymachus has a similar failing), and at 169c-d he is too ashamed to admit his own ignorance. At the end of the dialogue he and Charmides plot to *force* Socrates to share his charm. If Critias will not admit his own ignorance, then Socrates cannot educate him. Critias is an excellent example of someone whose bad tendencies ultimately are magnified because of a lack of education.[11]

The participants in the *Charmides* strongly resemble those of the *Lysis* and *Euthydemus*. Charmides, Lysis, and Cleinias all have a natural, untrained virtue. This natural virtue, with proper education, could become real virtue. Critias is similar to Ctesippus, Menexenus, and Euthydemus; they all represent base love, and the sophistic or poetic educational influence. Socrates must compete with these other men for control of the young men's souls, and Socrates is not very successful in this competition. Critias' influence on Charmides appears benign in the *Charmides*, but its ultimate result is not.[12]

Socrates is as steadfast in the *Charmides* as elsewhere; he can be tempted by physical beauty, but not diverted from his real goal which is the search for wisdom. Socrates, the real educator, channels the love for physical beauty into the love for *logoi*. The focus of the *Charmides* is on Charmides, and the main theme of the dialogue is education, and more specifically whose influence will control Charmides' *psychē*.

Charmides' Accounts of Temperance

Charmides has a headache. Socrates can cure it with a leaf remedy, but he must also apply a certain charm. Socrates has learned about this charm from certain esoteric and distant doctors (156d), but the charm is simply "words of the right sort" (157a-b). These words provide a therapy for the *psychē*, and one must treat the *psychē* before the body, since all good and evil for the whole person "springs from the *psychē* (156e). Charmides' headache is an opportunity for Socrates to get at his *psychē*. The proper charms (*logoi*) engender temperance in the *psychē*, and temperance provides health to the body (157b).

We may wonder whether Socrates really believes that all bodily disease and health comes from the *psychē*. But he makes this same claim in the *Republic* (403d), which supports an affirmative answer. Perhaps Socrates reasons as follows: The *psychē*, which is the erotic seat of desires, determines what the whole organism does or consumes. What we do or consume determines the health of our body. In any case, it is quite clear that intemperance causes some bodily diseases and headaches. Moreover, Charmides' headache occurs in the morning, and has a suspicious resemblance to a hangover![13]

Charmides submits to the charm, and Socrates twice directs him on how to seek for temperance (158e-159a, 160d). If temperance is in Charmides, then it will provide some perception of itself, and since Charmides speaks Greek he will be able to say what temperance is. Charmides is to look into himself, and see what quality temperance must have if it is to make Charmides good.

These are the only passages in the early dialogues which directly urge some type of introspection. But does temperance provide some appearance of itself to the temperate person who introspects?

Every virtue is both a psychic motive force for action, and an ability to state, clarify, and defend one's beliefs. Hence temperance is both an internal psychic state, and something which Charmides can articulate. But temperance does not have a characteristic appearance. I suggest the following interpretation of Socrates' instructions: Socrates asks Charmides to look inward for temperance both because temperance is an internal psychic state, and because *logoi* emerge from the *psyche*. Charmides is to dig deeply into himself for an account of temperance. When his accounts fail, we see that Charmides is vacuous; he is an empty shell of quiet behavior. Charmides is "good" through nature and accident, but there is nothing which grounds and holds his temperance.[14]

Charmides' first account is that temperance is doing everything orderly and quietly (159b). This definition specifies a group of actions which purportedly includes all and only temperate actions. Socrates always rejects this type of definition which specifies types of behavior either by showing that it is too narrow or too broad. In this case the definition is both. At 159b-c Socrates and Charmides agree on the regulatory premise that temperance is a noble (and hence beneficial) thing. Socrates then shows that quiet acts are no more good than bad; for some quiet acts are less desirable than quick ones. Hence this group of actions cannot define temperance.

Charmides' second account is that temperance is modesty, and modesty makes men ashamed or bashful (160e). This account picks out an internal psychic cause of temperate behavior, but it is the wrong cause.[15] Since Charmides is enamored of the poets, Socrates ironically quotes Homer who says that, "Modesty, no good mate for a needy man," and thus modesty produces both good and bad actions (161a-b).[16] Temperance is always good because its presence always produces good (161a-b), but modesty is good and bad because it has both effects.[17] Therefore modesty is not temperance. Charmides' two answers about temperance display both his lifestyle and his educational condition. Charmides is quiet and modest in whatever he does, even in intemperate drinking with friends![18] Since Charmides cannot sustain his answers, he shows that he does not know what temperance is, and hence is not really temperate.

Charmides exhausts his acquaintance with the superficial dimensions of natural temperance. He has heard his third account from someone else, and we soon learn that the person is Critias. Temperance,

Charmides says, is doing one's own business. Socrates treats this account as a riddle (161c, 162a), and thus raises the important question of how to interpret not only one's own words, but especially those of others. Socrates' interpretation is somewhat comical; since makings are a type of doing, and craftsmen make their own and other peoples' goods, they are not temperate. Craftsmen do (make) the business of other people. But a state in which each craftsman only makes his own goods is also unacceptable (161e). Charmides and Socrates are in a state of *aporia*, and they begin to doubt whether the author of this account knows what he means.

Socrates' interpretation of "doing one's own business" is as ironical as his treatment of Thrasymachus' "justice is the interest of the stronger," in the *Republic*. Since Milo the wrestler is "the stronger," and he eats meat, then meat is the interest of the stronger. But Socrates' ironical misinterpretations have an important function: they force the author of the account to clarify it, and this means that Critias must answer.[19] Socrates switches the conversation to Charmides' teacher. If Critias can be improved, then Charmides will also benefit, since Critias is both Charmides' cousin and his guardian.

Critias' Accounts of Temperance

Critias' clarification combines the "wisdom" of Hesiod (163b) with that of some sophist, perhaps Prodicus as Socrates suggests (163d). The mention of Prodicus marks a transition in the conversation. Charmides expresses views on temperance in accordance with how he lives, but Critias wants to win the sophistic contest of words.[20] Critias assigns implausible and even inconsistent meanings to "make," "work," and "do," and the upshot of his festival of words is that "the doing of good things is temperance" (163e). Socrates expresses some approval for Critias' statement, but he has one little question to ask: can the temperate be ignorant of their temperance? The "doing of good things" is a true statement about the temperate, but it gives only a *pathos* (effect) of temperance, not its *ousia* (essence or nature). Hence Socrates pushes Critias to explain the epistemic requirement for temperance.

Doctors, for example, do good things, but they may for some time be ignorant of their results. Critias is caught in a dilemma from which he never extricates himself. The only sort of benefit Critias is familiar with is found in the first-order knowledges such as medicine, moneymaking, cobbling, and the like. But if the temperate man produces this sort of product, then (1) temperance will not be always beneficial, (2) the temperate man will not know always that he is temperate—produces a good product, and (3) the temperate person will need to possess the first-order knowledges, since only these produce their specific products, medicine/health, cobbling/shoes, and so on. On the other hand, Critias senses that temperance is not like the other knowledges, but he has no notion of what it is about or what it produces.

Critias proclaims on the basis of the Delphic Motto "Know Thyself" that temperance is self-knowledge (164b). But for a Greek a cognitive power like knowledge is directed intentionally at something, and frequently has a characteristic *ergon* (result, 165d). "Knowledge" is also a success term. Knowledge just like sight is of or about something, or else there is no knowledge. With these characteristics of the Greek concept of knowledge, Socrates asks what the product of self-knowledge is. Critias correctly replies that some types of knowledge, for example geometry, do not have products, and self-knowledge is like geometry. But Socrates responds that geometry is, nevertheless, about lines, planes, points, and the like, which are distinct from geometrical knowledge. What, then, he asks is self-knowledge about? Critias is perplexed seriously since he senses that self-knowledge is not like the other types of knowledge, but he does not know what special benefit it provides. Moreover, the only goods he is familiar with are the products and objects of the first-order arts—health, shoes, and so on. In desperation he claims that self-knowledge is a second-order knowledge which is about itself and the other knowledges (166c). The knowledge of good and evil is also a second order knowledge which is over all other types of knowledge, and hence Critias' new account is a step in the right direction, but, ironically, Critias does not know anything about this.

Critias is frustrated, and he accuses Socrates merely of attempting to refute him. Here we see that Critias is more interested in the contest, and in saving face before the young men, than in the search for truth. Critias denies his own ignorance, and attributes his difficulties to Socrates. Socrates responds with his famous irony. He questions Critias only because he does not know the truth about the matter at issue (165b-c, 166c-d). But Socrates uses the regulatory premise to trap both Charmides and Critias, and he knows, as I will show, that only the knowledge of good and evil satisfies the regulatory premise. Does Socrates lie when he says that he does not know the truth? Gregory Vlastos in another context persuasively argues that Socrates does not. If "knowledge" is irrevisable, dogmatic belief, then Socrates does not have such knowledge.[21] But this is part of the poetic, sophistic concept of knowledge which Critias accepts. Of course Socrates could still have strong, justified beliefs about what temperance is, and use these beliefs to refute other accounts. But as long as these beliefs are revisable, they do not count as knowledge in the dogmatic sense, and hence Socrates does not lie.

Critias must first show that second-order knowledge is possible, and then that it is beneficial (167b). Knowledge, Socrates points out, is a *dynamis* (power, 168b), and powers are directed at certain objects or states of affairs which are independent of them. Sight sees color, hearing hears sound, love loves the beloved, and wish is of the future good. These powers do not appear self-reflexive, or else they would have the characteristics of their objects: sight would be colored, love beloved, and so on. Relations, moreover, cannot be self-reflexive; the greater is greater than the smaller, the double double of the half, and the like. A knowledge which is about itself appears impossible. But at 168e-169a Socrates concedes that some people would allow a motion which moves itself, and a heat which consumes itself. In fact in the *Phaedrus* (245c-e) Plato defines *psychē* as a self-moving mover. Is knowledge more like sight or motion? Socrates does not know.

Is self-knowledge, a knowledge of what one knows and does not know, beneficial? Socrates employs a masterful destructive dilemma to show that it is not. Either this second order knowledge is of what one knows and does not know, or it is only that one knows or does not know. On the former alternative one knows the content of all types of knowledge, on the latter one only knows that someone possesses some knowledge or other. Socrates rejects the first horn by arguing that only the special craftsmen know the content of their respective crafts (170cff.). Only a doctor knows about health, and a carpenter about wood. Socrates rejects the second horn because one would know only that someone possesses some knowledge or other (170d). But if one does not have first-order knowledge, then he cannot detect what specific knowledge is present. To simply know that someone possesses some knowledge or other is of little or no benefit.

At 170e-171a Socrates presents a paradox which hints at a solution to the *aporia*. The doctor *qua* doctor only knows medicine, and not second-order knowledge. But since medicine is knowledge, and the doctor does not have knowledge of knowledge, he does not know medicine. The temperate man knows second-order knowledge, but not the content of any knowledge. Hence he knows nothing of any use. A synthesis of second and first-order knowledge would solve these perplexities. But where are we to find such a synthesis? Moreover, how can the temperate person be aware of his temperance? This latter question started the discussion of self-knowledge in the first place.

Dialectic, I suggest, is the solution to the problem. For dialectic closely conjoins both first and second-order knowledge. Dialectic can reveal the proper use of each first order knowledge.[22] Certain rules and background conditions, as we will see in the *Gorgias*, define dialectic, and if one follows these rules, then a justified claim to knowledge can emerge from such a conversation. If one states, clarifies, and defends a belief in a dialectical conversation, then that belief becomes claimable as knowledge even if it is later revisable. Dialectic is the method for acquiring knowledge of good and evil, and if beliefs are tied down in a *psychē* by good reasons (cf. *Meno* 98a), then knowledge is present in that *psychē*. Moreover, anyone who submits to a dialectical test of his beliefs, if honest, will either survive the test or admit his ignorance. Therefore "Know Thyself" is, for Socrates, an exhortation to test dialectically one's beliefs.[23] The *Charmides* itself, as a dialectical discussion, is an attempt to know oneself. If the participants in the discussion either admit their own ignorance, or agree that some belief is correct, then they achieve self-knowledge. Thus we see in the *Charmides* a convergence of its major notions; dialectic is true philosophy, and the philosophical life is, at least, the road to temperance. Since Socrates is the true dialectician, he is also the man who approaches temperance.

The Real Nature of Temperance

Socrates asks Critias to imagine that self-knowledge is the infallible ability to pick out who has and who does not have some first-order knowledge. Error would then be abolished, but Socrates wonders, would we do well and be happy (172a)? At 172c Socrates states that their inquiry has been worthless, for he has a dream that the knowledge of what one knows and does not know does not make us do well and be happy. As is often the case, Socrates' dream intuitions introduce his most cherished thoughts, and there immediately follows one of the most important passages in the dialogues (173b-d):[24] Socrates depicts a technologically perfect state; only the real experts are at work in this state. All and only real doctors practice medicine, and likewise for each craft. Moreover, all and only real seers foretell the future; charlatans and ignorant pretenders are banished from this state. But will we do well and be happy in such a technologically perfect state? Critias and Socrates agree that we would not. One might accomplish what one desires, but one might not know what one ought to desire.

Socrates compels Critias to see, at least for the moment, that rule by the first-order knowledges does not make one do well and be happy. This is a common theme of other early dialogues. The *Laches, Meno, Euthydemus, Apology*, and *Gorgias* all distinguish the purported goods of the body and *psychē*, for example gold, health, boldness, and endurance, from what is really beneficial. All of these "goods" can be used either for good or evil. Critias admits that it is only knowledge about certain things which produces real benefit (173e). Critias and Socrates eliminate one knowledge after another until Critias, with unusual insight, sees that it is the knowledge of good and evil which is intrinsically beneficial (174b-c). We are brought back to Critias' earlier definition of temperance, "the doing of good things." We now see what makes one able to do good things: the knowledge of good and evil. Neither Charmides nor Critias have such knowledge, since they cannot say what temperance is.

Implicitly Socrates has a very simple argument in the *Charmides*:

    (1) Temperance is necessarily beneficial.
    (2) Only the knowledge of good and evil is necessarily beneficial.
∴ (3) Temperance is the knowledge of good and evil.

The same argument can be used *mutatis mutandis* for each virtue.

Socrates and Critias appear to discover what temperance is, but Socrates goes on to claim that this is not the case. He says that temperance is not the knowledge of good and evil because they agreed earlier that temperance is the knowledge of what one knows and does not know (174d). Moreover, since only the knowledge of good and evil is beneficial, and since temperance is not this knowledge, temperance is not beneficial. Critias, reverting to his earlier position, asks why the knowledge of what one knows and does not know is not beneficial (174d), and Socrates tells him. Critias' conversion to what is really beneficial is short lived.

The *aporia* (perplexity and lack of passage) at the end of the *Charmides* serves a typical Socratic educational function. Socrates does not want to close a conversation with a successful answer, especially since both Critias and Charmides need much more practice at dialectical inquiry. And even if Socrates were to say that temperance is the knowledge of good and evil, Critias would not understand what this answer means.[25]

The *aporia*, however, is breakable, if one pays close attention to the devious twists and turns of the conversation. Socrates and Critias only agree to test the claim that temperance is the knowledge of what one knows and does not know. This is a hypothesis, and Socrates emphasizes that it is a dubious hypothesis. Hence it does not provide any reason why temperance is not the knowledge of good and evil. As if to reinforce this solution to the *aporia*, Socrates emphasizes repeatedly at the end of the dialogue that temperance is a great good (175e). But only the knowledge of good and evil is intrinsically good, and capable of making other things good.

What, then, is temperance in the *Charmides*? My answer is that it is the knowledge of good and evil. But while dialectic is the way to acquire such knowledge, no one ever completes the acquisition. Hence no one, including Socrates, is ever temperate completely. But the extent to which one leads or does not lead a philosophical life determines the extent to which one does or does not approximate to temperance. Temperance, then, admits of degrees just as does the knowledge which is achieved through dialectic. Therefore Socrates' philosophical posture is that of the temperate man. It follows that temperance requires courage since it takes great courage to embrace a life like that of Socrates.

Conclusion

The conversation with Critias is very lengthy and difficult to follow. What can we grasp from it, as well as the conversation with Charmides, about Socrates' educational tactics? Charmides, who is accustomed to praise and attention, has considerable natural talent which could be developed into real virtue. Socrates employs with Charmides an unconcealed *elenchus* which is noteworthy for its lack of rancor and irony. The purpose of such an *elenchus* is to get Charmides to see, for himself, that natural temperance is not real temperance, and that he does not have the knowledge to possess the latter. The conversation then shifts to Critias because Critias is the most important influence on Charmides. Socrates' conversation with Critias is noteworthy for its numerous sophistical interchanges both about the nuances of words, and about the types of knowledge. These interchanges both expose Critias' educational background and show that for all his sophistic erudition, he does not know what temperance is. Socrates also practices *elenchus* and *psychagogia* with Critias, but the latter is subordinated to the former because Critias never admits his ignorance. Hence Socrates leads Critias to the claim that temperance is the knowledge of good and evil, but then he rejects this claim for no good reason at all.

At the end of the dialogue Charmides admits his ignorance, and says that he desires to be charmed by Socrates every day of his life. Critias praises Charmides for his choice. Is Socrates, then, responsible for Charmides' later tyranny? The *Charmides*, itself, suggests a negative answer. There is a startling hint in the last lines of the dialogue about what happens. Critias and Charmides plot to force Socrates to display his charm: "You [Socrates] must expect me [Charmides] to use force, he replied, since he [Critias] gives me the command: take counsel, therefore, on your side, as to what you will do." Charmides' evil mentor Critias becomes his guardian, and Socrates does not charm Charmides for very long. Critias makes Charmides the tyrant. But it is not simply the victory of one man over one man, for the beginning of the dialogue shows Charmides under the influence of his many admirers, and it is the conventional fame and goods which such people promise which ultimately wins Charmides.

5. Friendship and Education
in the *Lysis*

The purpose of the *Lysis*, some commentators believe, is to show both that friendship must be mutual, and that it must be between a wise man like Socrates and a willing student like Lysis. Some commentators also claim that the *Lysis* reveals that friendships should not be, in any sense, utilitarian. I will deny both of these claims.[1] I will show that a purpose of the *Lysis* is to convince us that interpersonal friendship, even when mutual, is not the final, complete, and most satisfactory form of friendship. Interpersonal friendship is only a means to a better goal. Our real friend and what is really dear to us is, I will argue, wisdom or the knowledge of good and evil.[2] The *Lysis* moves from friendship as a phenomenon between persons to an impersonal conception of what is really to our benefit — wisdom. Hence the *Lysis* is, in a sense, utilitarian, but Socrates urges us to distinguish the popular goods from what is really beneficial.

The *Lysis* intertwines the topics of friendship and education. The highest human friend is the real educator; for only the real educator can lead us to wisdom.[3] The dramatic features of the *Lysis* display to us the dynamics of education.[4] Each pair of lover and beloved represents, as I will show, not only a type of friendship, but also a type of education.[5] Moreover, each interlocutor has a distinct type of *psychē*, and Socrates fits his words (*logoi*) to the type of *psychē* which he addresses. Socrates uses either refutation (*elenchus*) or positive *psychē*-leading (*psychagogia*) depending on the type of *psychē* he wants to educate, and in each case he exhorts the *psychē* to wisdom.[6] True love is of wisdom, and the *Lysis*, itself, is a protreptic speech which urges us to become wise.

Before we start I will make some brief remarks about *philos* (friend, or what is dear), *eros* (love), and *epithumia* (desire), as well as cognate terms. Commentators try to discern distinct, although

69

related, applications for these terms. D. Hyland, for example, claims that *epithumia* more appropriately applies to the baser desires than the other two terms, and R. Hoerber says that *philos* is the generic term of which the other two are species.[7] I do not deny the accuracy of these claims for at least some contexts. What I want to emphasize is that all three terms have coordinate and overlapping applications.[8] There are base desires, lovers, and friends as exemplified in Hippothales, and there are true lovers, friends, and desires as instantiated in Socrates. Each type of desire has a coordinate type of lover and friendship as well as the converse.

I will discuss the *Lysis* in the order in which the argument occurs since each successive phase of the dialogue reveals to us more of Socrates' beliefs. I will also show that the unconditional friend—the friend which is not for the sake of any other friend—is not a Platonic Form; it is simply the Socratic knowledge of good and evil. Hence the *Lysis* clearly should be included with the other early Socratic dialogues.[9]

The Dramatic Setting and Participants

The first pages of this dialogue are filled with meanings which only later are amplified. In the opening paragraphs Plato twice emphasizes that Socrates goes straight from the Academy to the Lyceum (203a). Socrates has a single purpose from which he will not be deflected. He hurries from one place where men of all ages meet and converse to another such place. Socrates, we may speculate, did not find a suitable opportunity for conversation in the Academy, and so he goes to the Lyceum.

Socrates goes to the Lyceum by the road outside the town wall, and he meets his interlocutors near the spring of Panops (203a). These allusions to nature, like those in the *Phaedrus*, remind us that love, friendship, and desire are natural phenomena. Later in the *Lysis* Socrates tackles the natural philosophers' accounts of love and friendship as natural principles. He will reject their accounts, but not that *eros* is innate. Lysis and Menexenus, for example, have a natural, youthful friendship (211e-212a); they are naturally erotic.[10] But the direction of *eros*, how it is aimed and discharged, is due to education. This is why Socrates hurries to the Lyceum, to seek out erotic young men who need an education.

The door to the wrestling school is hidden and secretive (203e). Socrates has not even noticed the wrestling school before. Some forms of love must also be hidden — sexual intercourse, and what Hippothales feels for Lysis. This is why Hippothales blushes and dissimulates when his love for Lysis is revealed.

There is a brief mention of Miccus, an accomplished sophist, who presides in the wrestling school (204a). Miccus introduces another theme of the dialogue, eristic sophistry. The relationship between Ctesippus and Menexenus is founded on eristic.[11] In the *Euthydemus* Ctesippus learns to imitate the eristic brothers Euthydemus and Dionysodorus, and he passes on this acquired talent for the unserious use of words to Menexenus. Menexenus is as young and almost as handsome as Lysis, but unlike Lysis he is spoiled by having acquired from Ctesippus a skill in eristic combat. Lysis is pure and unspoiled since he has not given himself to an older lover; hence he has not been educated badly by another.[12] Socrates, as we will see, handles the two boys in very different ways.

Hippothales blushes when Socrates asks him to reveal who his beloved is (204b). Socrates notices that Hippothales is very far advanced in his love (204b). Hippothales blushes again at 204c. Hippothales is embarrassed by his love for Lysis, and he should be. His *eros* is excessive, and aimed in the wrong direction. Ctesippus, with malicious delight, relates how Hippothales treats his beloved. After a few drinks Hippothales repeatedly recites his compositions in praise of his favorite (204c-d), and Hippothales' friends become utterly tired of his saying "Lysis." Socrates does not want a recitation of these works, but he does want to know whether Hippothales knows what one ought to say to a favorite. Hippothales declines to speak, but Ctesippus does not. He relates how Hippothales profusely praises Lysis for his noble ancestors and possessions (205b-c). Hippothales is a flattering lover; his praise, if effective, would inflate Lysis and make him arrogant. Moreover, Hippothales is not concerned about Lysis' welfare since his praise is primarily about his ancestors. He also praises Lysis' possessions but not the knowledge required for their proper use.

Socrates admonishes Hippothales by the clever subterfuge of appealing to his self-interest. Hippothales' speeches will only make the boy more difficult to catch because they will fill him with pride (205e-206a). Hippothales is willing to hear "useful advise" from Socrates about how to capture Lysis. Socrates' advice, of course, will not at all address how to capture Lysis in Hippothales' sense; rather Socrates' words will really benefit the boy. Hippothales is a base lover; Socrates, as we will see, is a true one. But the true lover is the true educator, and thus Socrates is the true educator.

Lysis has a certain dislike for Hippothales perhaps because of his natural good sense. When the conversation begins, Hippothales conceals himself from Lysis because of the fear of incurring Lysis' displeasure (207b). Hippothales thus removes himself from the conversation, perhaps indicating that he is not educatable. Hippothales' overwrought *eros* may be beyond education. He will only react to the conversation with glee or embarrassment depending on how the *logoi* appear to favor his attempts to capture Lysis (cf. 210e-211a). When Socrates at the end of the dialogue says that the true lover must be befriended by his favorite, Hippothales in his delight turns all manner of colors (222a-b). But by 222a-b it is clear that he is not the true lover.

We receive a favorable impression of Lysis. We first learn that he is fond of listening to conversations in the gymnasium (206c-d). Lysis has a natural fondness for conversation which is as yet untainted by evil influences. When Lysis correctly interjects his correct opinion about a conversation, Socrates genuinely praises him for his taste for philosophy (213d). But Lysis only has the natual liking for conversation, and this liking easily could be perverted by bad influences. Lysis also is naturally modest and shy (207a-c, 213d), and there is nothing affected about his modesty. In summation, Lysis not only has a good appearance, but also he is noble and good in the manner appropriate to an untrained youth (207a). Lysis is a lesser Alcibiades with respect to natural qualities, but he also represents potential for good or evil. Socrates, Hippothales, Ctesippus through Lysis' friend Menexenus, along with Lysis' parents and *paidagogoi* all compete to influence Lysis. Lysis is the educational focus of the *Lysis*. He is worthy of a good education, and Socrates will attempt to show him what such an education is like.

Socrates' Hortatory Conversation with Lysis

Socrates' first conversation with Lysis (207d-210d) is a paradigm of a hortatory discussion. Socrates exhorts him to value and seek wisdom. Menexenus is called away to the festival rites, and this focuses our attention only on Socrates and Lysis in juxtaposition with Hippothales. Socrates' protreptic *logoi* are contrasted both with how Hippothales treats Lysis, and with how Socrates, himself, will treat the eristic Menexenus. Hippothales falsely praises the boy, but Socrates will humble him for Lysis' own benefit;[13] Socrates gently leads Lysis to an appreciation of wisdom, but he is sharp and even eristic with Menexenus. The boys' diverse *psychai* require different *logoi*, and Socrates fits the proper *logoi* to the *psychai*. Thus Socrates' first discourse with Lysis is juxtaposed both with what precedes and with what follows it.

Socrates poses a first-rate problem for Lysis. Lysis' parents desire for him to be happy, but they do not let Lysis do whatever he desires. Lysis even has some guardians who, while slaves themselves, nevertheless control Lysis. At the end of the dialogue these slaves force Lysis to go home; they symbolize the constraints imposed upon Lysis by his parents. Socrates gently pushes Lysis to understand the following difficulty: one cannot be happy unless one does whatever one desires, Lysis' parents desire Lysis' happiness, but they also keep him from doing whatever he desires. We can see the solution to this problem even if Lysis does not.[14] Socrates would claim that happiness or well-being is not doing whatever one desires. Doing whatever one desires could produce someone like Callicles in the *Gorgias*.

After Socrates stimulates Lysis with the purported problem, he leads him to a resolution. Socrates' benign and direct guidance of Lysis is only comparable to his similar treatment of the slave boy in the *Meno*, and Cleinias in the *Euthydemus*. All three boys are young and unspoiled. Lysis suggests that it is because he is not yet of age that his parents will not let him do what he desires (209a). Socrates shows him that this is not the correct reason, for they already permit him to do some things but not others. Socrates then leads Lysis to see that he must first be intelligent about something before he is permitted to do, use, or care for it (210a-b). Socrates also has Lysis see that only the wise and hence really useful will be beloved (210c-d). Lysis, of course, wants to be loved, and so he wants to acquire wisdom. Socrates stresses the beneficial aspects of knowledge at 209d-210d, and it is a common theme of the early dialogues that only the knowledge of good and evil is really beneficial (cf. *Meno* 88c-d, *Euthydemus* 281e). This is the sort of knowledge Lysis must acquire. Socrates finally humbles Lysis by getting him to see that since he does not now possess wisdom, he should not have a high opinion of himself (210d).[15]

Socrates uses both benign *elenchus* (refutation) and *psychagogia* on Lysis. Socrates employs a benign *elenchus* because Lysis is not stuffed with either purported knowledge or false beliefs. The *elenchus* is benign both due to its benevolent tone, and because Socrates does not really refute any of Lysis' beliefs; rather he sets an important problem for Lysis. Socrates immediately practices *psychagogia* on Lysis, and gets him to see that wisdom is what is important. A leitmotif of the *Lysis* is that wisdom is the highest object of love and our real friend; human friendships are good in so far as they foster the acquisition of wisdom.

Socrates' Eristic Conversation with Menexenus

Lysis playfully asks Socrates to speak with Menexenus so that he may see Menexenus trounced (211b). But Socrates' task may not be so easy since Menexenus is skilled at eristic; indeed, he is a pupil of Ctesippus (211b-c). Socrates says that there is one thing he desires to possess more than dogs, money, and distinctions, and that is a friend (211e-212a).[16] Menexenus and Lysis have so quickly, easily, and at an early age become friends, that surely Menexenus is able from this experience to say what friendship is (212a). Menexenus will prove unable to do this since he only has a natural, adolescent friendship with Lysis.

Menexenus is prepared to answer Socrates, but the conversation which follows is remarkable for its convolution and obscurity. I am not certain that I understand properly each twist and turn of the conversation, but its obscurity and complexity are, themselves, indicative of what Socrates tries to accomplish with Menexenus.[17] Socrates drives the young eristic to *aporia* (perplexity) by a series of sharp refutations which are stimulating, but also themselves sometimes eristic. Socrates uses Menexenus' own method—or at least those of Ctesippus—to refute him. At the end of the conversation Menexenus is tied in intellectual knots, and does not see any alternative for escape.

Menexenus claims that if A loves B, then A and B are mutual friends (212b). Socrates points out that even if A loves B, it does not follow that B loves A; B may not love A, or may even hate A. Experience should have shown Menexenus that although Hippothales loves

Lysis, Lysis does not even like Hippothales. Socrates concludes, *contra* Menexenus, that if the love is not mutual, then they are not friends (212c-d). But are there not lovers of things like horses, gold, and wisdom, where the objects of love do not reciprocate the friendship? Socrates and Menexenus agree that the objects of love are friends (or dear) to their lovers (212a-213a). But this leaves open the unacceptable possibility that some friends are enemies, and some enemies friends. Socrates seems to have in mind here the sorts of situations where we do not love what is really dear to us, or we love what is really detrimental to us. Socrates concludes that neither the lover, nor the loved, nor both together are the ground of friendship, and the conversation ends in *aporia*.

A number of important points emerge from this perplexing conversation. First the discussion is much more convoluted and obscure than my exposition makes it seem. Socrates' pedagogical point is to stun Menexenus, and to leave him no intellectual escape. Menexenus must be humbled in order to be purged of his eristic tendencies. Socrates uses sharp and sometimes eristic refutations to humble Menexenus. Second Socrates rejects mutual personal love as a necessary basis for friendship. He introduces another model where some person A loves not another person, but some object or state of affairs. The impersonal model of love displaces the personal model. The neutral "the dear" replaces personal love and friendship (212e-213a). Only on the impersonal model can wisdom become man's highest achievement; correct personal love is a means to this more important end. Third Socrates appears to reject the impersonal model because what we love can be really hateful and the converse. The conclusion to draw from this is that we ought to know what is and what is not beneficial, not that we ought to reject the impersonal model. In *Republic* I Socrates uses a similar argument to show that our purported friends may be our enemies and the converse (334c-e). Socrates' difficult discussion with Menexenus implies that the highest human desire ought to be for that wisdom which discerns what is really beneficial to us.

Socrates wonders whether there all along has been something wrong with the conversation with Menexenus, and Lysis, blushing, says that there is (213d). Socrates is delighted with Lysis' taste for philosophy— which reemphasizes the love for wisdom — and switches the conversation back to him starting from an entirely new point.

Socrates' Attack on the Poets and Nature Philosophers

Socrates leads Lysis to investigate the twin claims that like is friend to like and that unlike is friend to unlike. Socrates has two reasons for introducing these positions. His refutation of them permits him to attack especially the poets and then the physical philosophers as the educators and sources of wisdom in Greece.[18] The second is that the refutations of these extreme positions set up Socrates' more considered view that what is neither good nor bad is a friend to the good.

Let us first turn to "like is friend to like." Socrates quotes Homer as holding this view, and also mentions that certain physical philosophers also expouse it (214a-b). Socrates shows Lysis that the evil are not friends to the evil because nothing which produces harm is really a friend. Moreover, the evil are never even like, or in accord, with themselves. Our poet must, then, have some "hidden meaning" that only the good are friends to the good (214d). Socrates displays his typical posture towards poets in this passage; their sayings are inspired but obscure, and they require rational interpretation. But the good are not friends to the good either, for if one is completely good, then he does not need anything, and thus neither desires nor loves anything (215a-c). Moreover, the like cannot benefit like; what could the like man transmit to his friend that his friend could not provide for himself? But we do not cherish what is not of benefit to us (214e-215a). Socrates does not reject the "utilitarian" nature of love and friendship; we love and desire what we do not possess, but want. He does, however, reject conventional views about what is beneficial.

Socrates next tackles the position that unlike is friend to unlike. He attributes this position to Hesiod (215c), which raises the amusing specter of the major poetic educators of Greece disagreeing with one another. We see a similar spectacle in the *Laches* where the two expert generals disagree with one another about the value of fighting in heavy armor. Either Homer or Hesiod must be wrong; Socrates thinks that without considerable interpretation they both are. The claim that unlike are friends to unlike does fit some cases, since the poor befriend the rich, and the weak the strong; but it does not fit others because the loving are not friends to the hateful, the good to the bad, and the temperate to the profligate. Since polar opposites are unlikes, this account must be rejected.

Socrates immediately leads Lysis to an intermediate position which is considerably more promising: what is neither good nor bad is a friend of the good (216c). Socrates and Lysis agree that there are three kinds of things: the good, the bad, and what is neither good nor bad. By an elimination of other possibilities Socrates concludes that what is neither good nor bad is a friend to the good (216d-e).

At 216d Socrates boldly states that the good is beautiful. With one stroke he inverts the major assumption of base lovers like Hippothales. Hippothales desires beauty of physical form without concern for his own or his beloved's benefit. Socrates, on the other hand, implies that one must first discern what is really beneficial, and this is what is beautiful. Hippothales is deceived by mere appearance.

Socrates depicts his insight as a divination, something which is divinely inspired (216d-e). Often when Socrates introduces his highest principles, he attributes them to a dream or inspiration. Such an introduction lends to Socrates' positions an aura of divine authority not unlike the proem of Parmenides' poem on truth. We now enter the region of Socrates' own considerations about what is really dear and a friend.

The Highest Friendship

Socrates proceeds to explain his theory to Lysis. A healthy body has no need of health, and hence it is not a friend to the doctor. A thoroughly evil and sick body does not desire the good, and hence it is not a friend to the doctor. But a body which is only partially diseased is a friend to the doctor because of the presence of disease in it. The disease, however, cannot have made the body completely bad, or else the body would not desire health (217a-b).[19]

Socrates gives a second example (218a-b):

And consequently we may say that those who are already wise no longer love wisdom, whether they be gods or men; nor again can those be lovers of wisdom who are in such ignorance as to be bad: for we know that a bad and stupid man is no lover of wisdom. And now there remain those who, while possessing this bad thing, ignorance, and are not yet made ignorant or stupid, but are still aware of not knowing the things they do not know.

Socrates certainly agrees with these thoughts because they are also an important part of recollection in the *Meno*. Socratic *elenchus* with the slave boy produces the beneficial awareness of self-ignorance which causes the boy to seek for the correct answer. If the boy knew the answer, or if he were entirely ignorant of his own ignorance, then he would not desire to acquire wisdom. Thus a person who is neither completely good nor completely bad, but who is conscious of the bad present in him, desires the good.

Socrates, however, is dissatisfied with the above analysis, and he fears that their "new-gotten riches are all a dream" (218c). What follows does not repudiate the preceding schema, but rather emends it for a very special case. Socrates approaches his final statement in the *Lysis* about what is ultimately dear.

Lysis admits that when A loves B, then A loves B "for the sake of something, and because of something" (218a). In Aristotle's terminology we can say that there is both a final cause and an efficient cause of *eros*. Socrates immediately analyzes both types of causes. He asks Lysis whether A is a friend of B for the sake of another friend or not (218a). Lysis does not follow the question, and his puzzlement reveals that we are at a crucial transition in the conception of friendship. Lysis only experiences and understands interpersonal friendship, embodied in his friendship with Menexenus. Socrates reveals that interpersonal friendship should be a means to some futher desirable goal. A is a friend of B for the sake of C, where C is an impersonal good. Socrates implies this position earlier in the *Lysis* when he urges Lysis to acquire wisdom, and when he points to the "lover of *x*" model in his conversation with Menexenus. But now there is an explicit shift where states like health and wisdom are *philos* "a friend or what is dear." Socrates transcends interpersonal friendship as only a means — perhaps a necessary means — to even greater benefits.[20]

Socrates then asks whether the new friend will also be for the sake of a friend and so on in an infinite series. He comments that unless there is some final friend, a final *archē* (principle) which is not for the sake of some other friend (219c-d), then we will become tired trying to traverse an infinite series. If there were no final friend all of our labor would be in vain. This final friend is the real and true friend, and all other friends are mere *eidola* (phantoms or ikons) of this one true friend (219c-d). This final friend is that in which all other friends terminate (220a-b).

Some commentators believe that the final friend is either a reference to the middle-period transcendent theory of Forms, or a stage in that direction.[21] For phenomena are called *eidola* of the Forms in the *Timaeus*, and the real and true Forms are contrasted with their deficient ikons. But there is a contextually better interpretation of this passage. The final friend is contrasted with health and gold (219c, 220a), but Socrates in the early dialogues frequently contrasts wisdom with these other contingent goods (cf. *Apology* 30b, *Meno* 88c-d, *Euthydemus* 281e). Only the knowledge of good and evil is intrinsically valuable, and it is that on account of which other possessions of the body or *psychē* become valuable. Wisdom is the only true or real good, and when other things incorrectly replace wisdom as the highest objects of our desire, then they are mere ikons of wisdom. This analysis also connects the final friend with Socrates' exhortation to Lysis to desire and seek wisdom. Just as Lysis sees that no one is loved unless they are wise, so too wisdom emerges as the final friend, as what is most dear to us. Thus my interpretation produces a unity in the dialogue that is missing on the transcendent Form view, where the Forms would enter the dialogue in only one brief passage. We should not, then, see this passage as a reference to transcendent Forms.[22]

Socrates next attends to the efficient cause. If our love for the good is caused by evil, then when evil is removed we no longer desire or love the good (220b-d). This makes our need for the good dependent upon our possession of evil, but this is not correct, because the good (what is good) should be valued for its own sake (220d-e). Socrates' problem is that his model of desire, love, and friendship presupposes the lack of what is loved or desired, and this appears to be a positive evil. Men love wisdom because they possess ignorance, and they love health because they possess disease. Socrates points out, however, that while desires like hunger are bad because of their concomitant bodily depletions, they can also be beneficial to the organism. Thus these desires are neither good nor bad, nor are they abolished when evil is destroyed. Socrates concludes that not all love and desire is caused by evil, that desire is the cause of friendship, and that the desiring thing is a friend to what it desires (221b-d).

The *Lysis* then concludes by overturning all of its claims, and it leaves the participants in *aporia* (lack of passage).[23] Even when Socrates reaches his own position on a topic, he does not want to put a closure on a conversation, since he might then appear to be the new authority who replaces the poets. The continual practice of dialectic is as important as any positive conclusions which may emerge from it, since only dialectic can renew, tie-down, and test beliefs. Hence Socrates does not permit a certainty which closes conversation.[24] What is unusual about the contrived fallacies at the end of the *Lysis* is their convoluted and obscure nature.

If I interpret him correctly, Socrates first puns with *oikeion* (one's own or one's possession, or what is proper to one). He says that the true lover is deprived of what is proper to him—wisdom and other good things (221d-e). But then Socrates, to the discomfort of Lysis and Menexenus, argues that the beloved belongs to his lover, and is thus possessed by him (221e-222a). "What is proper to one" has shifted to "what one possesses or controls." The lover possesses the beloved, in which case Hippothales possesses Lysis! Then Socrates concludes that the beloved is a friend to his lover (222a-b), in which case Lysis is a friend to Hippothales. This severely discomforts Lysis since he neither desires to control Hippothales—although his slightest wish does—nor to be his friend. What then happens is quite amusing (222a-b):

> Then the genuine, not the pretended, lover must be befriended by his favorite. To this Lysis and Menexenus gave but a faint nod of assent; while Hippothales, in his delight, turned all manner of colors.

The quoted passage is amusingly ambiguous. Hippothales is not a true lover, nor are the objects of a false lover's attention his friends since they do not benefit him. Hence Lysis need not befriend Hippothales. The objects of the true lover's love, however, do benefit him and thus are his friends. Wisdom is the final friend of the wise lover. An apparently unacceptable consequence turns out to be, upon analysis, quite satisfactory to both Socrates and Lysis, although the latter does not understand the matter.

A second false *aporia* can also be solved by close analysis. Socrates asks whether the good belongs to everyone, or whether the good belongs to the good, the bad to the bad, and what is neither good nor bad to what is neither good nor bad (222b-c). They agree on the latter alternative which implies that like is friend to like. But they have already rejected this view, and so their choice fails. There are ample clues that the *aporia* can be solved from material within the *Lysis* itself. At 219b Socrates indicates that simply because like, in some sense, is friend to like does not count against a position.[25] We should remember Protagoras' witty comment in the *Protagoras* (331d-e) that everything, in some way, is like everything else. Second, *oikeion* is again ambiguous. The good does belong to everyone; that is, it is what is proper and appropriate for everyone. On the other hand the good are good by the presence of good things, and the bad bad by the presence of bad things. Thus the good, in fact, possess good things and the bad bad ones. Both *aporiai* at the end of the Lysis emphasize the distinction between what really is proper and beneficial to one, and what people actually possess.

What has Socrates done to educate the boys since his divination? He has led them to the correct conception of love and friendship which must include the best object of love, wisdom. The boys do not resist this conclusion. But Socrates must overturn even the correct view, and to do this he uses contrived *aporiai* whose solution can be seen by unraveling the complexities of linguistic meaning.[26] Why does Socrates overturn even the correct view of love? He does not want to become the new authority, the new Homer or Hesiod. There must be a reversal which activates the dialectical process, for only through dialectical conversation can beliefs be tested and tied down in the *psychē*, and only tied down beliefs should be claimed as knowledge.

Conclusion

In conclusion: The love of Hippothales for Lysis symbolizes a base type of love. Hippothales is not concerned with what is really beneficial either for himself or for his beloved. The liaison between Ctesippus and Menexenus represents another form of base love. Ctesippus transmits a false semblance of dialectic to Menexenus and makes him an eristic. The friendship between Lysis and Menexenus is youthful and attractive, but it is at the stage of mere potentiality. Lysis could become good or evil. Since Menexenus is already an eristic, the dangers to Lysis are great. Only Socrates is the true friend and lover. His love leads beyond the personal to what is unconditionally beneficial and dear — wisdom. The different *logoi* Socrates uses with the boys reflect his educational goal. To quote P. Friedländer: "Lysis loves Socrates. Socrates loves truth. Love tends upward."[27]

6. Force and Persuasion
in *Republic* Book I

Socrates successively talks in *Republic* book I with three interlocutors, and this arrangement of discussants is different from any we have studied so far. Later we will see a similar arrangement in the *Gorgias*. Is there any significance to the order of interlocutors, and do we learn anything about education from this arrangement? From the standpoint of education other questions also occur: Why does Socrates permit Cephalus to leave the conversation and how is Socrates to educate someone like Thrasymachus? To approach these questions will require a close scrutiny of the interlocutors' characters.

Before we begin let me say something about both the explicit topic of *Republic* I, justice, and Socratic definition. The meaning of "justice" is up for grabs with the stresses and strains of the Peloponnesian War. The Homeric and Hesiodic notions of excellence no longer sway the minds of men, and there is a vacuum of viable conceptions of excellence. This chaos is reflected in *Republic* I. Cephalus hints that justice is fairness in business transactions, Polemarchus believes that it is helping one's political friends and harming one's political enemies, and Thrasymachus thinks it to be the interests of the *de facto* rulers. Socrates will argue that justice is the art of living and doing well. He also will develop new notions of benefit and self-interest. Socratic definitions are not, then, reports of the ordinary meanings of words, nor are they analyses of demotic concepts.[1] Socrates attempts to persuade us of a new notion of justice; his definitions are persuasive and normative. Thrasymachus also attempts a persuasive definition of justice. Both men, we will see also vie for the allegiance of their listeners with distinct versions of educational persuasive — dialectic for Socrates, and force for Thrasymachus.

The Introductory Paragraphs

The dialogue opens with Socrates reporting that he went down yesterday to the Peiraeus, the port of Athens (327a). There is symbolic significance to this journey. The Peiraeus, the seat of naval power, is a source of degenerate tendencies in Athens; it is also the source of Athenian imperialism as well as the introduction of new, novel foreign beliefs, customs, and gods. The goddess Bendis, whose festival Socrates and Glaucon go to celebrate, is one of these new foreign imports. The descent to the Peiraeus symbolizes Socrates' going down to discourse with those political and intellectual elements in the state who will be hostile to him. The hostility is first in beliefs and later in demeanor. Cephalus, Polemarchus, and Thrasymachus are all, I will show, examples of degeneration; Cephalus, we shall see, causes it, Polemarchus epitomizes it, and Thrasymachus is the ultimate effect of it. Socrates descends to talk with those who neither will understand nor ultimately listen or sympathize with him.

Visual terminology is prominent in the opening lines of the *Republic*. Socrates will *see* how they conduct the festival to the goddess (327a-b, 328a), and he later reports that he has *seen* the *spectacle* (327b). Plato high-lights the visual nature of the spectacle because it includes nothing less than the novel sight of a nighttime horseback race with torches. The riders will pass the torches on to one another as they race (328a). The themes of vision and spectacle are found frequently in early dialogues. Recurrent motifs of the *Hippias Major* and *Gorgias* are who will appear ridiculous, and who will present a spectacle, Socrates or his antagonists? Socrates makes a spectacle of himself before the many; Callicles and Thrasymachus are shamed at dialectic. Socrates' atypical appearance and discourse are a sight, a spectacle. Socrates also entertains the young men who enjoy seeing their elders discomfited (*Apology* 23c-d); he provides them with a festival. But, as we learn from the *Euthydemus*, the essence of a good Socratic conversation is moral seriousness. Thrasymachus misses this moral seriousness when he accuses Socrates of a festival feast at his, Thrasymachus', expense (354a). Thrasymachus believes that Socrates is merely giving a show, an *agon* (contest), but Socrates is not. For Socrates discourses with the serious intent of finding truth.

The festival sight also represents the present condition of the

Athenian state. Athens welcomes a foreign goddess, and reduces her to a mere festival, a religious triviality. Athens embraces the novel and new, and treats it all as a mere festival. The sight lovers of book I like those in book V are typical Athenian citizens; they immerse themselves in the phenomena *qua* phenomena. The many revel in the games and festivals provided by politicians to placate them.

A civic festival to a foreign goddess raises the interesting question of the charges against Socrates for impiety. The specific charges are that Socrates "does not believe in the gods the state believes in, but in other new spiritual beings" (*Apology* 24b-c). But the Athenians themselves introduce new gods, and hence Socrates, even if guilty, is only doing what is demotically popular. We see Socrates, moreover, paying his devotions to the goddess, and since her festival is part of civic ritual, Socrates overtly adheres to the rituals of the city. Socrates does not confront civic religion, even though it is far from what he takes to be true piety. There is a strong conservative tendency in Socrates, the moral revolutionary. In the *Euthyphro* Socrates rejects Homeric/ Hesiodic religion, and attempts to lead Euthyphro to the position that god is good (cf. *Euthypro* 13c, 14e-15a) rather than arbitrary and capricious. But Socrates is reluctant to act against conventional praying and sacrificing because it stands between civilization on the one hand and Callicles/Thrasymachus on the other. Socrates does not directly assault conventional religious observance, as personified in Cephalus, even though it does not have the intellectual basis to sustain a really just and pious society.

Two other themes are intertwined in the opening passages of the *Republic*: coercion vs. persuasion, and listening vs. not listening. After saying their prayers and seeing the spectacle Glaucon and Socrates start for town when Polemarchus sees them and *orders* his servant to run and *bid* them to wait (327b). The boy *grabs hold of* Socrates' himation (327b). When Polemarchus comes up he playfully threatens force to *make* Socrates and Glaucon stay. Socrates asks whether he might persuade them to let him go (327c), and Polemarchus replies that he cannot be persuaded because he will refuse to listen. The tone of the banter is light and playful, but its symbolic nature is significant.

Persuasion and coercion are central themes both in *Republic* I and in the whole work. Socrates tries to persuade through *logoi*; his persuasion is aimed at the core beliefs—those that are most important for defining who someone is—of those with whom he talks. Thrasymachus, on the other hand, tries to coerce the other participants; he hurls himself into the discussion like a wild beast, and tries to intimidate the others by the sheer force of his attack (336b-c). When Socrates does not accept his view Thrasymachus says (345b):[3]

> And how am I to persaude you? . . . if you are not convinced by what I just now was saying, what more can I do for you? . . . Shall I take the argument and ram it into your head?

Thrasymachus' entire posture is one of force, and when he cannot overcome Socrates in debate, he will take his position and "ram it into his [Socrates'] head." Therefore a major theme in book I is between Socrates' rational persuasion, and Thrasymachus' irrational force. Persuasion makes some headway in the dialogue; it keeps Thrasymachus in the conversation, and it later causes him to blush.

Socrates listens to Thrasymachus and understands his position, but he will not accept Thrasymachus' false views. Thrasymachus, at the end of book I, does not listen to Socrates at all; he simply agrees to answer Socrates, to do his bidding (351c-d). Thrasymachus acts as if he were conquered in battle and made a slave; he answers in a slavish way, and makes no attempt to understand Socrates. Listening is a necessary prerequisite for dialectical inquiry, but Thrasymachus lacks this characteristic, and hence cannot be a fit dialectical partner.

Cephalus

Plato presents his characters in a well-contrived order. Cephalus is an old man with oligarchic tendencies, Polemarchus the democratic, and Thrasymachus the tyrant. Cephalus, I will show, is both the biological and the intellectual father of Polemarchus, and Polemarchus, through his careless views, makes possible Thrasymachus. Hence *Republic* I has as a major theme how one type of bad education breeds another. To see this we will need to look closely at the characters of each man.

Cephalus seems to be a decent person. Indeed, he is a man of demotic virtue and piety. Cephalus praises with many words the tranquility and temperance which comes with old age (328cf.) He is also moderate in his quest for wealth, being content to bring his legacy somewhat past his own inheritance from his father (330b-c). Cephalus appears to be a man of moderation. He also enters the conversation from praying and sacrificing, and he leaves to do the same, which shows his adherence to civic piety.

Demotic virtue, however, is not good enough for Socrates, and Socrates reveals the intellectual and moral decay behind the facade. First Cephalus admits that the desire for and pleasure in conversation has only recently come upon him with the decay of bodily satisfactions (328d). This admission suggests that while the bodily satisfactions were great, Cephalus looked to them, and cared little or nothing for discussion. Socrates notes that it has been a long time since he has seen Cephalus (328c), and Cephalus shows no ability for dialectical conversation. Socrates extracts an account of justice from Cephalus' vague remarks, and quickly counterexamples it (331b-d). More than likely Cephalus has no clear views on justice at all. Cephalus leaves the discussion as soon as he can—even though he proclaims an increased desire for it—and goes to the sacrifices. Cephalus' entering the discussion from ritual and prayer, and his leaving for ritual and prayer shows that he prefers the certainty of ritual to open, unpredictable discussion. He is old and set in his ways, and really has no desire for dialectical discourse. Socrates permits him to leave with no attempt to hinder his escape.

Cephalus says some revealing things about the use of money. With increasing age he becomes more concerned about the tales of the after life, especially how men may have to pay the penalty there for what they did here (330d-e). One may well wonder what it is about his previous behavior that so worries him. But wealth is the answer to the problem. At 331a-b Cephalus says:

> It is for this, then, that I affirm that the possession of wealth is of most value, not it may be to every man but to the good man. Not to cheat any man even unintentionally or play him false, not remaining in debt to a god for some sacrifice or to a man for money, so to depart in fear to that other world—to this result the possession of property contributes not a little.

The possession of money, according to Cephalus, removes the need to cheat! Socrates points out in the *Apology* (40c-41c) that the fear of death is irrational, if one has been a good man. Evidently Cephalus has some reason for his fear. But he solves the problem by praying and sacrificing—a bribing of the gods—in the tradition of Euthyphro who sees our relation with them as a sort of barter. Cephalus tries to influence the gods by ritual actions, and to Socrates this is the false pretense of piety. We thus see behind the veneer of appearance that Cephalus is of dubious intellectual and moral character.

The demotic virtue of Cephalus only is a pale shade of the real thing, and it cannot be transmitted (*Meno* 99e-100a). Demotic virtue is a divine knack or chance occurrence which is easily upset by other motives. In Cephalus' case he probably would not be virtuous if he were poor. Most important, Cephalus cannot give, clarify, and defend an account of his life and his ways. Cephalus' thoughtless views on justice, piety, and the use of money cannot withstand even momentarily a Socratic attack. Cephalus symbolizes how a society gets itself into trouble. When its practices and beliefs are, for the most part, indefensible, then they cannot sustain that society through periods of stress and strain. Men like Cephalus could not sustain Athens through the eruptions of the Peloponnesian War. The excesses of a Thrasymachus are the result.

Socrates' rejection of the account he extracts from Cephalus' remarks is a classic example of *elenchus* (refutation) by counterexample. The account is that justice is truth telling and paying back what one has received (331b-c). Socrates points out that one ought not return a knife to someone who has gone mad. Hence the actions which instantiate Cephalus' definition turn out to be both just and unjust (331c-d). A satisfactory definition of justice would be, presumably, neither too narrow nor too broad, but would include all and only just acts. I have argued elsewhere that given Socrates' assumptions one cannot find a satisfactory definition of justice in terms of just acts.[4] For Socrates is after a strict principle of justice, not a *prima facie* one, and any account of sufficient generality is likely to admit of counterexamples, especially since Socrates allows madmen and the like to count as such examples. I believe that it is for this reason — because behavioral accounts of a virtue invariably fail — that Socrates ultimately locates justice in the *psychē*.[5]

Cephalus hands over the conversation to his son, Polemarchus, who is his heir in all things. The ritualistic life of Cephalus makes possible the poetic and sophistic education of Polemarchus. The man of demotic virtue gives a typical Athenian education to his son. But why does Socrates let Cephalus escape the conversation without forcing him to defend his life and ways? Socrates probably sees Cephalus as uneducatable; Cephalus was a man of great desires, and now he is a man of ritual. Moreover, Cephalus is old, and age can retard the educational capacity. So Socrates lets Cephalus go, but Socrates also treats him with a certain decency and respect due to his age and position. Nevertheless, Socrates the "professional" educator replaces the father; he shelves him, but does not insult or dialectically assault him. Socrates' replacement of Cephalus symbolizes the conflict between the old and a new type of education, where Socrates represents the new education of the professional.

Polemarchus

Polemarchus inherits the discussion, as well as his education, from his father. He has made every effort to memorize the poets and retain their wisdom. Polemarchus will prove to be more pliable than his father; he will accept revisions, changes, and modifications of his basic theme, that justice is giving to each his due. Such pliability, however, is not a sign of wisdom; rather it represents the democratic tendency to move with whatever wind is pushing you. Polemarchus represents the pliable man, the man of affairs in the city, and his account of justice is tailored to the political battles in such a state.

Polemarchus has heard from the poet Simonides that justice is rendering to each his due (331d-e). Since Polemarchus symbolizes the poetically educated man, let us look at Socrates' attitude towards poets. Socrates says that Simonides is wise and inspired (331e), but that what he means by "the due" is quite unclear, which is typical of statements by the poets (332b). Socrates clarifies "the due" and draws one of its consequences which is that the just man is a thief (to be discussed below). He then says (334a-b):

> A kind of thief then the just man it seems has turned out to be, and it is likely that you acquired this idea from Homer. For he regards with complacency Autolycus, the maternal uncle of Odysseus, and says he was gifted beyond all men in thievery and perjury. So justice, according to you and Homer and Simonides, seems to be a kind of stealing, with the qualification that it is for the benefit of friends and the harm of enemies.

After Socrates refutes the view that a really just man would harm anyone, he says that "no truly wise man" would claim this (335e). He and Polemarchus must, then, fight against anyone who attributes such a false view to a poet (335e). Socrates' claims about poets are, indeed, confusing.

Socrates objects to the preeminent position of the poets in education.[6] Poetic education is, for the most part, rote memorization and recall of poetic material. The many think that poets are experts about many subjects. If a young Athenian gentleman wants to know what to do in some situation, then he consults his memory for the proper poetic advice. Socrates denies that the poets are a repository for either moral or practical wisdom. Most important, poetic education is authoritarian; it emphasizes passive listening, singing, memorization, and mere recall. The performance aspects of poetry, as sung, also foster the noncognitive activities rather than thought, questioning, and analysis. Poetic education takes from the individual the moral responsibility to test his beliefs, and come to see for himself what the truth is.[7] Socratic dialectic fosters the opposite effects. Thus Socrates opposes the poets as educators.

But why, then, does he say that the poets are inspired? Is Socrates sarcastic? Perhaps his view is this: There is something in poetic madness, perhaps it comes from a *daimon*. In any case, the poets say some interesting things. Moreover, poetry is a powerful and alluring educational tool which can neither be ignored nor successfully suppressed. Let us praise the poets but always reserve the right, indeed the duty, of interpreting them to philosophy (also see *Apology* 22b-c). Socrates, then, insists that poetic inspiration must be subordinated to philosophical analysis and interpretation. The poets' words are vague like those of the Delphic oracle, and they require an interpretation to give them meaning. Socrates does not yet entertain the case where the poets' words are clear, and clearly pernicious. Socrates does say that we should never attribute a morally pernicious meaning to a poet.

Socrates helps Polemarchus interpret Simonides' obscure saying. They agree that "to render to each his due" means "to benefit friends and to harm enemies" (332d). Socrates' refutations of this account are among the most unusual, and the most revealing, in all the early dialogues.

Socrates first wants to know what benefit justice renders to a friend (332df.). The physician produces health, the navigator safety at sea, and the general victory in war, but what does justice produce? Polemarchus replies that justice is of use in business engagements and dealings (333a-b). Socrates asks just how justice is of use in these matters. A horse trainer is of use if one wants to buy a horse, and a stockbroker if one wants to invest, but when is justice useful? Polemarchus offers that justice is of use when money is to be deposited and kept safe (333c). Socrates paradoxically concludes that "in the use of each thing justice is useless but in its uselessness useful" (333d).

The first refutation of Polemarchus/Simonides involves an *ad hominem* argument. Polemarchus assumes that justice has a specific product exactly like any other *technē*. The argument which follows presupposes this assumption and treats justice as if it were one among the many arts. Of course it is hard to specify what the product of justice is. Hence Socrates reduces the account to the absurdity that justice is useful only when other things are useless. This absurd conclusion should motivate us to wonder what has gone wrong. The argument invites us to identify and analyze the presuppositions of the refutation; the important presupposition is that justice, just like any other art, has a specific product. I will look at this presupposition after the second refutation.

In the second refutation Socrates employs what I will call the bivalence principle:[8] an art which makes one good at φing also makes one good at the opposite of φing. For example, the doctor who is good at producing health can also use his knowledge to poison someone; the cobbler who is good at making shoes for the care of the feet can also use his knowledge to cripple someone. Given the bivalence principle, the just man who is good at guarding money is also good at stealing it (334a). The just man, is, then, he who is gifted above all others in thievery and perjury just as the poets say (334b)!

Polemarchus admits that he no longer knows what he meant by "the due," but he still believes that justice benefits friends and harms enemies (334b-c). Socrates' dialectical method presupposes that if one knows something, then one can state, clarify, and defend it. Polemarchus does not quite feel the sting of Socratic refutation because he does not admit his ignorance.

In the second refutation Socrates also uses an *ad hominem* argument to produce a *reductio ad absurdum*. Polemarchus continues to assume that justice is exactly like any other art, and since other arts admit the bivalence principle, so too does justice. That the just man is the expert thief is absurd; it is so outlandish that it motivates us to look and see what has gone wrong. The proper question is whether justice is just like any other art.

The answer is no. In the *Laches* (195c-d) Nicias correctly distinguishes between the medical art which only knows how to heal or hurt, and a master art which knows what, in any situation, is best to accomplish. Only the knowledge of good and evil gives one the latter ability (cf. *Laches* 199bf.). In the *Charmides* (173aff.) Socrates depicts a technologically perfect society where the experts are all in their proper positions. Steersmen are at the helms of ships, prognosticators are predicting the future, and cobblers are making the city's shoes. But, Socrates asks, where in all of this is human well-being? Only wisdom or the knowledge of good and evil can produce this (*Charmides* 174b-c).

Justice, the knowledge of good and evil, does not instantiate the bivalence principle. Socrates holds the psychological premise that all men desire their own good (*Meno* 77b-78b, *Gorgias* 467b-468b). Hence each person acts on their conception of the good, and ignorance is the only thing that makes us miss the mark. Thus, as Socrates claims at *Republic* 336e, "it is unwillingly that we err." Therefore the bivalence principle does not apply to the art of justice; he who has the knowledge of good and evil would not willingly misuse such knowledge. This is not the case with the subordinate arts like cobbling and medicine.

Justice is the master art which ought to rule over all the other arts. It should rule over them by setting the goals they ought to seek. When justice infuses the other arts, then they are always used for the good of their subject matter. In the *Gorgias* Socrates tries to get Gorgias to see this very point. Rhetoric is a powerful tool, either for good or for evil. Unless it is controlled by virtue, it will undoubtedly cause harm. Hence a true rhetorician must also be a teacher of virtue; in fact, rhetoric must be used to teach virtue.

Socrates' third refutation leads us to see the importance of knowledge for justice. Socrates asks whether we are to benefit those who really are our friends or those who seem so, and whether we are to harm our real enemies or those we think to be our enemies (334b-c). Polemarchus chooses the latter alternative in each case, and Socrates concludes that for those who err it is, on Polemarchus' view, just to harm their real friends and benefit their real enemies (334c-e). The importance of knowledge is clear. If one is to help one's friends and harm one's enemies, then one needs to know who are one's real friends and enemies. This knowledge is not the full knowledge of good and evil, but it is a step in that direction. A major theme in the rest of book I is the disclosure of the role of knowledge in justice. Socrates shows Thrasymachus that the ruler must know what is really to his benefit, and at 351a Socrates blurts out that "if justice is wisdom and virtue, it will easily, I take it, be shown to be also a stronger thing than injustice, since injustice is ignorance—no one could now fail to recognize that— . . ." Socrates just about says that justice = virtue = wisdom, but by this time Thrasymachus has stopped listening; he only responds yes or no.

Socrates' fourth refutation of Polemarchus is entirely done with Socratic meanings for its key concepts. Socrates argues that a good and just man will never harm anyone (335b-d). For real harm hurts the proper virtue or excellence of a thing, and in the case of man his specific virtue or excellence is justice (335c). Socrates then asks (335c-d):

> By justice then do the just make men unjust, or in sum do the good by virtue make men bad? . . . It is not, I take it, the function of heat to chill but of its opposite . . . nor of dryness to moisten but of its opposite . . . nor yet of the good to harm but of its opposite?

Elsewhere I argue that Plato often presupposes the causal principle that a cause must have what it produces in something else.[9] Given the causal principle a just man can no more make one unjust than moisture can make something dry. I suggest that Socrates' fourth objection should be interpreted as follows: the just man, whose desires are moderate and ordered, knows that it is best to produce people like himself, and hence he would not voluntarily make someone unjust (cf. *Apology* 25c-26a). The argument explicitly employs Socrates' notion that the specific function of man is justice, and his premise that no one errs willingly.

There is a persistent belief among commentators that Socratic education mainly is negative refutation. On this model Socrates refutes each definition for the sole purpose of engendering the beneficial awareness of one's own ignorance. This model is, I believe, too simple because it overlooks how Socrates rejects some accounts. His rejections sometimes are extremely paradoxical—contrary to the intuitions of an interlocutor—as in the conclusion that the just man is the expert thief. Such conclusions motivate both the interlocutor and the reader to wonder at what went wrong. We then need to look at the presuppositions of the argument. In the conversation with Polemarchus the major presupposition is that justice is just like any other art, and we are invited to investigate this presupposition.

I conclude that Socratic education sometimes has two parts: (1) *elenchus* (refutation), and (2) *psychagogia* (soul-leading). *Elenchus* and *psychagogia* often, as in the conversation with Polemarchus, occur together. The former attempts to produce the awareness of self ignorance, and the latter attempts to draw one to the correct conclusion. Socrates uses *psychagogia* because he will not teach by telling or imparting information to the listener. Polemarchus, with his poetic education, would not learn to think for himself, if Socrates used a more direct educational method.

When Polemarchus leaves the conversation we do not know to what extent, if any, he responds to Socratic *elenchus* and *psychagogia*. We can see, however, how Polemarchus' education and beliefs create Thrasymachus. It is a short step from "Justice is helping one's friends and harming one's enemies," to "Justice is the interest of the stronger." If one misconstrues one's real interest, then the latter position could require the former. Morever, a standard poetic education would make it very difficult for one to argue against Thrasymachus' position, even if one were unsympathetic with it,

Thrasymachus

Thrasymachus represents force and coercion. Those sitting next to him restrain him from breaking into the conversation, but when his opportunity arrives he hurls himself upon the discussion like a wild beast (336b). He attempts physically to intimidate the other participants, and when Socrates tries to placate him with irony, Thrasymachus unmasks the irony and abuses Socrates. He claims that Socrates does not have the force to beat him at argument (341b), and at one point he offers to ram the argument into Socrates' head (345b). But Thrasymachus, the man of force, is persuaded to remain in the argument, and he is beat in the debate with Socrates.

Thrasymachus lacks the prerequisite character traits — knowledge, good will, and frankness (*Gorgias* 487a) — which are necessary for a good answerer in a Socratic discussion. Thrasymachus' lack of knowledge manifests itself quickly both in his inability to sustain his account, and in his vacillations and contradictions (cf. 340c-d). At 345b-c Socrates says to him, ". . . when you have said a thing stand by it, or if you shift your ground change openly and don't try to deceive us." Thrasymachus, seeing the discourse as a debate, and not a search for truth, is less than frank and honest. For example, he first agrees that the rulers are fallible, and then denies that he meant any such thing (340c-d). It is essential to Socratic dialectic that an answerer be honest and frank so that he is committed to his answers, then to their defeat, and hopefully to his own ignorance. Thrasymachus' lack of honesty and frankness renders impossible these stages of Socratic education. We should not be surprised, then, if the discussion degenerates into a series of fruitless, hostile clashes.

Thrasymachus eventually answers just to please Socrates. First he says that it makes no difference to him if he believes what he says (349a), and then he says just what he thinks Socrates desires to hear. His goodwill and frankness have entirely dissipated; Thrasymachus responds to defeat by slavish withdrawal in all but the physical sense. All that Socrates can do in the end is to lecture and cajol Thrasymachus in the hope that embarrassment and shame will improve him. Thrasymachus views the entire discussion with Socrates as Socrates' agonistic festival at his, Thrasymachus', expense (359a), and hence there is little chance for a genuine conversion to occur.

There is also an important difference in the tone of conversation compared with previous discussions. Socrates immediately opposes Thrasymachus with heavyhanded irony (336e, 337a, 337e-338a), and the irony only gives way to an equally heavyhanded sarcasm (340e, 351c). Socrates does not do these things with the previous interlocutors. For his part, Thrasymachus consistently responds to Socrates with insults: Socrates is a pettifogger (340d, 341a), a shyster (341c), and a snot (343a). Thrasymachus also resists answering Socrates, and Socrates must force Thrasymachus' responses (344d, 346c, 350d). When Socrates crushes Thrasymachus' resistance, Thrasymachus feigns being a slave. The entire conversation is a contest between opposing forces, and Socrates, distastefully, defeats Thrasymachus again and again. Finally Thrasymachus is beaten to the point where he blushes (350d) from shame. Has Socrates lowered himself to Thrasymachus' level, or is there a pedagogical purpose in how he handles Thrasymachus? After I briefly describe the debate we will return to this question.

At first Thrasymachus wants Socrates to answer, and to say what justice is. But he will not let Socrates say that justice is the beneficial, useful, profitable, gainful, or advantageous (336d). These answers, Thrasymachus claims, are nonsense. Socrates twice says that he desires to give one of the forbidden answers (337c-d, 339b), and of course Thrasymachus also holds that justice is the advantageous — what is of advantage to the rulers. Both men are locked on the issue of "the advantageous."

The frequency with which advantage is mentioned signals its central role in the debate. Indeed, the debate between Socrates and Thrasymachus is a microcosm of the larger political debates seen in Thucydides. At a certain point in the Peloponnesian War Thucydides vividly displays how advantage is the only criterion in debate. For example, both the Athenians and the Melians agree that they must appeal to the advantage of Athens, who is the stronger, they simply disagree about what is to the advantage of Athens. So too Socrates and Thrasymachus agree that justice is advantageous, but they understand this claim in very different ways.

Socrates' moral revolution and Plato's great dramatic art is to take a position such as Thrasymachus' "Justice is the advantage of the stronger," and infuse it with an entirely different meaning. Both men agree that the statement is true, but they disagree about what "advantage" and "stronger" should mean. Socrates transmutes Thrasymachus' politically strong man into one who controls his desires, and external wealth becomes an internal harmony of the *psychē*. There is considerable reason for these men to disagree totally.

Thrasymachus' definition of justice is that it is the advantage of the stronger (338c). He also claims that the stronger are the ruling political party in a state (338d-e). His position, at least in first formulation, is distinct from that of Callicles in the *Gorgias*. For Callicles the strong are in some sense naturally so, while for Thrasymachus the strong are simply the *de facto* rulers. Socrates, however, might well see these positions as basically the same, since he attacks Callicles' application of the nature/convention distinction (*Gorgias* 489a-b), and could argue on similar grounds that the *de facto* rulers are the "naturally" stronger.

Socrates forces Thrasymachus to admit that the rulers sometimes mistake their own advantage (339c-d), and in conjunction with the admission that it is just for the subjects to obey their rulers, Socrates compels the conclusion that justice is sometimes to the disadvantage of the rulers. Again we have a hint about the necessary role of knowledge in justice; the knowledge in this case is the recognition of one's real advantage. Thrasymachus immediately dissimulates, and denies that he ever meant that a ruler *qua* ruler could err (340c-d).

Socrates is delighted to speak precisely with Thrasymachus about the practitioners of an art (340e). Precisely speaking, Socrates says, it is essential to the practice of an art that it is for the good of its subject matter; it is accidental to such a practice that the artist is benefitted. For example, someone practices medicine when he heals, not when he receives a fee for it. By analogy Socrates then claims that one practices statecraft when one acts for the good of one's subjects, not when one receives pay. But does one not practice rhetoric even if one's speech is not for the good of the listeners? Socrates is not simply analyzing the prevailing notion of an art; he wants all real arts to be guided by virtue, and this is why he claims that each art must act for the real good of its subject. Without this assumption the bivalence principle would reenter the picture, and Socrates' analogy would collapse. The doctor could use his art to heal or kill. Socrates tries to legislate what a real art is, and Thrasymachus will have none of it.

The rest of book I is a series of arguments against some claims Thrasymachus endorses for the unjust and injustice: the unjust are wise, they are strong, and injustice is advantageous (348a-b). Socrates rejects the first claim by saying that the unjust man will attempt to overreach both his like and unlike, but a just man does not desire to exceed his like. But a wise craftsman also does not want to overreach his like; the just man, then, is more like the wise than the unjust is (350c). We see in this analogy that injustice is an overreaching, an excessive striving to do or obtain what is beyond the appropriate mean. We also see a close connection, for Socrates, between justice and wisdom.

Socrates denies that the unjust are strong because if, for example, a band of crooks were completely unjust, then they would not keep their hands off one another (351c-e). Complete injustice causes total social disintegration. Justice now manifests itself as the glue of social harmony, and injustice as the source of enmity and hate.

Finally Socrates tries to show that justice is beneficial because it is the proper function of man. He says at 353d-e:

> The soul, has it a work which you couldn't accomplish with anything else in the world, as for example, management, rule, deliberation, and the like; is there anything else than soul to which you could rightly assign these and say that they were its peculiar work?

Justice is the virtue or excellence of a *psychē* (353e), and hence a just *psychē* will rule well, and a just man will live well and be happy (353e-354a). This argument posits justice as the distinctly human excellence, but it leaves many questions unanswered.

Conclusion

The conversation with Thrasymachus, like that with Polemarchus, uses both *elenchus* and *psychagogia*. Each time Socrates refutes Thrasymachus we learn something positive about justice or the just. For example, the just are wise, they are strong, and their possession of justice is to their benefit. But the tone of Socrates' conversation with Thrasymachus is very different from earlier discussions. Their conversation is a clash of hostile forces. But a wise educator fits his *logoi* to the condition of the interlocutor's *psychē*. Socrates has little chance to have a successful *elenchus* with Thrasymachus, for Thrasymachus will not engage in an honest conversation, much less admit his own ignorance. In this context, Socrates uses the only option available; he opposes force to force. Thrasymachus must be beaten and humbled before he can be made a suitable dialectical partner. Thus Socrates engages in pre-dialectical education with Thrasymachus; he attempts to shame Thrasymachus. But is Socrates successful in even this preliminary activity? Thrasymachus blushes once, but there is no evidence of any further change much less a permanent one.

What about Plato who is the silent author behind the dialogue? What does he think about the conversation, and what does he want us to think about it? The most compelling conclusion is that Socrates fails to educate Thrasymachus. Thrasymachus neither changes his beliefs, nor his behavior, even though he is thoroughly beaten by Socrates. Socrates' attacks fail, but why do they fail? Plato surely asked himself this very question, because the rest of the *Republic* tries to answer it. Perhaps Thrasymachus' *eros* is not philosophically inclined, or his false beliefs were set long before Socrates talks with him. Thrasymachus should be a member of the spirited class whose actions are governed by true beliefs instilled through moral training. In any case, Thrasymachus desperately needs a basic education in music and gymnastics like that adumbrated later in the *Republic*.

7. To Keep the Conversation Going in the *Apology* and *Crito*

The *Apology* is Socrates' justification for his life; Socrates' life is the life of philosophical activity, and this activity is essentially educational. Hence the *Apology* is also a justification for how Socrates educates the Athenians. The *Apology* is, in part, a metaeducational dialogue. Socrates explains how he comes to do dialectic, the sorts of people he talks with, and the effect he has on them. He announces why he does dialectic—the unexamined life is not worth living—and he characterizes himself as the educational gadfly of Athens. Socrates also explains why his dialectical refutations engender hostility in his interlocutors.

All of the important actions in Socrates' life, including his staying in prison and drinking the hemlock, attempt to foster the growth of rational, civilizing *logoi*.[1] Socrates' only goal in both the *Apology* and *Crito* is the continuation of dialectic question and answer. Just behavior promotes or tends to promote such *logoi*, and unjust behavior has the contrary effect. One ought not commit an injustice because it discourages the give and take of *logoi*, and as Socrates says, "the unexamined life is not worth living" (*Apology* 38a).[2] When we see what Socrates' ultimate aim is, then we will understand his actions in both the *Apology* and *Crito*, and see that these actions are consistent.

Social and Political Background

The Peloponnesian War between Athens and Sparta, which began in 431 B.C. and with some uneasy periods of peace lasted until 404, is the most important influence on Socrates and the jurors. In 431 Athens was a great power, proud of her intellectual and mercantile accomplishments; but by 404 all is in ruins. Athens' imperial influence and democratic institutions are swept away by Spartan victory. Sparta garrisons Athens, and helps to install the ruthless dictatorship of the thirty oligarchs. These tyrants eliminate without trial large numbers of their opponents, but are in turn driven out in 403. Democracy is restored, but it is under the new democracy that Socrates is brought to trial.

The events of the war have a subtle influence on Socrates' fate. Early in the war two devastating plagues carry off large segments of the population including Pericles and his successful defensive military policies. Thucydides gives us a vivid picture of the effects of the plague. People lived only for the present since the future is most uncertain. Standards of virtue and excellence ceased to exist; people grasped the pleasures of the moment. Piety also is shaken; either the gods have been terribly offended, or else they are unjust, or may not even exist. When traditional norms dissolve, there is a tendency for both conservative and radical elements to fill the gap. We see many of these people in the early dialogues; Callicles, Thrasymachus, Critias, and Euthydemus, among others, represent various types of radical responses to the crisis, while Cephalus and Anytus are examples of a conservative reaction. The latter want to return to the authority of the poets, and oligarchic decency. We see the same conflict between the speeches of the old and new educations in Aristophanes' *Clouds*.

A second influential event of the war is the infamous double sacrilege: the profanation of the Eleusian mysteries and the mutilation of the hermae. On the eve of the military expedition to Sicily, drunken revelers mutilate the hermae—roadside gods of protection— which is a sacrilege. Alcibiades, a friend of Socrates and a general in the contemplated expedition, is implicated, perhaps unfairly, in the sacrilege, and escapes punishment by leaving Athens, later to join Sparta. Subsequent investigation reveals other profanations. Athens generally is permissive about the variety of religious rituals and beliefs, but the gods have their limits, and these have been transgressed. Socrates, through his friendship with Alcibiades, is implicated vaguely in the profanations.

Sacrilege guarantees the failure of the Sicilian expedition, and Athens is defeated. She eventually surrenders to Sparta, and Sparta helps to install the thirty tyrants. Few regimes are as ruthless and bloodthirsty as this one. Moreover, two of Socrates' students, Critias and Charmides, are among the tyrants, and Critias is the most ruthless of them all. Furthermore, his religious cynicism matches his politics; he is reported to have said that men make the gods in order to keep other men in bondage. Again Socrates' associations connect him vaguely with impious, antidemocratic elements.

The thirty are driven out in 403, and democracy restored. The democracy declares a general amnesty for its political enemies, and the amnesty is enforced. It does not, however, prevent Socrates from being indicted, but it does insure that his political associations are no official part of the indictment.

Let us now look at the legal system which prevails in Athens. There are no public prosecutors, and hence private citizens must bring their charges to the proper authorities. Meletus, the good and patriotic, charges Socrates. Since Socrates is charged with a public indictment for impiety, a preliminary hearing is held at the bench of the King Archon. The *Euthyphro* depicts Socrates before the doors of this judge. The King Archon, who is charged with the protection of religious matters, makes a preliminary determination of both law and fact, and decides whether the case will go to trial. Socrates is permitted to answer the charges at this stage, but evidently he is unsuccessful.

Socrates' trial is before a jury of 501 citizens. Each receives three obols for a day's jury service — a poor hired man's wage. The jury probably is composed disproportionately of the poor who want the money, the old who desire the entertainment, and the civic-minded wealthy.[3]

The jurors, although untrained in law, are both judge and jury. They will decide both law and fact.[4] The prosecution and defense present their own cases; they make their own speeches, although they can employ professional speechwriters. Each side introduces law and fact, and there are stiff penalties for introducing nonexistent laws, and for perjury. The prosecution speaks first, and then the defense, and the only control on relevance is time, which is measured by the waterclock. The defense can crossexamine the accusors and ask the jurors to testify to one another. We see Socrates do both of these things in the *Apology*. After a guilty verdict there is a second vote on the penalty; the defense and prosecution each recommend a penalty to the jury, and the jury must select one of these recommendations. The jury cannot choose their own alternative.[5]

The jury is like any other large crowd. It can be attentive, angry, boisterous, and so on. Socrates frequently asks the jury for attention and silence; the jury sometimes reacts violently to what he says. Athenian courts are more akin to political rallies than to our modern, more controlled proceedings.[6] Such a context places a high premium on rhetoric. One successfully attacks or escapes through persuasion of the jury. Gorgian speechmaking persuades or fails to persuade the multitude of jurors.

Socrates is very clear that he is forced to speak in such a context (*Apology* 19a). He does not believe that real education can occur in such a short time (a day), and before such a large number of people. In the *Gorgias* he makes a sharp contrast between philosophical dialectic and rhetorical persuasion. The latter persuades of mere belief, and its home is in the assembly and law court — wherever there is a crowd. The former can produce knowledge — justified, tested beliefs — in the one on one of question and answer. Socrates is a dialectician, not a rhetorician; he is out of his element before the court. But he gives a speech, the only sort of speech he knows how to give, one which only tells the truth no matter what the effect on the jurors.[7] Socrates' speech is rhetorical anti-rhetoric. I will have more to say on this later.

M. I. Finley describes three facets of ancient Greek piety: The first is that Greek religion "had become very complicated over the centuries, with a great variety of gods and heroes who had numerous and crisscrossing functions and roles." The second is that "religion had little of what we should call dogma about it, but was largely a matter of ritual and myth." and the third is that Athenian religion is intimately associated with the family and the state. The first two points reinforce a claim which R. E. Allen makes about the charge of impiety against Socrates: the charge is very vague.[8]

The jury will decide if Socrates is guilty of impiety even though there are no clearly delineated boundaries to the law against impiety. Most jurors can agree on paradigm examples of impiety, as in the double sacrilege, but in the absence of a clear paradigm — which Socrates seeks in the *Euthyphro* — the application of the law is vague. If a law is vague, then it is difficult to deny the charge of having violated that law.[9] Indeed, Socrates does not deny straightforwardly the charges against him. He cannot rebut definitively a vague charge. Rather he tries to educate the jurors about his values, character, and philosophical mission. The issue becomes the sort of person Socrates is, not whether he breaks some law.[10] The jury will judge Socrates' character.

Is the *Apology* an accurate statement of what Socrates actually said? Socrates of course did not write anything, nor were the proceedings taken down except for the charge and the verdict. Thus it is very difficult to settle the above question with any confidence. Callicles claims in the *Gorgias*, and Socrates agrees with him, that if Socrates were to be hauled into court, then he would have nothing to say before the court (486a-b, 521d-522a). These statements started a tradition that Socrates is mute at his trial. But they imply no such thing. Callicles and Socrates are inversions of each other; Socrates cannot speak in a court with the same effect as Callicles. Socrates cannot give a Gorgian speech before a jury, but he is forced to give a speech (19a). Socrates speaks the truth, but the truth may not acquit him; it may even offend the jury, and result in his conviction. From Callicles' perspective such a speech is no speech at all. It is tantamount in ineffectiveness to silence.

The *Apology* is not a stenographic transmission of what Socrates says at his trial. But is it accurate about the tone, content, and effect of Socrates' words if not about their every detail? Vlastos and Allen think so, although they admit that their arguments are not conclusive.[11] Vlastos believes that the *Apology* basically is accurate because Plato is not able to defend Socrates before an audience, many of whom were at the trial, with an inaccurate depiction of events. Allen notes that Isocrates' *Antidosis* imitates Plato's *Apology*. But Isocrates compares himself to Socrates not to Plato's portrait of Socrates, and Isocrates is of an age to know what happened at the trial. Hence the *Apology* is a reasonably accurate account of what Socrates says. I agree with these arguments even though there is room for skepticism about their conclusion.[12]

The Causes of Socrates' Indictment and Conviction

The causes of Socrates' indictment and conviction differ in degree of temporal proximity to their effects, and are also of different degrees of importance. No single cause explains Socrates' predicament; rather it is their accumulative weight which has explanatory value.

The charge of impiety against Socrates is vague, and the reasons for the charge are also unclear. Aristophanes' *Clouds* is an influential cause of the charge. Aristophanes depicts Socrates as a physical philosopher who humorously replaces Zeus with the convection principle. The *Clouds* is a cause of the charge, but there are still puzzles. I will show that Socrates may well have studied physical phenomena in his

youth, but there is reason to believe that his youthful investigations
are not conspicuously public in nature. Socrates, as we will see, probably does not teach them to others. Furthermore, even though physical
philosophers can be theological revisionists—identifying some physical
element with the godhead—this does not preclude adherence to civic
religious rituals; if we can trust the opening paragraphs in the *Republic*,
Socrates adheres to the civic religious festivals even when they honor
a foreign Goddess! Twenty five years before the trial Aristophanes in
the public mind associates Socrates with the physical philosophers, and
these philosophers with impiety. The associations are outside of comedy
unfair, and they are influential in Socrates' indictment and conviction.

Socrates' *daimon* is another possible source of the charge of impiety. Socrates' *daimon* usually holds him back from some course of
action, but Socrates also has dreams which command him to do certain things such as "Make music" (*Phaedo* 60d-61a). Some philosophers
want to see the *daimon* as nothing more than a reference to conscience,
or even as a mythological way to give authority to the results of rational deliberation. But I believe that there is more to the *daimon* than
that. A man who has dreams and trances (cf. *Symposium* 220c-d) is
also capable of hearing voices. Socrates' examination of Meletus reveals
more about the *daimon*. He claims that since he believes in *daimones*
he also believes in gods since *daimones* are, in some way, the children
of gods. This argument has, I suggest, interesting implications. If
Socrates' *daimon* is the offspring of a god, then the appearance of the
daimon probably is not within his control. The *daimon* is a foreign
voice which takes control of Socrates. It is because this voice is not within
his control that he must attribute its source to something else.

Does Socrates' *daimon* support a charge of impiety? I do not think
so. In Homer, for example, voices and apparitions purportedly caused
by the gods are common occurrences. With respect to the *daimon*
Socrates is an archaic man, not a theological revolutionary. Moreover,
in a period of social stress and strain such as the Peloponnesian War,
soothsayers and diviners are common phenomena. Socrates' references
to his *daimon* produce neither curiosity nor even great interest.

Perhaps Socrates' private *daimon* is in conflict with civic piety.
But I see no evidence for this; the *daimon* does not hold Socrates back
from public worship, or from going to his trial. Socrates interprets his
dream to "Make music" as an exhortation to do philosophy, and here,
if anywhere, is the offense.

Socrates' *daimon* is unusual because it is subject to rational interpretation and scrutiny no less than the Delphic oracle. If Socrates is impious, then it is his relentless practice of philosophy which gives offense. To see how this might come about, let us place Socrates within the development of Western thought. From the seventh to the fifth century B.C. Greece emerges from a predominately oral culture. An oral culture prefers songs and verse to prose, and verbal performances to written performances. We need only recall that the Homeric epics are sung long before they are written down. Such poems are easy to memorize because of the verse and formulaic language. But the difference between an oral and a written culture is not only in the mode of expression, but also in the manner of thought. In an oral culture wisdom comes from authority — the voices one hears or recalls. Poems are the repositories of public wisdom, and one is wise insofar as he can recall the accumulated, public wisdom. Education is predominately by means of memorization. A written culture, on the other hand, obviates the emphasis on memory since the documents are ready to hand. One can check and recheck what is said. More important, there is room for the development of ratiocination. One can stare at a text, and then think about it.

Socrates is a deeply oral man who, nevertheless, reflects the chief value of a written culture — rationality. He attempts to preserve the best of both cultures, but satisfies neither. His practice of philosophy is oral; question and answer uses no stenographers, and is done face to face. But the very practice of dialectic destroys authority; for it presupposes that each person has the obligation to state, clarify, and defend his beliefs.[13]

Socrates' attack on authority should not be confused with his appeal to experts. All forms of inspiration — poetic and Delphic — must submit to the standards of rational interpretation and examination. Inspired sources may be inspired but they cannot give a defensible account of their own utterances. The Delphic God does not lie, but his human repositories are obscure. Expert craftsmen, on the other hand, can give an account of their methods and procedures. Given their ends, craftsmen know how to achieve those ends. Hence Socrates emphasizes in the *Apology* that craftsmen, unlike poets and oracles, do know some things (22d).

Socrates conventionally is impious because he launches an attack on the received sources of wisdom. Corruption of the youth springs from the same source.[14] But does Socrates corrupt the youth? An answer to this question hinges on what counts as corruption. If to undermine parental authority is corruption, then Socrates is guilty. His guilt comes about in the following way. Traditional education in Ancient Greece is handled in the home — frequently by a household slave — or by actual experience in the *polis*. The head of the house arranges for the proper education, and this responsibility is part of his authority. The rise of sophists — professors — in fifth century Greece changes all of this. They lure the young men away from parental authority by providing them with a specialized education which is needed in their increasingly complex society. The sophists compete with the fathers for influence with the young men, and they are winning. Socrates denies that he is a sophist because he does not charge fees, and he does not teach. I will discuss these claims below. But even if Socrates is unlike the sophists in these respects, he is like them in that he provides an expert service which lures the youths from their parents' authority.

Socrates only asks questions and hears answers, but he does this better than others, especially better than the young men's parents. Socrates admits that the young men collect around him, and imitate his method (23c-d). He draws the young men from the traditional studies of the poets, and from parental authority. Therefore if Socrates corrupts the youth, then he does it for the same reason that he is impious: dialectic challenges the prevailing authorities. Socrates, who refuses to preach any position, becomes the new anti-authority authority.

At 33b Socrates says:

> I ask questions, and whoever wishes may answer and hear what I say. And whether any of them turns out well or ill, I should not justly be held responsible, since I never promised or gave instruction to any of them . . .

Socrates forces Gorgias to admit that if a student comes to him to learn rhetoric, but does not know virtue, then Gorgias will teach him virtue (*Gorgias* 460a). He wants Gorgias to see that any art must be guided by virtue, if it is to be really beneficial. Is there any relevant difference between the two men so that Socrates is not responsible for how his students turn out but Gorgias is? The difference is in their conceptions of teaching and learning. Gorgias teaches by a transmission or giving over of set material to his students. The students learn by ab-

sorbing the material. If one can teach in this way, then one is responsible for the content of what is taught. Socrates, however, doubts that
virtue can be taught in this way. If it could, then fathers would make,
or hire sophists to make, their children virtuous; but even though fathers
desire to make their children virtuous, they usually do not. Hence virtue is not taught by transmission (cf. *Meno* 93af.). Socratic question
and answer, on the other hand, places the responsibility for learning
on the learner who must undertake the activity himself. Someone cannot be forced to do dialectic or to use his mind, and while Socrates
may persuade and cajole someone to continue talking, he will not and
cannot force them to do so. Socrates tells them about the value of dialectic: the unexamined life is not worth living; and he tries to sting people into action, but he cannot coerce rationality. Thus he is not responsible for how his listeners turn out; they are responsible for themselves.
Alcibiades, Critias, and Charmides turn out poorly, and since the many
think that Socrates teaches like a sophist, they also believe that he corrupts his pupils.

There is a final reason why Socrates is convicted, and this is his
demeanor at the trial. Socrates appears arrogant, but I do not see how
he could appear otherwise. The appearance is due to the juxtaposition between telling the truth and expected courtroom behavior. Socrates states the truth even if it angers the jury. A normal speech seeks
only acquittal, and it flatters the jury. The jurors expect flattery and
praise, but Socrates does not give them what they expect. Socrates
changes a potentially entertaining day for the jury into a moral lecture, and in the process is convicted.[15]

The Opening Scenes of the *Apology*

Socrates distinguishes the persuasive speeches of his accusers from
his own poor ability to speak well (17a-d). His accusers speak so persuasively that Socrates almost forgets his own identity (17a). Given
standard Athenian legal practice, Meletus has just completed his ac-
cusatory speech with all the expected rhetorical embellishments, when
the *Apology* opens. Socrates insists that he is not a clever orator, at
least after the fashion of Meletus (17b). He will not present to the
jurors carefully arranged words, but rather they will hear "things said
at random with the words that happen to occur [to Socrates]" (17b-c).

Socrates' unadorned words will express only the truth (17b, 18a).

R. E. Allen argues that Socrates' feigned inability to make a well-composed speech is ironical.[16] Socrates' speech is very well-composed; in fact it is an anti-rhetorical parody of set courtroom rhetoric. Socrates' very mention in the introduction of his advanced age, unfamiliarity with courts, and inability to speak, mimics standard defense orations. Allen convincingly shows that the different stages of the *Apology* parallel set Lysian/Isocratean courtroom speeches: there is a well-formed exordium, a statement of the case and plan of the plea, a refutation—first against the old accusers who started the prejudice against Socrates and then against the actual charges—and finally a speech to convince the jury of Socrates' nobility. But Socrates' speech is an anti-rhetorical parody of rhetoric because it inverts the customary purpose of courtroom speeches. These speeches are given to achieve acquittal or conviction; Socrates will tell only the truth to the jurors no matter what the effect on the jurors. Socrates turns a tool that is used for one purpose to a very different purpose. He does not speak well by received criteria, but he speaks very well given his criterion. Most people would agree with Socrates that he does not speak well, but he does not agree with them! Callicles is right that Socrates will not have a word to say before the bar, but he is wrong if he implies that Socrates will not speak. Socrates makes a speech, but it is unlike other speeches.

The Old Accusers

Only Aristophanes is identified by name among this group, but he wrote the *Clouds* twenty-five years before Socrates' trial, so why does Socrates unearth ancient history? His explicit reason is to recall an old but lasting prejudice against him. Unless Socrates disarms this prejudice, he cannot escape the new charges. Furthermore, the new charges are vague, and this tends to make the issue more about Socrates' character than about whether he breaks the law. The *Clouds* has a lot to do with the perception of who Socrates is.

At 18b-c and 19b Socrates lists the old accusations. The central charges are that Socrates: (1) investigates things beneath the earth and in the heavens, (2) makes the weaker argument appear the stronger, and (3) teaches these same things to others. Related accusations are that he is a wise man, criminal, and busybody. (1) suggests that Socrates does not believe in any gods, and (3) conjoined with (1) or (2) implies corruption of the youth. The old accusations are all found in the *Clouds*. (1) is the stock charge of studying nature, and (2) is the stock charge of practicing sophistry. Socrates does these things in the *Clouds*, and he teaches them to others.

Socrates denies that he is a *physiologos* (a student about nature). He knows nothing about these things, and has nothing to do with them (19c). He does not dishonor such knowledge if others have it, but he has no such knowledge of nature. Socrates asks the jurors to inform one another if they have ever heard him converse about such matters (19c).

Are Socrates' denials honest? In the *Phaedo* he admits that he studied physical philosophy in his youth (95ef.); moreover, West suggests that Socrates may well have studied nature prior to Chaerephon's visit to the Delphic oracle.[17] Socrates only sets out to puncture purported wisdom after he hears the declaration of the oracle that he is the wisest of humans. Is Socrates lying to the jury? I do not think so. Socrates never denies studying about nature; he does deny that he has any knowledge about these things, and that anyone has heard him discourse about such matters. The *Phaedo* confirms the first denial; following Anaxagoras Socrates did believe that like produces like, but when he tried to extend this explanation he ran into paradoxes: the same cause can have opposite effects, and opposite causes the same effect (96cff.). To resolve these paradoxes Socrates recurred to *logoi* rather than the direct investigation of nature. Socrates does not have knowledge about nature just as he claims in the *Apology*.

Socrates does not, then, have anything to teach others. Nor is there any evidence, besides the *Clouds*, that Socrates teaches natural philosophy. Unlike dialectic, the study of nature does not require either a partner or a public setting. Socrates could easily do the research of an Anaximenes or Anaxagoras in private, or with a few close friends. If Socrates through the study of physical philosophy becomes impious, then probably it is a private impiety.

Socrates also denies that he teaches others, and hence by implication that he corrupts the youth. It is a fine thing, he sarcastically says, to be able to teach like Gorgias, Prodicus, and Hippias, and receive a fee for it (19d-e). Hippias can transmit the geneologies of the gods and heroes, but the sophists do not teach anything as important as virtue. Taking a fee seems to be only an accidental distinction between

Socrates and the sophists. It seems that Socrates has a perverse preference for poverty where the sophists do not. But the question of fees is more important than it seems. The sophists teach to obtain a fee, and the bigger the fee the better. Teaching is a mere means to a fee just as class work is for some students a mere means to a grade. Sophists whose eyes are on their fees must pander to the students, and give them what they want, or risk the loss of the fee. Socrates does not take a fee, and hence he is free to tell the truth, even if the truth angers others. Thus Socrates, unlike some sophists, can practice an art which aims at the good of its subject matter.

Socrates tells how he met Callias who has spent more money on sophists than anyone else (20a-c). Callias has two sons, and he engages the sophist Evenus for their instruction. 20a-c is a very ironic passage. Socrates reiterates that Callias has two sons; he does not need to mention to the jury that the first is by his wife and the second by his wife's mother. First Callias swears that he only has one son, then he swears that he has two. Since Callias has spent more money on sophists than anyone else, the sophists must be responsible for his scandalous behavior, or so Socrates insinuates. Socrates agrees that sophists corrupt, but he is not a sophist. He does not accept any money from Callias, or anyone else.

The Delphic Oracle

Socrates then attempts to explain the origin of the prejudice against him, for he does do something which is out of the ordinary. He describes Chaerephon's visit to the Delphic oracle. Chaerephon asks the oracle whether there is anyone wiser than Socrates, and the oracle replies that there is not (21a). Socrates does not understand what the oracle means, and so he sets out to prove that the oracle is wrong (21b-c). He tests the politicians, poets, and artisans who are thought to be wise, but they are not, nor are they aware of their own ignorance (21c-d). The poets are inspired like prophets and givers of oracles, and they make carefully constructed poems, but they know nothing about the fine things which they say (22b-d). The artisans know some things in their specific arts, and because of this they think that they know more important things, but they do not (22d). Socrates is wiser than the artisans because he is not deceived about his own ignorance.

People hate Socrates because of his examinations. Nobody, especially somebody who thinks he is wise, likes to be refuted, especially not in public before young men. Socratic *elenchus* (refutation) causes great enmity against Socrates (23c). He is also despised because he appears wise in those matters in which he refutes others (23a). If Socrates can refute others then, presumably, he knows what the correct answer is. Socrates ironically feigns ignorance, and then refutes someone; this is the ground of the charges of "wise man," and "arrogant" against him.

Socrates replies that he has only human wisdom; others may have a wisdom which is greater than human, but not he (20d-e). Socrates is the wisest of people because he alone recognizes that he is not worthy with respect to real wisdom (23b). How are we to interpret these obscure claims? Certainly Socrates is not better than others because he knows that he holds false beliefs while they do not. A common interpretation is that Socrates knows that he does not know anything, and this implies that the early dialogues are totally aporetic. Socrates refutes others, but he neither states, nor implies his own positions, because he does not have any.[18]

Whether Socrates knows that he does not know anything depends upon what is meant by "know." An interpretation of Socrates' ignorance must satisfy two conditions: (1) "Knowledge of ignorance" must not be rendered inconsistent or paradoxical, and (2) it must explain Socrates' strong beliefs in the *Crito* (49a-d) that one ought never commit an injustice, or return an injustice with an injustice, as well as his strong beliefs in other dialogues (cf. *Meno* 86b-c, *Gorgias* 508e-509a).

To understand what human wisdom is, we need to know what it is contrasted with—divine wisdom. Divine wisdom is absolute, closed, and unquestionable. One does not question the authority of Homer or a dream from god. Divine knowledge is dogmatic. Human knowledge, by contrast, is revisable; no matter how strong the arguments in favor of some belief, that belief can never be closed to further inquiry.[19] It is always open to further evidence, and more dialectical investigation. Socrates knows in the sense of "revisable knowledge" that he does not possess absolute knowledge. This is consistent with Socrates strongly believing some things, those which have survived dialectical inquiry.

Socrates' posture towards the Delphic oracle is confusing. First he says that the god does not lie, and then he sets out to prove that the oracle is wrong (21b-c). We must, I think, distinguish between the god and his oracle. The god cannot lie, but the oracle can be misinspired; at the least the oracle is aphoristic and paradoxical. Socrates flirts with impiety by questioning the oracle, but he does not question the veracity of the god.

Socrates' attempt to refute the oracle turns into a service to the god at the god's behest (23b). The god stations Socrates at his philosophical post with the duty to examine others (23e-29a). What starts out as Socrates' self-initiated testing of the oracle ends as a command from the god to examine others. Once Socrates sees what human wisdom is, it is reasonable for him to want others to see it too; but there is no explanation in the *Apology* for how the god commands Socrates to examine others. Socrates' *daimon* holds him back from doing something, and the oracle only said that he is the wisest of men. I suggest the following solution to this problem. Socrates gradually replaces reference to the Delphic god by mention of simply "a god," and then at 33c he says, "But, as I believe, I have been commanded to do this by the god through oracles and dreams and in every way in which any man was ever commanded by divine power to do anything whatsoever." It sounds like one and the same god speaks through the different media; the Delphic oracle, Socrates' *daimon*, and his dreams are all messages from a single source. A single source for different voices would explain why Socrates is vague about which god he refers to after the Delphic story, and why the god exhorts Socrates to do philsophy; for in the *Phaedo* (60e-61a) a dream urges him to "Make music," and he interprets this foremost to mean that he should do philosophy. If the same god speaks through both the dream and the oracle, then the Delphic god also urges Socrates to do philosophy. Socrates would then think that his philosophy is in obedience to the command of the Delphic god.

Socrates' service to god in the *Apology* (cf. 30a) is the same as that hinted at in the *Euthyphro*. There we are to imitate the gods by doing good things, and knowledge of good and evil is needed for such action.[20] But Socrates also believes that the knowledge of good and evil can be found only through dialectic. To do dialectic, then, is to serve the god in the *Apology*.

The Official Charges

The official indictment brought by the self-styled "good and patriotic" (24b) Meletus with the aid of Anytus and Lycon is as follows (24b-c):

Socrates is a wrongdoer because he corrupts the youth and does not believe in the gods the state believes in, but in other new spiritual beings.

Socrates summons Meletus for interrogation. He makes a counter accusation against Meletus: Meletus jokes and pretends to be concerned about things which he is not concerned about at all (24c). Meletus is not really serious or concerned unless he can state, clarify, and defend his accusations. Socrates has high standards for the morally serious life, and Meletus does not meet these standards. Meletus' bad *logoi* reveal his lack of moral seriousness.

Socrates first attacks Meletus' democratic bias; he gets Meletus to claim that everyone else in the state benefits the youth, and only Socrates corrupts them. Socrates compels Meletus to see that the experts in all other areas who benefit their subjects are few, while the charlatans and pretenders are many. Socrates' implied conclusion—another example of his arrogance—is that he alone benefits the youth while the democratic majority—including the jury—corrupt them. He does not flatter the jury by this implied conclusion.

Socrates next turns to the charge of corrupting the youth. He forces Meletus to consent to the following argument; if Socrates corrupts the youth, then he makes them bad. If he makes them bad, then he surrounds himself with bad persons who will, in turn, make him worse (25d-e). Nobody suffers harm voluntarily, and since Socrates knows that if he corrupts the youth then they will harm him, he does not corrupt them voluntarily. Therefore either he does not corrupt the youth, or if he corrupts them, then he does it involuntarily. In the latter case what he deserves is private instruction and admonition (25e-26a).

Socrates does not deny directly the charge of corruption. The charge is vague, and there is no point to deny a charge whose tentacles spread out to all facets of one's life. Also Socrates probably is guilty by conventional norms; he leads the young men away from the authority figures in the *polis*. Finally a straight denial does not educate either Meletus or the jury, but Socrates is always an educator. Hence he forces Meletus into a dilemma; either Socrates does not corrupt the youth, or if he corrupts them he does it involuntary. On the first horn he denies the charge; on the second he denies the point of bringing him to court. In court, just as in his everyday activities, Socrates forces people to think by his strange claims. Two of these claims are: to harm a fellow citizen by making him worse is to harm oneself, and doing wrong is involuntary and should be remedied by education. The second claim presupposes that wrongdoing is due to ignorance.

Meletus claims that Socrates corrupts the youth by not believing in the gods which the state believes in, but in other new spiritual beings (26b). Socrates asks Meletus whether he, Socrates, believes in some gods, and is not altogether godless, or whether he does not believe in any gods at all (26c). Meletus unexpectedly chooses the latter alternative because Socrates believes, or so Meletus claims, that the sun is made of stone, and the moon of earth. These positions are known to belong to Anaxagoras, and Socrates simply denies that he is Anaxagoras. It appears that Plato foists an *ignoratio* on Meletus: the charge is that Socrates believes in gods other than those of the *polis*, not the stronger claim of atheism. But he refutes the stronger not the weaker claim. This charge, I believe, is unfair to Plato. Meletus states the only plausible charge he can make—that Socrates is an atheist. For in *Republic* I we see Socrates abide by the public modes of worship, and there is nothing impious or even unusual about his *daimon*. All that Meletus can say, relying on Aristophanes' association of Socrates with the physical philosophers, is that he is an atheist. That this charge is also weak reflects Meletus' lack of seriousness.

Since Meletus' official charge is that Socrates believes in some *daimones*, but not those of the city, Socrates uses this concession to show that he believes in gods. Since Socrates believes in *daimones*, and since *daimones* are in one way or another the children of gods, he also believes in gods (27d). Socrates reaffirms that a god is behind his dreams, internal voice, as well as the inspiration of the Delphic oracle. Hence he concludes his defense as follows:

> . . . for I do believe in them [the gods], men of Athens, more than any of my accusers, and I entrust my case to you and to god to decide it as shall be best for me and for you.

At 28b Socrates rhetorically asks whether he is not ashamed to do what he does. He compares himself with Achilles who also does what is noble but at a great price. The god, so Socrates claims, stations him to do philosophy (28e-29a), and Socrates would wrong the god if he were to desert his post, and cease from interrogating others (29b). He imagines a conditional court release where the court would let him go on the condition that he cease from philosophy (29c-d).[21] He would refuse such a release. This refusal, as well as two events described below, are sometimes thought to conflict with the position of the *Crito*. I will show that they do not.

Socrates' Disobedience

Later I will defend the claim that Socrates' position in the *Crito* is that one ought to abide by the laws provided that they are just (50a). The question is what "provided that they are just" means. The context implies that the principle that one ought never commit an injustice takes precedence over any other principle (cf. 49af.). Obedience to the law is, then, a secondary principle which must conform to the previous one: one ought to obey the law unless it requires one to commit an injustice. Suppose that Socrates would act as he hypothesizes; is refusing the conditional release inconsistent with the position of the *Crito*? No, and for several reasons. Let us suppose that obedience to the law also requires obedience to court decisions. An offer is still not a judgment and Socrates can refuse any offer the court makes. Moreover, it is a procedurally irregular offer since only the defense and prosecution can offer penalties.[22] But Socrates must reject the offer in any case, for to accept it would be to commit an injustice.

There are several reasons why Socrates would commit an injustice. He would disobey the god (29d). The god is better than Socrates, and he commands him to do philosophy; to disobey the god would be to wrong him (not necessarily harm him), by disobeying his command.[23] Second Socrates would withhold a great benefit from the city (30a), and from himself. For the unexamined life is not worth living (38a), and dialectic is necessary for the examined life. Third we must understand the close association between intelligent *logoi* and the *polis*. The city is the home and father of civilized *logoi*, and such *logoi* in turn create a civilized city. The city educates us, among other things, to speak, and we later become educators in the city. If Socrates were to quit speaking, then he would banish himself from the civilizing influence of the city, and from his part in the process. He would deny his own achieved humanity by ceasing to speak. This he will not do. He will reject any option which forces him outside the city, or requires him to be silent — the two are close to the same thing.

Socrates relates how his *daimon* prevents him from partaking in politics since a just man cannot survive in it (31e-32a). Socrates illustrates the perils of politics with two examples which are thought to conflict with the *Crito*. The first occurs under the democracy and the second under the thirty oligarchs; hence a good man cannot survive either regime!

Under the democracy Socrates is chosen by lot a prytane of the assembly when the mob wants to collectively, not individually, try the ten generals who failed to gather the slain after a naval battle. Socrates refuses with "law and justice" on his side even though the mob howls at him. Socrates abides by the proper legal procedure, while the mob does not. If Socrates were to give in to the mob, then he would wrong the laws by failing to abide by their procedurally fair application.[24] He would also wrong the generals and harm them by denying them an adequate, individual defense. The *logoi* of each general are silenced by a collective trial; they are not individually permitted to persuade the court of their innocence. Again Socrates refuses to commit an injustice, and protects the civilized *logoi* of the state.

In the second case the thirty oligarchs command Socrates to bring in Leon of Salamis for execution. Others went to arrest Leon, but Socrates went home and awaited his fate. Government with all its power could not make Socrates commit an injustice. But what is the injustice here? It is not just the harm to Leon's body, but most important the denial to him of a trial and defense. The oligarchs would dispatch Leon without a trial and defense, and this is the greatest injustice to him. Again Socrates preserves the civilized *logoi* of the city. Hence neither of the above cases is incompatible with my interpretation of the *Crito*. It is doubtful whether Socrates breaks a law (or disobeys a legitimate government) in either case, and even if he does, obedience to a law would require him to commit an injustice which violates his major principle that one ought never to commit an injustice.

Conclusion

Socrates ends his defense to the jury by affirming his piety to the god, a piety which far exceeds that of his accusers. Socrates' speech is honest and truthful, and it frequently offends the jurors. He is convicted by a margin of thirty votes, and then there is the separate question of the penalty. The procedure is that the prosecution and defense each offers a penalty, and the jury must accept one or the other offer. The prosecution offers the death penalty, and then it is Socrates' turn.

Socrates continues to maintain that he is the city's greatest benefactor, and in consistency with the services he renders he should receive free maintenance at the Prytaneum (36d)—something like our equivalent of the athletic training table. Since he never voluntarily harms another, he will not choose what he knows to be an evil for himself. He refuses exile since if his own countrymen cannot tolerate his conversations, others are unlikely to endure them, and he refuses to be driven from city to city (37c-d). Socrates refuses to be silent, for exile involves silence. He also refuses to leave the court, go home, and be silent (37e). His answer is the same as before: silence is to disobey the god, and to wrong himself and the city (38a).

Socrates' final counter-offer is to pay a fine of thirty minas (38b). Smith and Brickhouse argue that this is no small sum of money—it is enough to build and equip a warship.[25] Is Socrates trying to buy his way out? Smith and Brickhouse go on to argue that money means little or nothing to Socrates. To pay a fine neither wrongs nor harms anyone. Socrates would like to avoid the death penalty, and a fine provides the jury with a graceful way to release him.

The jury votes for death by a somewhat larger margin than the previous vote.

The *Apology* is a great educational work. Except for a small section, it does not show Socrates at his dialectical task; rather Socrates states his values. Money is not the greatest value, death should not be feared, and the unexamined life is not worth living. Plato not only wants us to see Socrates, but also he wants us to think about these values.

CRITO

Initially it appears that the *Apology* and *Crito* are inconsistent.[26] Indeed, the two dialogues differ in emphasis and tone. In the *Apology*

Socrates will obey the god even if he must reject a court offer of freedom on condition that he cease from dialectic; in the *Crito* the personified laws claim that Socrates is their slave. He must obey them. But I will show that there is no substantive inconsistency between the *Apology* and *Crito*. The most important moral principle in the *Crito* is that one ought never commit an injustice (do wrong). The arguments of the *Crito* require us to obey the laws unless the laws ask us to commit an injustice. If the laws require us to commit an injustice, then we must disobey them. But this is as far as Socrates' position on civil disobedience goes; if one breaks a law, even one which requires us to do an injustice, then one must either persuade the court that disobedience is justified, or accept the court's penalty.[27] Socrates acts as if the laws have two levels: the first prescribes or forbids some behavior, and the second consists in the sanctions for disobedience. Morality may require one to disobey the first level of law, but not the second, unless a punishment requires one to commit an injustice. Socrates would be a destroyer of law, the laws will claim, if he were to escape, since he then would deny the authority of law to punish him. The *Apology* and *Crito* are consistent because: (1) In both dialogues Socrates refuses to do wrong, and (2) In the *Apology* he does not break a law unless it requires him to commit an injustice. (And Socrates may not have broken any laws in that dialogue in any case.)

The *Crito* not only provides interesting arguments for obedience to the laws, but also it is the only explicit example of the knowledge of good and evil in application to a complex situation.[28] We already have seen that Socrates identifies each virtue with the knowledge of good and evil, and we know that this knowledge is about what it is best, on the whole, to do. The *Crito* shows Socrates taking the previous results of dialectic, and applying them to the problem at issue. The *Gorgias* principle that one ought never commit an injustice is an example of a premise which is justified by previous dialectical inquiry. Crito and Socrates agree that there is no need to reinvestigate this principle (49a-e), and they proceed to apply it to Socrates' decision. The *Crito* also depicts Socrates acting in harmony with the best results of dialectic — his words and deeds chime in harmony together. He does not commit suicide, not even judicial suicide.[29] He only does what the *logoi* (arguments) tell him that he ought to do. Socrates could be wrong, for all human knowledge is revisable, but one must act on those beliefs which at the time are fastened as well as one can.

Crito's Arguments for Escape

As the dialogue opens Crito finds Socrates in prison sleeping sweetly (43b). He reports that Socrates always was of a good disposition, but never more so than now even though death awaits him. Socrates' sweet sleep is symbolic both of death, and that death is not to be feared. In the *Apology* (40c-41b) Socrates asserts that either death is a long dreamless sleep, or it is a dialectical heaven where he can examine those who have gone before him. In either case we should not fear death as some evil about which we have knowledge. The opening of the *Crito* is essential for understanding Socrates' later arguments; Socrates does not view death as an evil, nor does he think that the laws wrong him because they require his death.

Socrates reports to Crito a dream which he has just had: a beautiful maiden, dressed in white, comes to him and says, "Socrates, on the third day you will come to fertile Pythia" (44a-b). This dream assures Socrates that death is not an evil; in fact, for him it is a great benefit. Socrates will not wrong himself if he drinks the hemlock. The jurors who voted against him do treat him badly, but he will not treat himself in that way.

Crito sees Socrates' impending death as a great misfortune (43b). That Socrates will die in a few days is sad news to him (43c). Crito is, I think, something of an intellectual puzzle. He is an associate of Socrates, but he only agrees with some of Socrates' assumptions, and he views Socrates' death as a tragedy. Socrates' strictures against fearing death do not influence him at all. Is Crito simply a poor student who is drawn to Socrates because he discerns him to be a decent man, or is Crito judiciously influenced by some but not all of Socrates' beliefs? Does the speech of the personified laws, as has recently been suggested, overexaggerate the laws' claims on Socrates in order to persuade a dull Crito who is not capable of Socratic dialectic?[30] This last claim cannot be dismissed entirely, although it would be odd for Socrates to pedagogically overexaggerate, when the circumstances call for the unbiased pursuit of nothing but the truth.

Crito gives several reasons why Socrates should escape from prison, but it is not clear whether these reasons are prudential or moral ones.[31] Crito probably intends for them to be a mixed bag, and Socrates does not make much of a distinction between the prudential and the moral. For Socrates living well and living right are the same (48b). Socrates' cavalier dismissal (48c) of Crito's reasons is also perplexing. Socrates seems to dismiss even questions about the eventual fate of his children. But Socrates is not as callous as he appears. He responds to several of Crito's reasons, and the rest have clear Socratic answers. However, Socrates does consider Crito's reasons to be peripheral to the main issue — whether he does wrong by escaping. However, some of them — for example the future of his children — are not so peripheral.

At 44b Crito opens by urging Socrates to save himself. This exhortation highlights the values which Socrates rejects. Crito wants Socrates to choose life, with all its desires and urges, even if it must be a life without philosophy. Crito urges Socrates to live rather than to live well. To choose those desires whose satisfaction is only available to the living may be wrong, if it requires as a necessary means the commission of an injustice.

Crito's first claim is that if Socrates stays in prison and is executed, then he will loose an irreplaceable friend (44b). Socrates does not answer this claim directly, but he has an answer. Nor is Crito unreasonably selfish; Socrates ought not deprive him of a valuable friendship, if he can avoid it. For part of Socrates' gadfly mission to Athens is to benefit Crito who is a fellow citizen. Crito justifiably should not want to be deprived of this benefit, although there is some doubt about whether he recognizes its nature or not. This is why Socrates is an irreplaceable friend. But let us suppose that Socrates escapes. He can no longer be the gadfly of Athens, and if he went into exile he believes that he cannot continue dialectic. With the reputation of a law destroyer he will be ashamed to carry on his accustomed conversations (53b-c), nor will foreigners be likely to tolerate his conversations. Escape precludes Socrates from being the true friend of the *Lysis*; for a true friend leads the *psychē* through dialectic to the truth. This is Socrates' indirect but firm reply to Crito.

Crito's second reason is that he will gain the odious reputation of valuing money more than his friend's safety (44b-c). Socrates replies that Crito should only be concerned about intelligent opinions. Behind Socrates' elitism is a good reason to reject Crito's claim. The many hold inconsistent opinions, and their opinions fluctuate. If Crito does nothing, some will condemn him; and if he helps Socrates escape, others will condemn him. One cannot win against uneducated opinion.[32]

Socrates also rejects public opinion because it can accomplish neither good nor evil (44d). To understand this reply we must remember that for Socrates knowledge is the only intrinsic good, and ignorance the only intrinsic evil. Public opinion cannot generate knowledge, only dialectic does that. Public opinion cannot create ignorance; it cannot loosen beliefs which are tied in the *psyche* by dialectic. Public opinion does not create ignorance, but it is a form of ignorance. To that extent we should fear it.

Crito claims that it is right for him to risk the loss of property, money, and other things by helping Socrates to escape (44e-45a). Socrates replies that he is considering this point and other things (45a), and later the personified laws at 53b confirm the risk which Socrates' friends will incur if they help him escape. They risk, among other things, banishment and the loss of their property. It may be right for Crito to run such a risk, but it is wrong for Socrates to accept it.

Crito offers to help Socrates escape to Thessaly; he has friends there who will protect Socrates (45b-c). Thessaly is a symbol of why Socrates refuses exile either as a possible punishment or as a result of escape. Thessaly, as the laws later point out (53d) is full of disorder and lawlessness; it is also the home of the notorious Meno. Thessaly is good for raising horses, but it is not a civilized state, Socrates cannot do dialectic there; he can only feast and drink! Socrates also refuses to go to well-governed states like Thebes and Megara, if he must go to them as a lawbreaker and enemy of the *polis* (53b-c). Socrates refuses exile as a punishment in the *Apology* because such a punishment would be an admission of guilt, and a harm to him even though he has done no wrong; he refuses exile in the *Crito* because he would be an enemy of any civilized state, and unable to do dialectic in any state. Thus he rejects Crito's offer of Thessalian hospitality.

Crito gives two final reasons why it is wrong for Socrates to remain and be executed (45c). The first is that he will betray himself, and bring upon himself what his enemies want. Woozley cogently argues that even if it is wrong for someone to bring about a certain result, it need not be wrong for another to bring about the same result.[33] Socrates' accusers treat him badly by how they bring about his death; it does not follow that Socrates acts badly by failing to avoid execution. The accusers bring about his death through unfair accusations; Socrates dies believing that death is no evil, but to escape from prison is.

Crito's last argument is that if Socrates does not escape, then he will abandon his children when he might bring them up and educate them (45d). Crito also claims that Socrates' children probably will meet with the bad treatment which generally comes to orphans in their destitution (45d). Let us look at the second claim first. Socrates need not deny that orphans are treated badly, only that his children will be treated like most orphans, and will be worse off if he does not escape than if he does. The personified laws argue on Socrates' behalf that the children will not be worse off if he stays. Should Socrates take them to Thessaly to educate them, and make exiles of them (54a)? This is unacceptable. Furthermore, Socrates' friends will care for his children just as much if he goes to the dwelling of the dead as into exile.

At 48c Socrates seems to dismiss his responsibility to educate his children:

> But the considerations you suggest, about spending money, and reputation, and bringing up my children, these are really, Crito, the reflections of those who lightly put men to death, and would bring them to life again, if they could, without any sense, I mean the multitude.

As Woozley claims, Socrates has a distasteful detachment from his children.[34] He appears unconcerned about his obligation to educate them. I know of no textual evidence which rebuts this charge. But Socrates can explain why escape will not help him educate his children. If escape is wrong, and Socrates escapes, then he will only be an evil influence on them. Also he is not able to do dialectic in exile, and thus he is not able to educate his children in exile. In the *Apology* (39c-d) he projects, with what may be more than a mere wish, that his death will unleash a host of dialecticians upon Athens — young men whom he previously restrained. His children would certainly benefit from this dialectical swarm. We do not know whether Socrates would apply these arguments to the education of his children, but he could.

Crito is ashamed of Socrates and their friends, and he fears that people will think that the whole affair, from indictment to execution, is conducted with cowardice (45e). Crito agrees with the many that Socrates' trial defense is cowardly and ineffectual. We saw in the *Apology* that Socrates inverts the normal purpose of a courtroom defense; instead of acquittal at any price he tells the truth whatever the effect on the jury. Crito is as intellectually distant from Socrates on this issue as the rest of the many; he does not understand why Socrates acts as he does. Socrates must lead Crito back to follow the *logoi*, and not mere opinion.

Socrates' Major Assumptions

We next enter a phase of the dialogue where Socrates prepares Crito for the speech of the laws. Socrates asserts that they must examine the question dialectically, *for Socrates will only act on the considerations which seem best to him* (46b).[35] He will not discard those conclusions which survived previous dialectical assault, unless they are now defeated (46b). He must respect his previous views, unless his prior activity was mere play (46d); a morally serious person, however, must look at the arguments. Socrates then recalls for Crito the following claims:

(1) They ought to esteem good but not bad opinions (47a-c).
(2) The *psychē* is more valuable than the body, and harm to it makes life less worth living than harm to the body (47e-48a).
(3) Not living, but living well, is what is important (48a).
(4) Living well and living justly are the same thing (48a).
(5) Wrongdoing harms the *psychē*.
(6) We ought never do wrong, or return a wrong with a wrong (49a-b).

(1) - (6) embody numerous difficult Socratic positions, but I want to focus on the notion of "doing wrong." What does Socrates mean by this? If *A* wrongs *B*, then *A* either harms or attempts to harm either *B*'s body or *psychē*. *A* harms or attempts to harm *B*'s *psychē* by promoting or attempting to promote those desires which impede *B*'s rationality. Since virtue is knowledge, and knowledge comes through rational dialectic, desires which impede *B*'s rationality harm *B*'s virtue. This analysis can be extended from persons to laws. The laws of a city are identified closely with that city, and a city is the father and *locus* of rationality. One harms the laws and the *polis* if one effects the laws in such a way as to decrease rationality within the *polis*.[36] This, I suggest, is part of what Socrates is getting at in the *Apology* and *Crito*. In the context of these beliefs he asks whether it is right for him to escape from prison.

The Speech of the Laws

The personified laws, speaking for themselves and for Socrates, present two related arguments for why Socrates should not escape. The first I will call the "argument from agreement," and the second the "argument from harm." I will refer to these arguments by their key premises, and later present them *in toto*.

At 49e and again at 50a Socrates states the argument from agreement:

> . . . must one do what he has agreed to with respect to just things, or may he violate his agreements?. . . if we go away from here without the consent of the state, are we doing harm to the very ones to whom we least ought to do harm, or not, and do we remain with those things we agree are right, or not?

Both quotes illustrate that the argument from agreement has an important proviso: one ought to abide by one's agreements *about or with respect to just things*. We must first see what the accusative of respect refers to. At 52e the laws state that Socrates did not agree to abide by them through either fraud or compulsion, in which case the agreement would not be binding. But there is no evidence, direct or contextual, at 49e-50a that this is what Socrates has in mind. What precedes the above quotes, however, is Socrates' repeated assertion that one ought never commit an injustice. "Concerning just things," I submit, refers to this highest principle.[37]

Agreements must be kept unless they require one to commit an injustice. Socrates apparently believes that one can agree to do an injustice, but that such an agreement should not be kept. Thus he maintains in the *Crito*, as he does in the *Apology*, the supreme prohibition against wrongdoing.

The argument from agreement is subordinate to the principles of right and wrong action, whatever they may be. One must first see whether keeping an agreement requires one to do a wrong action; if it does not, then one must abide by the agreement. We can also see how the arguments from agreement and harm are distinct but connected. The former requires us to abide by our agreements to do right or morally neutral things; the latter forbids us to do harm, and one type of harm arises from breaking agreements which do not require wrong actions. This is why the laws intermix both arguments in the text. Socrates could not harm the laws unless he is under their authority, and the argument from agreement establishes this authority.

The argument from agreement in premise conclusion form is as follows:

    (1) One ought to abide by one's agreements unless they require one to commit an injustice.

    (2) Socrates has agreed to abide by the laws of Athens, and by the law that judicial decisions be carried out.

    (3) Socrates will not commit an injustice either to himself or to another by not escaping from prison, and by being executed.

∴ (4) Socrates ought to stay in prison.

Let us first look at premise (3). Socrates is not concerned about the conceptual problem of whether one can wrong oneself, nor will I be. In both the *Apology* and the *Crito* Socrates' only practical alternatives are death and exile. To recommend anything less than exile to the jury is certain to invite the death penalty, and this is precisely what happens. Socrates consistently rejects exile; he cannot live well in Thessaly or some other foreign place. But what about death; is it not a great evil for Socrates, and will he not wrong himself by not fleeing it? We have seen that this is not the case from the introduction to the dialogue.[38] Socrates not only believes that death is no evil, but also that it is a great benefit. For these reasons he does not think that he wrongs himself by accepting the decision of the court. Moreover, as we have seen, he does not think that he wrongs either his children or his friends. Hence Socrates believes that the third premise is true, and this belief is reasonable and intelligible in light of his other beliefs.

We may, of course, disagree with Socrates' view of death. In the *Apology* he describes death as either a long dreamless sleep or a dialectical heaven where he can continue to question others. We may not share Socrates' pleasure in the anticipation of a possible unending, dreamless sleep. We can also disagree with Socrates' pessimism about the possibility of philosophy in exile. His pessimism is due to two considerations: (1) Strangers are less likely to tolerate his questions than his fellow citizens, and (2) If escape wrongs the laws, then he will not only have a reputation as a law destroyer which will result in his being driven from city to city, but also he will be ashamed to continue his accustomed conversations about virtue (53c). The first reason is weak empirically and the second depends upon the argument from harm. The Athenians take quite a long time to silence the gadfly, and while foreigners may silence him faster, he would still have some time in which to speak.

Let us look at premise (2). Has Socrates agreed to abide by the laws of Athens, in particular the "law" that the decisions of courts be carried out? This "law" amounts to the notion of authority in a legal system. Laws are authoritative only if decisions made under them can be applied.[39] The personified laws spend a large proportion of their speech attempting to persuade Socrates that he has agreed to abide by them. They claim that Socrates "agreed, not in words, but by acts, to live in accordance with us" (52d). As a native citizen Socrates has not made an explicit agreement with the laws, but his actions, so the laws claim, imply his agreement with them.[40]

The laws use the following points to support their claim:

(1) The laws used neither fraud nor force to obtain Socrates' agreement and continued residence in Athens (52e).
(2) Socrates had seventy years in which to judge the laws; he saw how they administer justice and the state, and still he did not leave Athens. Moreover, the laws allow anyone to take his possessions and leave the state, and to go to another county or to a colony (51d-52e).
(3) Socrates does not find fault with the most important laws in the state (50d-e).
(4) Socrates more than most people was pleased with the state. He seldom left it, and begat children in it (52b).

The laws have powerful claims to support an implied agreement. There are however, at least four objections against their conclusion:

(A) In many early dialogues, especially the *Gorgias*, Socrates is bitterly critical of Athens. Hence he does not imply agreement with the laws because he explicitly criticizes them. But what is Socrates critical about? He condemns the politicians, sophists, and poets, as well as on occasion the administration of the laws, but not the laws themselves. Socrates never questions the excellence of the laws or of a particular law—at least in the early dialogues.

(B) Socrates imagines the following objection (50b-c): "The state wronged me and did not judge the case correctly." His accusers and the jurors who vote against him wrong him, so why should he suffer a wrong decision? But Socrates knew full well how the laws are administered, and that bad judgments could be made in their name. There is nothing wrong procedurally with Socrates' trial and indictment, and hence he is not wronged by the laws. Furthermore, given his prior knowledge of how decisions are reached, Socrates still agreed to abide by the procedurally correct verdicts of the courts (50c), not just those he agrees with.

(C) Certainly one can imply general agreement with the laws

which in turn does not imply agreement with each and every law. The law against impiety is vague, and for this reason alone it is a bad law. Socrates does not agree to abide by bad laws. This objection has force, but it is not applicable to Socrates. Nowhere does he argue against the law against impiety; in fact, he seems to approve of this law. I suggest that Socrates' attitude is due to the following: he sees the close connection between the health of the *polis* and the vigor of civic religion, and yet Athens justifiably permits a wide and flexible variety of religious practices. In this context it is better to leave the law vague, and allow a jury to decide when impiety has occurred.

(D) Cannot someone live in a state, accept its benefits, and serve in its offices and still not imply an agreement to obey the laws? What about the thoughtless person or the reformer who works within the system? This sort of objection must be met on a case by case basis. Socrates is not a legal reformer, although Plato later is in the *Republic* and *Laws*. Nor is Socrates the sort of thoughtless person who can live in a system and never consider its excellence. The sort of behavior described above does not invariably imply agreement, but in Socrates' case there is good reason to think that it does.

The argument from agreement places the emphasis on agreement, not the special case of agreement to obey the laws. One ought to abide by any agreements unless they require an injustice. But why in the *Crito* does Socrates emphasize keeping agreements when he barely mentions the matter in other dialogues? The key is again, I suggest, language—the civilizing art. Socrates emphasizes the need for consistency between word and deed; if the deeds do not fit the words, then we will not trust the words (cf. *Laches* 188ef.). Socrates, himself, will act in accordance with the arguments. Keeping agreements is a type of harmony between word and deed. If we break agreements, then language becomes untrustworthy. If language becomes untrustworthy, then it cannot fulfill its civilizing function in the *polis*.

Let us now turn to the argument from harm. This argument is an application of Socrates' major premise that one ought never do an injustice to his treatment of the laws, if he escapes. In premise conclusion form the argument is as follows:

(1) One ought never commit an injustice.
(2) If Socrates escapes from prison, then he will harm the laws.
(3) To harm the laws is to treat them unjustly.
∴ (4) Socrates ought not escape from prison.

The argument from harm is subordinate to the argument from agreement. Socrates could not harm the laws unless he is under their authority and the argument from agreement establishes this authority.

The crucial premise is (2); we need to know what "harm" means. Both Allen and Woozley distinguish two uses of "harm": "injure," and "treat badly."[41] On the first Socrates' escape literally will weaken the effectiveness of the laws perhaps by causing disrespect for them. Socrates sometimes talks as if his escape would injure, and even destroy, the laws. The second starts from the personified laws' accusation that if Socrates escapes, then he is "intending by this thing you [Socrates] are trying to do, to destroy us, the laws, and the entire state, so far as you are able" (50a-b). On this view Socrates' escape actually will not harm the laws, but he will, nevertheless, wrong them. He acts as a law destroyer, even if he in fact does not harm the laws.[42]

The first interpretation of "harm" makes the truth of premise (2) an empirical matter. Will Socrates weaken the laws if he escapes? He is a moral force in Athens, and sets an example for many young men; his escape could weaken respect for the laws. On the other hand many convicted prisoners escape from prison, and their escapes do not weaken respect for, enforcement of, or obedience to the laws. The laws of Athens might even benefit from Socrates' escape, since they will not be blamed, in posterity, for his death. Hence it is unclear whether Socrates actually will harm the laws.

If Socrates does not weaken the laws in fact, then how can he be the sort of person who is a law destroyer? He knowingly acts in such a way as to harm them, even if a single escapee cannot achieve this result. Socrates also displays his disrespect by breaking his agreement to obey the laws, even if his action does not weaken agreement keeping in general. The arguments from harm and agreement conjoin at this point; an enemy of the state attempts harm and breaks his agreements.

The Conclusion

The *Apology* and *Crito* are consistent in substantive doctrine. Each dialogue subordinates legal obligation to the principle that one ought never do an injustice. One ought not obey a law if it requires one to commit an injustice. The *Crito* also shows us a Socrates who seeks for the knowledge of good and evil with respect to a specific problem. Socrates argues that he ought to stay in prison and drink the hemlock, and these beliefs are tied down in his *psychē* by reasons and replies to objections.

What does the *Crito* have to say to us about Socratic education? Socrates' philosophical activity is his educational activity. In the *Apology* and *Crito* Socrates always acts to further the opportunity for him to do dialectic; hence he acts to maximize his philosophical and educational function. Socrates does not believe that he can continue to philosophize if he escapes from prison; he cannot continue in Athens and foreign cities would not be hospitable to him. But Socrates also believes that there is a good chance that he can continue to do dialectic in heaven. Hence to permit his execution need not stop Socrates from his educational task.

8. Socratic Education
of the *Psychē* in the *Gorgias*

The explicit topics of the *Gorgias* are rhetoric and justice. For this reason Socrates talks with Gorgias, Polus, and Callicles, all of whom represent, in some way, the teaching or use of rhetoric, as well as different conceptions of justice.[1] The *Gorgias*, like other early dialogues, has different levels at which it presents its topics. There are the explicit arguments and speeches, and what is shown or displayed in the dialogue. I am concerned primarily with the latter. Here Socrates shows what he believes by how he conducts the argument, and by how he treats the different interlocutors.

While the *Gorgias* discusses overtly true and false rhetoric, it is itself an example of diverse discussions, and in these discussions Socrates states numerous rules for dialectic.[2] I first will focus on the rules for dialectic. Socrates seems to contrast dialectic with rhetoric; the former may produce beneficial refutation of an interlocutor, and justified claims to knowledge; the latter can at best persuade one to accept true beliefs and at worse crush one with the weight of false witnesses. But Socrates gives speeches, and he ends the *Gorgias* with a lengthy speech in which he threatens Callicles with failure at his last judgment. Does Socrates renounce his own educational views? Some commentators believe that Socrates is no better than Callicles because they both use bad rhetoric merely to persuade.[3] I will investigate this serious charge against Socrates.[4]

The Opening Sections

Gorgias has just given a lengthy display or exhibition when Socrates and Chaerephon arrive. Chaerephon assures Socrates that Gorgias will give him another display if Socrates desires. Gorgias' display will be one of rhetoric. His finely tuned words and phrases capture the attention of his listeners for the purpose of persuading them. A good rhetorician makes a fine rhetorical display.[5]

One's educational level determines the kind of display one gives.[6] Gorgias, Polus, and Callicles will all give displays, but they will be displays of ineptitude at dialectic. Callicles predicts that Socrates will also give a display, a display of ineptitude if he is required to defend himself in court (486a-b). Socrates, presumably, will be as inept at persuasive speeches to the many as the three rhetoricians are at dialectic. But the *Gorgias* concludes with Socrates giving a great speech, and a very fine display it is. Socrates not only gives a rhetorical display, but also he returns to Callicles a threat for a threat: Socrates may be judged guilty in the city's courts, but Callicles will not survive the divine judgment. Socrates' great speech is a counterweight to Callicles'. Why does Socrates in the end give a speech? Is he converted to the mere knack of rhetoric?

Other themes are hinted at in the opening lines. The first line, which is put into the mouth of Callicles, illudes to warfare and battle. Socrates, I will show, does not refute Callicles, but rather there is a battle or contest between them. Ideological blows are delivered, but there are no honest, philosophical conversions.[7] Socrates and Callicles pour their positions on one anothers' ears, but they do not discourse. We will want to see whether Socrates betrays his own educational principles when he exchanges blows with Callicles.

Another motif is hinted at by the contrast between the free discussions in the marketplace, and the confines of Callicles' house. Socrates has been discoursing in the market place, a symbol of free and open discussion; he is invited to Callicles' house where the enclosure is inhabited by sophists and their prospective students. Socrates will be constrained by those with whom he speaks; their natures will determine the sorts of *logoi* (words, statements) which Socrates must use.[8] Moreover, the audience—composed of young men—will place constraints on what Socrates can accomplish. Polus and Callicles will not be shamed easily before such an audience, and Callicles will refuse to answer to save face.

Arts and Knacks

Socrates argues that there is a distinction between real arts and mere knacks. We need to understand this distinction so that we may evaluate what Socrates, himself, does in the dialogue. An art satisfies the following three conditions (464b-465e): (1) it discerns the nature of its subject, so that (2) it may see the good of its subject, and, then, (3) it seeks the best means to achieve its desired end which is the good of its subject. An art must satisfy each of these conditions, and a knack fails to satisfy at least one of them. The knacks Socrates identifies in the *Gorgias* are not concerned with the good of their subjects which causes them to fail some or all of the above conditions. Hence an art aims at the good of its subject, while a knack does not.

Socrates claims that rhetoric, as some practice it, is a mere knack. A mere knack does not aim at the real good of its subject, but rather attempts to persuade of the apparent good. The apparent good tends to be the immediately pleasant, and thus false rhetoric titillates its subjects by urging them to immediate pleasures, or by telling them what they want to hear. Dialectic, on the other hand, aims at the good of its subjects. Hence dialectic is an art. The dialectic art is the art of Socratic question and answer. Socratic question and answer aims at the good of its subject by first refuting the erroneous definitions which refutations hopefully engender an admission of self-ignorance. Admitted ignorance is a necessary propaedeutic for the positive acquisition of knowledge, and the knowledge of good and evil is essential for living well.[9]

We cannot conclude, however, that all rhetoric is false rhetoric or that all question and answer is an art. It is possible for some types of rhetoric to satisfy the conditions of an art. Although it is true that no rhetoric can benefit a soul by producing knowledge in it—for speeches do not provide the dialectial testing of their claims—there can be other forms of educational benefit which rhetoric can accomplish. For example, rhetoric might be used to placate or to humble an interlocutor in order to make him amenable to dialectic.[10] Such educational aims are propaedeutics for the dialectical acquisition of knowledge. Dialectic question and answer, on the other hand, can degenerate into eristic. Contentious dialectic is eristic because winning the contest, and not the search for truth, is its aim. Callicles practices eristic not dialectic.

Rules for Good Dialectic

The nature of a *psychē* may be such that cajoling or threatening speeches are required for its benefit. Not all answerers, we will see, are prepared to admit self-ignorance. Callicles, in particular, lacks some character traits which are prerequisites for a good Socratic discussion, and Socrates must have recourse to something other than question and answer with Callicles. We cannot, then, assume that a philosopher/true rhetorician/educator will always practice dialectic question and answer; a good artist fits his method to the nature and condition of his subject matter.[11]

The leitmotif of the *Gorgias* is the distinction between the knack of rhetoric and the art of dialectic. During Socrates' conversations with all three interlocutors he introduces numerous rules for the practice of dialectic and character traits for good dialecticians.[12] He introduces these rules and character traits in the actual discussions with each answerer, often to comment on their behavior, or to highlight it for the reader. Hence Socrates tells us a lot about how he views the abilities and characters of Gorgias, Polus, and Callicles. In short we come to see how each of them fails to be a good dialectician.

I divide Socrates' comments into practice rules and character traits. Other of his comments I place under the headings of contextual features, and the *ad hominem* nature of Socratic dialectic. Socrates contrasts the interlocutors' defects with ideals for how to be a dialectician and do dialectic. The material which follows describes the rules and conditions for the best educational method—dialectic question and answer.

Practice Rules: some rules which regulate the proper asking and answering of questions:

(1) At 448d-e Socrates observes that Polus simply does not answer the question which he is asked; instead he gives a speech. Polus is evidently more practiced in speeches than question and answer. The rule is that an answerer ought to answer the question which is asked.

(2) At 451d-e Socrates says that Gorgias' answer is unclear and ambiguous. Gorgias has just said that rhetoric deals with the greatest and best of human affairs. The rule is that an answer ought to be clear and unambiguous.

(3) At 461d Socrates says that an answerer can revoke at pleasure anything which he thinks has been wrongly asserted. Each successive answerer is permitted to revoke previous admissions with which he does not agree. The questioner permits this so that an answerer is committed to each premise. The rule is that an answerer should be and is

responsible for only what he consents to, as well as the implications of these claims. Commitment is important, we will see, because admitted self-ignorance can only be about beliefs which are one's own.

(4) At 462d-e Socrates says that both the questioner and answerer should understand each other before they proceed to other questions and answers. The rule would have the same content as the above statement.

(5) At 489e Socrates accuses Callicles of uttering mere words. The rule here is not simply that an answerer should be clear and unambiguous in what he says, but also that the answerer should mean what he says.

(6) At 453c and 454c Socrates says that although he knows what Gorgias will answer, Gorgias must make his own answer in his own way. The rule is that an answerer must complete his answer as he desires. The purpose of this rule is, as in (3) above, so that the answerer is committed to his answer, as well as the orderly and deliberate completion of the argument. Socrates aims at an answerer's core beliefs, those that are central to his self-image and life.[13] In order for Socrates to defeat these beliefs, an answerer must state them, and mean what he states. At 454c Socrates says that his questions are not aimed at Gorgias, but there is very little difference between a person, and a person's core beliefs. As we shall see below, the *ad hominem* nature of dialectic is both one of its strengths and weaknesses.[14]

(7) At 462c-d Socrates implies that questions should be in the proper logical order. Polus wants Socrates to say whether rhetoric is fair or foul before they know what rhetoric is. But one cannot determine some characteristics of something until one knows what it is (cf. *Meno* 71a-b). The rule is that questions ought to be asked in a proper logical order.

(8) A 466b Socrates asks Polus whether he is asking a question or making a speech. Polus is unable to play the role of a questioner, because he always makes declarations and does not ask questions. A questioner should ask questions, and not give speeches.

(9) At 466c Socrates declares that he cannot tell whether Polus is asking a question or making a declaration. The rule is that a questioner ought to ask questions and not state opinions.

(10) At 466c Socrates accuses Polus of asking two questions at once. The rule is that one ought to ask only a single question at a time; also questions should not have loaded presuppositions.

Character Traits for Good Dialecticians

(11) Preparatory to closing the trap on Gorgias, Socrates declares that he debates only from a desire for knowing the truth, and he trusts that Gorgias has the same desire (453b). The *elenchus* (refutation) only can be beneficial to someone if they have a genuine desire for truth; otherwise, the refutation will generate hard feelings against the questioner, and not the beneficial acknowledgment of one's own ignorance.

(12) At 457e Socrates states not only that he is glad to refute another, but also that he is even happier to be refuted. To be purged of one's false beliefs is the greatest benefit which can happen to someone. (12) is closely connected with (11), but it emphasizes the attitude one ought to take to being refuted. One ought to embrace refutation as a great benefit. (12) presupposes the Socratic position that all men desire their own well-being, and that only ignorance makes them miss the mark. Furthermore, refutation is the first step in removing ignorance.

(13) At 457d and again at e Socrates warns Gorgias that he is not refuting him out of a spirit of contention, but from a desire for the truth. Participants in a dialectical discussion should not engage in an *agon* (contest) where victory is the dominant purpose. (13) is a corollary of (11). When one enters discussion with a desire for victory, not truth, then the beneficial effects of refutation cannot occur.

(14) Just after Gorgias agrees that refutation is a great benefit, he tells Socrates that the listeners may be too tired to continue since they have already heard a lengthy display (458b-c). A new conversation would seriously protract the sitting. Chaerephon and Callicles urge Gorgias to continue, but Gorgias values rest over truth. At this point in the discussion, but interestingly not later on, Gorgias lacks that crucial aspect of courage which is endurance in the search for truth (cf. *Laches* 194a).[15]

(15) At 487a Socrates ironically states that Callicles will be a good test for the rectitude of his life because he possesses the characteristics of knowledge, goodwill, and frankness. I will show later that Callicles is woefully deficient in all these traits, which is why his conversation with Socrates breaks down.[16] These traits are necessary for a successful Socratic discussion. By "knowledge" in the above context Socrates means roughly the following: an answerer sufficiently should have thought out his position so that he is not easily defeated. If an answerer is easily refuted, then he lacks even the rudimentary knowledge necessary to

be a good opponent in a dialectical test. A poorly defended position receives no good test. Callicles is not a fit opponent for Socrates because Socrates easily refutes his nature/convention distinction (489a-b).

Part of what Socrates means by "goodwill" can be seen from Callicles' behavior. Callicles eventually answers Socrates only to please Gorgias; he answers in a hostile manner, and he intersperses his replies with threats at Socrates. Callicles thinks Socrates to be contentious, and returns blow for blow. At 481c Callicles even doubts whether Socrates is serious about the things he says. We cannot expect goodwill or agreement among men as opposed as these.

Callicles is not frank with Socrates because he only desires to win the *agon*. To achieve a victory, Callicles does not answer honestly. He attempts to be consistent even at the cost of not saying what he means (495a-b), and he accuses Socrates of doing the same. Callicles also feigns that he does not hear Socrates, and finally he simply refuses to answer him. The above indicate that Callicles is utterly deficient in frankness.

(16) At 482c-e Callicles inadvertently implies an important character trait of any learner—shame. He recounts how both Gorgias and Polus were shamed into admitting concessions which caused their downfall. Callicles, however is utterly shameless; he will not be ashamed to flaunt received beliefs.[17] Since Callicles neither respects genuine consistency nor concedes received moral intuitions, there is no easy way for Socrates to shame him. Socrates also will not be shamed by the laughter, jeers, or testimony of the multitude. He refuses to concede the result of Polus' attempted reductions to absurdity because he does not agree with the many that the conclusions are absurd (463bf.).[18] Socrates cannot be shamed by reference to the opinions of others; he shares this much with Callicles. But Socrates would admit defeat, if his mutually supporting positions were shown to be inconsistent.

Contextual Features of Dialectic

At 455c-d Socrates states that he asks Gorgias what rhetoric is because there are a number of Gorgias' potential pupils observing the discussion who may be too embarrassed to ask Gorgias this question. Socratic conversations are frequently surrounded by onlookers who are often young men. An audience is sometimes useful in facilitating the conversation; at 458d-e Gorgias is shamed by the audience into continuing, and he later persuades Callicles at least physically to remain in the conversation.

Socrates often will refute an interlocutor by pressure from the audience; refutations sometimes, we may surmise, depend on the frowns and glances of the audience. On the other hand Socrates is oblivious to such pressure; he is not persuaded by the mere fact that all others disagree with him. Socrates, then, has a decided advantage over most of his opponents; he can refute them by one means more than they can refute him. Callicles will be an exception to this.

The audience can also turn a conversation into an eristic *agon*. The older discussants often wish to impress the young bystanders, especially given their homosexual tendencies. This introduces considerable tension into the conversation. Gorgias, Polus, and Callicles are all concerned with the audience, and want to make a good appearance before them. At 497b Gorgias tells Callicles to keep answering because it is not Callicles' "credit that is at stake." But Callicles' reputation is at stake, and he knows it. Callicles chooses embarrassing silence to the shame of further refutation by Socrates. The audience is, then, both a benefit and a hindrance to a dialectical discussion.

In the *Gorgias* we receive a picture of what I will call the *ad hominem* nature of Socrates' method. Socrates does not abuse an answerer, nor does he impugn what the answerer says by pointing to his circumstances; rather he attacks the core beliefs of an answerer, those beliefs that form one's self-image, and motivate action. Socrates' method is *ad hominem* because it attacks the core beliefs in an interlocutor's soul, and these beliefs are closely connected with the identity of an interlocutor.[19] Gorgias sees himself as a rhetorician, and Callicles sees himself as a naturally strong ruler.

When we focus on the *ad hominem* nature of *elenchus*, a number of Socrates' moves take on new significance. We saw earlier that Gorgias must complete his own statement in his own way. Gorgias must be committed to his answers to be affected by their defeat; it must be Gorgias' beliefs which are refuted. Even though Socrates assures Gorgias that he is not aiming at him (454c), the refutation of Gorgias' beliefs is *a fortiori* a refutation of his life, since the beliefs make the life. The personal nature of the *elenchus* is only partially hidden by Socrates (cf. *Laches* 188c-e).

At 455e Socrates claims that speeches cannot produce knowledge, they can only persuade of beliefs. Speeches present a plethora of claims without an opportunity to interrogate and test them individually; also speeches give over their opinions to the inactive listener, and hence they do not commit the listener to what is heard. The material of a speech does not belong to a listener; one is not responsible for the *logoi* given to one. Hence refutation (*elenchus*) cannot occur. Finally, speeches do not take into account the diverse intellectual capacities of their listeners, and thus they do not foster the habit of dialectical testing. Speeches do not have the *ad hominem* thrust of question and answer. We cannot, however, conclude that speeches have no proper educational role.

From 471-476 Socrates contrasts his method with that of the law courts. Socrates believes that the law courts with their use of speeches are useless for getting at the truth. False witnesses may convict, but they cannot compel consent, and they may crush the truth with perjury. Only a good dialectical opponent will not perjure himself, and Socrates is only interested in this witness, the person with whom he talks (472b-c, 474a). Socrates will be completely satisfied with the sole assent of the answerer.

Socrates uses the *ad hominem elenchus* to force assent. At 474b he insists that Polus really believes what Polus denies that he believes; Socrates often claims that Callicles yields a point when Callicles denies that he does. Socrates is enforcing rationality in these cases. He forces an answerer to assent to what purportedly is implied by his previous admissions. At 508b-c Socrates tells his listeners either to concede his paradoxes or refute them. Socrates here compels consent by an appeal to rationality; a rational person believes what repeatedly survives *elenchus*.

Polus tries three "refutations" on Socrates, and Socrates rejects them all. Polus produces witnesses against Socrates (472b-c), tries to make Socrates' flesh creep (473c-d), and laughs at his position (473d-e). Socrates says about the last: "Here we have yet another form of refutation—when a statement is made to laugh it down, instead of disproving it!" Socrates' positions are inversions of common sesnse, but Socrates never previously consented to common sense! Polus fails to refute Socrates because while the conclusions Polus displays are implied by Socrates' positions, Socrates does not deem them absurd; moreover, nothing Socrates has consented to implies that the conclusions are absurd.

Socrates is "shameless" in refutation. At 471d he refuses to admit "a single point in what you [Polus] say," even though the whole world agrees with Polus. Polus does not really argue against Socrates on Socrates' terms, but unabashedly appeals to received opinion. But Socrates cannot be refuted in this way because he does not accept such opinion. Socrates' definitions and principles are normative; they do not describe existing phenomena, but rather how things ought to be. True rhetoric, for example, ought to be for the real good of its subject matter. Socrates cannot be refuted by *de facto* existence anymore than by received opinion.

Gorgias, Polus, and Callicles all delight in giving speeches. Socrates wants to practice dialectic question and answer. A tempting conclusion is that question and answer is the only good educational method. This conclusion is not correct; dialectic is the best educational method, but it is not the only one. For what should Socrates do to educate an interlocutor who is defective in one or more of the personality characteristics required for a serious dialectical discussion? We will see that Socrates tries different educational techniques—even threatening speeches—when he finds people like Callicles unwilling and perhaps unable, due to prior bad education, to participate in dialectic.

The Goal of Dialectic

Epistēmē (knowledge) is the ultimate goal of dialectic. Knowledge is stating clearly one's beliefs, and defending them against a dialectical attack.[20] Knowledge is, for Socrates, a matter of degree; at some point one's beliefs have received enough defense to become knowledge, but they can always admit of more need for defense.[21]

At 508e-509a Socrates says:

> All this, which has been made evident on the lines I have stated some way back in our foregoing discussion, is held firm and fastened—if I may put it rather bluntly—with reasons of iron and adamant . . . which you or somebody more gallant than yourself must undo, or else find you cannot make a right statement in terms other than I now use. For my story is ever the same, that I cannot tell how the matter stands, and yet of all whom I have encountered, before as now, no one has been able to state it otherwise without making himself ridiculous.

There are two key claims in this paragraph. The first is that Socrates' positions are firmly fastened with reasons; the second is that Socrates does not really know how matters stand. The first connects with Socrates' humor, at Callicles' expense, that Socrates always says the same things about the same things, and Callicles never the same (490e, 491b). Socrates is consistent, and consistency is a test for truth. Moreover, we may well imagine that Socrates frequently has discussed and defended his positions in the past, and that they always have survived objections. Socrates has not yet encountered an unanswered objection to them. His positions, then, are tied in the *psychē* with reasons of iron.

But is Socrates' claim that he does not know how the matter stands consistent with the above? I believe so. Socrates does not have knowledge if by "knowledge" is meant something certain and irrevisable; Socrates does not have the absolute knowledge of God. All of Socrates' strong beliefs are revisable in light of future objections. Thus Socrates can have strong, well-founded beliefs even if he does not know how matters stand. He later says to Callicles that if they go over the same things again and again, then Callicles may well be convinced by the truth of what Socrates says (513c-d). In the *Meno* (85c-d) Socrates emphasizes that true beliefs become knowledge when they are turned and tested from a number of different perspectives. It is important to understand that dialectic is an ongoing process which accumulates evidence for or against a position, but which never permits closure.

Gorgias

Gorgias brags to his audience that he will answer any questions which they want to ask (447c), and he means that he will answer them to their satisfaction. Gorgias modestly adds that nobody has asked him anything new in many years (448a). Gorgias is very confident about his verbal dexterity to answer any question; he has heard them all before, or so he thinks. In the mouth of Gorgias these words are heavily ironical; for he has never met a questioner like Socrates. Socrates quickly will find some important questions which Gorgias has not heard before.

Gorgias is more concerned to advertise his skill to the audience— he claims to be a good rhetorician—than to tell Socrates what rhetoric is (449a). He declares himself to be both a master of lengthy speech, and of short speech; indeed, he claims to be able to express himself in briefer terms than anyone else (449b-c). However, it takes some effort for Socrates to elicit Gorgias' brief responses; for Gorgias strongly desires to play to the crowd of potential pupils who are gathered around. Socrates eventually pries Gorgias away from the audience and to the *logoi* at issue. Nevertheless, Gorgias displays the rhetorician's focus which is constantly on the praise or blame of the audience.[22]

Once Gorgias' attention is turned to the conversation, he manifests adequate good will and frankness. As Callicles later points out, Gorgias is shamed into admitting that he will not give over such a powerful tool as rhetoric to someone who does not possess virtue. Gorgias will teach them virtue. This admission is highly ironic because Gorgias elsewhere believes that virtue cannot be taught (cf. *Meno* 95c). Gorgias, as we will see, also represents a mere technician; he is in love with rhetoric, itself, as a powerful tool. But Gorgias does recognize and admit his refutation, and when the discussion passes to Polus and Callicles, his posture is to facilitate the conversation (497b-c, 506a-b). It is almost as if Gorgias really wants to wait and hear what real rhetoric is, and whether or not he practices it. Gorgias appears to be a basically decent person, who begins with bravado, admits defeat, and develops an appreciation for at least listening to dialectical discussion.

But this appraisal is much too generous to Gorgias; Gorgias is not as innocent as he appears. He is very much aware of the power of rhetoric, and even boasts about it (452e, 455e-465d); a rhetorician can accomplish many things where other experts fail. But Gorgias has never considered that rhetoric must be guided by virtue—the knowledge of good and evil—to be a genuinely valuable art. This is a serious defect. Gorgias is not basically decent because he is thoughtless. He has not investigated what any purported *teacher* of a subject ought to investigate, and this makes him a corruptor of others; Polus and Callicles symbolize Gorgias' corrupting influence.

Gorgias appears decent when compared with Polus and Callicles. But the interlocutors appear in a premeditated and significant order.[23] Each successive answerer is more intractable and immoral than his predecessors, but each predecessor establishes the educational conditions for those who follow. Gorgias, just like old Cephalus in the *Republic*, is the source of the rot. Gorgias is the mentor of Polus, either in fact or in spirit. Gorgias' emphasis on the mere techniques of rhetoric both spawns textbooks on rhetoric like those of Polus, as well as Polus' praise for tyrants. Gorgias views rhetoric as a mere tool for power, and this is the message in his teaching of rhetoric. Polus, for all his praise of tyrants, is as I will show a proponent of received belief and convention. Convention is weak, and inconsistent; it even carries the seeds of its own destruction in that it holds that a tyrant who usurps the laws and escapes punishment is the happiest of men. Callicles correctly sees the indefensible nature of conventional belief, and boldly asserts that the natural man should take power. The moral and intellectual failures of Gorgias and Polus create Callicles.

Let us now see how Socrates educates Gorgias. Socrates asks Gorgias what rhetoric is, and this question goes to the heart of Gorgias' self image. Gorgias sees himself as a rhetorician, and as a rhetorician he should know what rhetoric is. If Gorgias knows what rhetoric is, then he is able to say what it is (cf. *Laches* 190c); if he cannot say what it is, then he does not know. Saying what rhetoric is involves both stating a clear definition of rhetoric, and defending that definition against a Socratic attack. If Gorgias fails to say what rhetoric is, then he fails to uphold his own self-image. Socratic dialectic is an attack on how an interlocutor leads his life.

Socrates, with great difficulty, forces Gorgias to clarify and refine his *logoi* about rhetoric. At last Gorgias makes the following statement (454b):

> Well then, I mean that rhetoric is about that kind of persuasion, Socrates, which you find in the law-courts and in any public gatherings, . . . and it [rhetoric] deals with what is just and unjust.

Gorgias claims that rhetoric is persuasion about (*peri*) the just and unjust. All Gorgias means by this is that rhetoricians discuss what ought or ought not to be done, and "ought" does not here have even a distinctly moral as contrasted with prudential sense. We will see that Socrates makes much more out of Gorgias' answer than Gorgias has in it.

Gorgias proceeds to praise the persuasive power of rhetoric. Rhetoric alone, he claims, makes a man a match for all other professionals (456b-c), but we ought not blame the teachers of rhetoric for what their pupils might do with it (456e-457c). Here Gorgias envisages rhetoric as a mere technology divorced from any value considerations. A mere technology is a set of rules or procedures for accomplishing some end divorced from considerations of virtue and the good which is to be achieved. Gorgias is a proponent of mere technology for the sake of technology; he is fascinated with the power of his technique.

But there is another side of Gorgias which becomes concerned about the possible misuse of such a powerful tool. Socrates uncovers this side by the following question (459d-e):

> Does he [the rhetorician] not know what is really good or bad, noble or base, just or unjust, but has he devised a persuasion to deal with these matters so as to appear to those who, like himself, do not know to know better than he who knows? Or . . . must anyone who intends to learn rhetoric have a previous knowledge of these things when he comes to you? Or if not, are you, as the teacher of rhetoric, to teach the person who comes to you nothing about them—for it is not your business. . . ?

At 460a Gorgias responds that "if he [the pupil] happens not to know these things [just things] he will learn them too from me." Gorgias is shamed into admitting that a student of rhetoric who does not possess justice would learn justice from him.[24] Socrates now closes the trap. He reminds Gorgias that Gorgias had said that rhetoric is about the just and unjust, and he forces Gorgias to agree that this implies that the rhetorician knows what justice is. Socrates gains Gorgias' assent to the following premises:

    (1) Rhetoric is about just and unjust things.
∴ (2) The rhetorician knows about justice and injustice.
∴ (3) The rhetorician is a just person, and hence will act justly (460b-c).

Gorgias assents to (1), and Socrates insists that (1) implies (2) and (2) implies (3). (2) implies (3) only on the Socratic assumptions that: (a) all men most desire their own happiness; (b) he who knows what justice is knows that justice is necessary for happiness; and (c) one acts on one's estimate of what produces happiness. Gorgias concedes (2) and (3), but only because he is very confused, and Socrates, under the pressure of circumstances, makes him think that (1) implies (2), and (2) implies (3). If dialectic were a purely logical activity, then Socrates would be quilty of grievous errors. But dialectic is not a purely logical activity. What is essential for dialectic is that the answerer concede the premises which lead to his refutation.

Socrates convicts Gorgias of the following contradiction: a rhetorician need not be just, and a rhetorician must be just. The former claim emerges when Gorgias says that one should not blame the teachers of rhetoric for the misuses of rhetoric by their students. Presumably these students use the "art" of rhetoric for unjust purposes. The latter claim is the result of (1) - (3) above.

Socrates may twist Gorgias' words to get a contradiction, but he does not practice eristic. Gorgias' claims are vague; he does not know what he means, or what he implies by what he means. Socrates educationally exploits this unclarity. Also Gorgias freely assents to how Socrates develops the argument. But most important, Socrates makes Gorgias aware of a serious, indeed, essential problem for a rhetorician; he also makes Gorgias acutely conscious of the fact that he does not know the answer to this problem. The issue is ultimately whether a true technology can be a mere technology, or in other words, whether a real art can be practiced without virtue. Socrates believes that an art like rhetoric, to be an art at all, must be subordinate to the master art of virtue, i.e., the knowledge of good and evil.

Educationally Socrates practices both *elenchus* and *psychagogia* on Gorgias. These two aspects of dialectic occur at the same time. Gorgias both has his definition of rhetoric refuted, and indirectly learns that true rhetoric must involve virtue. Socrates is more successful with Gorgias than with just about any other non-youthful interlocutor in the early dialogues. Gorgias' early bravado gives way to *aporia* and to a genuine desire to know what real rhetoric is. Thus Gorgias continues to facilitate the discussion. But why does Socrates stop conversing with Gorgias? Gorgias is old like Cephalus in the *Republic*, and Socrates stops conversing with Cephalus because Cephalus is set in his ritualistic ways. Cephalus enters the conversation from praying and sacrificing, and he returns to these activities. But Gorgias is not rigid like Cephalus, and he seems to have a genuine curiosity to learn. I *think* that Socrates drops Gorgias as an interlocutor for two reasons: (1) Gorgias himself needs to proceed to the next educational stage where he thinks over his perplexity, and (2) Gorgias needs to see in Polus and Callicles the effects of mere rhetoric, i.e., the effects transmitted by him as a teacher.

Finally we should note that Socrates is as successful as he is with Gorgias because while Gorgias does not have knowledge, he does have goodwill and frankness. The latter two character traits permit a successful *elenchus*; their absence in Callicles, as we will see, makes it impossible for Socrates to practice *elenchus* with him.

Polus

Polus immediately dismisses Gorgias' shame in admitting that he would teach virtue to rhetoric students who do not know it; he also denigrates the "little inconsistency" which Socrates pushes Gorgias into (461b-c). We see that Polus will be harder to shame than Gorgias and that Socrates will have more difficulty in refuting Polus.

Polus is the archtypical rhetorician, but he is not as versatile as Gorgias.[25] Gorgias can answer long or short, but Polus only knows how to give speeches. Polus, at the beginning, cannot do question and answer at all. At the opening of the dialogue he answers Chaerephon's questions with speeches; when Socrates gives him an opportunity to ask questions, he is utterly incompetent to do so (462aff.). Whether Polus asks or answers, he gives speeches. I will pursue the implications of this defect when I look at Socrates' educational tactics.

The tone of the conversation is very interesting. Socrates engages in unremitting sarcasm about Polus. At 461c he says that it is a good thing that he and Gorgias have a young man like Polus to set them straight. At 463e he says, straight out, that Polus is "so young and fresh," and at 467c Socrates mocks Polus' rhetorical style. Socrates' heavy sarcasm is distasteful, and it appears detrimental to the progress of the discussion. But the sarcasm is justified. Polus is young and fresh; he is also arrogant.[26] Socrates' sarcasm is an attempt to "take Polus down a peg or two" in order to make him amenable to *elenchus*.

Behind Polus' shield of rhetorical bravado, we can see that Polus represents received opinion. He represents such opinion so well that he displays one of its major incoherences. On the one hand Polus praises tyrants (466c-d, 471a-c). He does not praise them for reasons like those of Callicles, but on the ground that if someone can break or usurp the laws and escape the penalty, then this person is better off than the law abiding citizen. Plato attributes this same position to the many in the second book of the *Republic*. On the other hand Polus concedes that doing wrong is fouler than suffering it (474c). The many judge that doing wrong is fouler presumably because of its base making characteristics. When we conjoin these two views we see, then, that the tyrant is better off because of some base making characteristic, given the uncontroversial premise that tyrants do unjust things. Socrates loses no time in exploiting this paradox in received belief. Polus symbolizes the false rhetorician who panders to thoughtless opinion; he flatters his hearers by telling them what they already believe. Such untested beliefs prepare the ground for a real tyrant, or a Callicles, by among other things extolling the benefits which accrue to tyrants.

Socrates uses both speeches and short wiry arguments to attack Polus. Polus is unable to ask or answer questions. Socrates sarcastically remarks that Polus has "a good training in rhetoric, but seems to have neglected dialectic" (471d). What is Socrates to do with someone who can neither ask nor answer questions? He gives a speech. He cogently distinguishes in his speech true arts from mere knacks (464b-466a). Socrates comments on his speech (465a-466a):

> However, I can fairly claim indulgence [for giving a speech]: for when I spoke briefly you did not understand me; you were unable to make any use of the answers I gave you, but required a full exposition. Now if I on my part cannot tell what use to make of any answers you may give me, you shall extend your speech also. . . .

Socrates has not become a false rhetorician. He sees that Polus' *psychē* needs a speech to make it listen. Hence a speech at this point is what is most beneficial to Polus. Also Socrates' speech does not compel us to conclude that he has abandoned the thesis that only dialectic produces knowledge. The speech may be only a propaedeutic to education. Polus must listen, and he must listen to a compelling denial of his fondest beliefs.

Socrates forces Polus to agree that the rhetorician is powerless, but right afterward (468e) Polus acts as if he never made any of the previous admissions. He sneers that Socrates would certainly accept the liberty of doing what he thinks fit (even if he is ignorant of what is really beneficial). Socrates must force Polus to recognize his own admissions, and not ignore them. To do this Socrates returns to a coercive *elenchus* which forces Polus to assent to question after question. Socrates repeatedly tells Polus that he only wants him as a witness (471eff.), and Socrates proceeds to get him. He compels Polus to concede the Socratic paradoxes.

Socrates uses both speeches and elenctic arguments with Polus. The former force Polus to pay attention; they also attack directly his views about the nature and value of rhetoric. Socrates' speeches are the use of forceful persuasion to attack engrained attitudes. They are not the method to educate someone, but make possible the use of *elenchus*. The *elenchus* is, at least on the surface, successful with Polus. Polis is tamed sufficiently by Socrates' speeches that he answers the questions with great brevity, and is "shamed" into a refutation. Unlike Callicles, Polus admits refutation because he is frank. He answers as seems correct to him, and hence he is committed to whatever unacceptable conclusions result from his answers.

But is Polus led to beneficial perplexity? We cannot be sure. Just after Socrates drives Polus to the last paradoxical result—that the wrongdoer should use rhetoric to accuse himself (480b-d)—there is the following exchange (480e):

> Pol. An extraordinary result, Socrates, it seems to me, though perhaps you do find it agrees with what went before.
> Soc. Well, either that must be upset, or this necessarily follows.
> Pol. Yes, that certainly is so.

Polus' adherence to received opinion makes Socrates' arguments extraordinary in his eyes. Polus' earlier value training probably makes it impossible for him to reject his entrenched beliefs. Hence even though Polus concedes the logical compulsion of Socrates' words, he does not seem perplexed about them. The *elenchus* is not sufficient to convert Polus.

Callicles

I will emphasize two points about this discussion. The first is that Socrates and Callicles have radically opposed positions; they are so opposed that there is not sufficient common ground for argument, much less mutual understanding and respect. Dialectical discussions must fail when the participants do not share key beliefs in common (see *Crito* 49c-d). Socrates can refute Callicles' words, but he is never able to change his mind (513c). The second is that Callicles does not have the character traits which are necessary for a good dialectical conversation: shame, knowledge, goodwill, and frankness. In the absence of these traits one can expect a bitter and fruitless exchange between these antagonists.

Callicles signals his radical disagreement with Socrates the instant he enters the conversation. Callicles has just heard Socrates defend his paradoxes, and his first response is to ask whether Socrates is serious

(481c). If what Socrates says is true, then life must be turned upside down. But Socrates is serious; he is the serious man who is after the truth.[27] Callicles is not.

A recurrent theme in the discussion is who will appear ridiculous. Callicles introduces this theme in his great speech (494d-e):

> So when they [philosophers] enter upon any private or public business they make themselves ridiculous, just as on the other hand, I suppose, when public men engage in your studies and discussions, they are quite ridiculous.

Callicles denigrates philosophy; it is all right to practice it as a young man, indeed, it is liberal to do so; but to practice it into manhood is perverse; it is to neglect what is important for a real man (484c-d). Callicles thrice predicts that Socrates would be ridiculous in court if he were accused before the Athenian *demos* (486c, 508d, 509a). Socrates would prove defenseless, and not have a word to say before the bar. Socrates agrees that if he were forced to defend himself before charlatans and pretenders, then the truth would appear ridiculous (521d-522a). On the other hand Callicles proves to be ridiculous at dialectic; Socrates refutes his contentions with little or no difficulty. Callicles is so embarrassed that he eventually refuses to answer. Socrates also gives a great speech which balances that of Callicles. In this speech, at the end of the dialogue, he threatens Callicles with the specter of appearing ridiculous, not to say wicked, when he appears naked before the judges after death. Callicles' *psychē*, stripped of its fine adornments, will be seen to be base and wicked. Socrates returns threat with threat. Callicles is ridiculous in dialectic and laughable in the final judgment; Socrates appears ridiculous in public transactions, and before the assembly. Both men have complete disdain for one another.

They ground this disdain in fundamentally opposed views. Callicles praises the man of natural justice who "tramples underfoot our orders and juggleries, our charms and laws" (484a), and who "lets his desires be as strong as possible and does not chasten them, and he should be able to minister to them when they are at their height by reason of his manliness and intelligence" (491e-492a). Socrates, on the contrary, is the champion of *cosmos* (order / harmony). The *cosmos* in something is the cause of its *aretē* (virtue / excellence), be it in a house, ship, soul, or world (503eff). These fundamental metaphysical differences cause equally fundamental political ones. Socrates states that the true rhetorician or statesman engenders *cosmos* in the souls of his listeners (504d-e), and in an uncharacteristically frank statement Socrates asserts that he is the only person in Athens who practices the true political art (521d). Callicles, on the other hand, praises the rulers who stuffed the city with walls, arms, and other such accoutrements. Pericles was most proficient at this.

Even though Socrates does not drive Callicles to an admission of defeat, I believe that Socrates wins the "debate," but by default. Callicles is not a fit partner for dialectic because of character flaws which make him unable to abide by the rules of dialectic. Plato, I believe, intends for us to see these flaws in Callicles, and to see how Socrates handles them.

At 482c-e Callicles analyzes the defeats of Gorgias and Polus as due to an excess of shame. They were shamed into admissions which caused their defeat. Callicles implies that he cannot be shamed especially by an appeal to received morality. Callicles, like Socrates, cannot be embarrassed by a divergence from received opinion. Indeed, even when defeated in argument, Callicles does not admit error. Callicles nominally values consistency, but he also values any unscrupulous means of maintaining it.

At 486d-e Socrates ironically claims that Callicles is the proper test or touchstone for Socrates' *psychē*. If he and Callicles were ever to agree on something, then there would be no need of a further test (487e). Socrates is ironic because we are about to see that Callicles lacks the necessary character traits to be a good dialectical opponent.

Socrates then says that unlike his predecessors Callicles is a man of knowledge, goodwill, and frankness (487a). Earlier I showed why these three characteristics are essential for a good dialectician. Now we will see why Callicles lacks each of them.

Callicles first reveals his ignorance. In several short moves Socrates demolishes Callicles' nature/convention distinction which is the keystone of his position (489a-b). Callicles then begins to constantly change his position in order to save it. He accuses Socrates of always saying the same picky little things about the same things, and Socrates rejoins that Callicles, on the contrary, never says the same things about the same things (490e-491c). Callicles vacillates and is easily refuted each time; these are clear signs that he lacks knowledge.

Callicles' frankness is the next to go. At 495a he answers as he does simply to be consistent. He does not say what he believes, but only tries to keep from being refuted. Callicles, as Socrates notes, is no longer a fit partner in discussion. Callicles, then, pretends not to understand Socrates (498c), and at 489c he misleadingly says that he has made only a verbal slip. Then at 499b-c Callicles admits that he does not really believe the position he gave. His frankness finally is gone totally when he refuses to answer Socrates.

Callicles' good will also vanishes. He complains of Socrates' petty, unimportant questions (497b), and then refuses to answer (506c). He charges Socrates with pure contentiousness (515b); Callicles believes that Socrates only wants to win the *agon*.

How is Socrates to educate Callicles? First we should notice that the tone of their conversation is very different from what precedes it. Socrates is firm with Gorgias and sometimes admonishes him, but there is always a basic respect and concern between these interlocutors. Socrates is sarcastic with brash Polus; the young colt needs to be fenced in with ridicule. In contrast Socrates meets Callicles with unmitigated ironical opposition. Callicles needs to be beaten, even humiliated, before dialectic with him is even possible. Socrates' posture towards Callicles is suited educationally to the task even if it does not work, since no other posture would work.

Socrates indicates earlier in the *Gorgias* that dialectic is the ideal educational method. One should react with surprise, then, at Socrates' rhetorical attempts to persuade Callicles. Socrates uses (1) persuasive images (e.g. the soul as a sieve, the power of order (cosmos) in the world, and the like), (2) the great speech of final judgment at the end of the dialogue, and (3) a monologue completion of the argument (506cff). He constantly asks Callicles, "Do I now persuade you?" (see 493d, 494a). None of Socrates' stories move Callicles. But at 513c Callicles admits that there is something correct in what Socrates says, but he still does not believe Socrates. Socrates diagnoses Callicles' resistance to him as the "love of demos" in Callicles' soul. The only way Socrates could break down such a strong resistance is by persuasive words not *elenchus*. For Callicles does not have the values which permit him to engage in *elenchus*. Persuasive stories are, indeed, a second best method which at best prepares one for dialectical education. But there is no indication in the *Gorgias* that Socrates' stories convince Callicles, or that Callicles is made more amenable to dialectic. Socrates' educational methods, while suited to the nature of Callicles, are nevertheless inadequate to the task.

One might object to my intepretation that Socrates is no better than Callicles in the end. Rhetorical persuasion has no proper educational function, and Socrates uses rhetorical persuasion. But I believe that there is evidence in the text that Socrates uses his rhetorical persuasion to make Callicles better—whether or not he succeeds. At 503a-504e Socrates distinguishes true and false rhetoric. True rhetoric meets the conditions of art. Then at 505b Socrates states that true rhetoric must restrain the desires in a bad soul, and that it must correct such a soul.[28] Immediately thereafter Socrates lectures Callicles about his condition! At 513d Socrates distinguishes flattering speech from that which aims at the best. Socrates, then, berates Callicles in a most unflattering way. At 519e Socrates justifies his extended speeches on the ground that Callicles will not answer. The last fifth of the *Gorgias* alternates between Socrates theorizing about what a good rhetorician/ ruler would do, and then doing it to Callicles.

Conclusion

A major theme of the *Gorgias* is the contrast between dialectic and rhetoric. Dialectic is the ideal educational method, while rhetoric as practiced by Gorgias, Polus, and Callicles does not educate. Nevertheless Socrates adapts different methods to the different natures of his interlocutors. In particular he uses persuasive speeches and images in his fight against Callicles since Callicles is unable to engage in dialectic. But we must conclude that Socrates does not correct either Polus or Callicles; he does not make them dialecticians. Hence Socrates fails as an educator. But the *Gorgias*, more than any other early dialogue, displays the reasons for Socrates' failure. Gorgias, Polus, and Callicles already have found their loves; their value structures and personalities are established. The *Gorgias*, I suggest, stands on the threshold of the *Republic*. The *Gorgias* displays a need for a predialectical training in music and gymnastics, and the *Republic* explains how this need is to be fulfilled.[29]

9. Educational Theory in the *Meno*

The *Meno* raises many, difficult questions. To open the dialogue Meno asks (70a):

> Can you tell me, Socrates, whether virtue can be taught or is acquired by practice not teaching? Or if neither by practice nor by learning, whether it comes to mankind by nature or in some other way?

Meno's question is a series of loose disjuncts, and he assumes that virtue or excellence comes through one and only one means — teaching, practice, or nature.[1] What does Meno mean by these notions, and does Socrates share Meno's conceptions?[2] Does Socrates also believe that virtue comes through a single means — perhaps dialectic? Also Socrates' denial in the *Meno* that he teaches is very puzzling. Finally the conclusion of the *Meno* is hard to accept — that virtue is true opinion which comes through divine dispensation or luck. Is this really Socrates' position?

Teaching, Practice, and Nature

Meno is a student of Gorgias, and Gorgias is a well-known rhetorician. Gorgias symbolizes the type of teaching which Socrates rejects. Oral modes of communication are still influential in fifth century Greece. The epic poems of Homer are sung and read, and their poetic meter and repetitive phrases facilitate their oral execution and memorization. Poetic education consists in: (1) singing or reading a poem, (2) memorizing its moral and exemplary content, and (3) acting on the precepts so memorized. The rhythmic nature of a poem would aid in memorizing it as well as diminish cognitive activities such as analysis, criticism, and the like. This education is authoritarian and nonrational. It does, however, help train the memory.

151

Socrates, with considerable justification, assimilates poetic and rhetorical teaching. Rhetoricians like Lysias, Isocrates, and Gorgias take over much of education from the poets. A man makes his mark in the assembly, and other public places, by speaking; and while a professional might write the speech, the speaker would deliver it himself. If attacked in a civil or criminal suit, one would have to defend oneself. Hence teachers of rhetoric are in great demand, and the demand for them increases as society becomes more complex. Rhetorical education makes one strong in the assembly and law courts; indeed, such an ability in the popular mind comes to be called virtue or excellence. Speeches like poems are delivered, heard, and their content is often memorized; they too do not facilitate the analysis of specific claims. Thus Socrates rejects this conception of excellence and the education which creates it.

But what are Socrates' own educational goals? He believes that a proper education should: (1) instill the desire to seek truth, and (2) give one a method by which truth may be sought. Given these goals, Socrates has a strong case against poetry and rhetoric. Rhetoric, just as poetry, emphasizes the memorization of its contents. In the *Phaedrus* we see the young man Phaedrus memorizing the speech of the rhetorician Lysias. Phaedrus does this both to learn what a good speech is like, and to learn its contents. Such memorization is nonrational. Rhetoric also is nonrational because it appeals to the emotions of an audience to persuade or move them. Hence in the *Gorgias* Socrates dismisses one type of rhetoric as a mere knack for persuasion, Rhetoric pours a large number of claims on its passive recipients without an intermission for reflection and questioning. When there are questions, as in a modern presidential news conference, there is not sufficient time for detailed investigation and follow-up questions. Socrates believes that for clarity and truth to emerge there must be many questions and answers on a single topic. Speeches, by their multiplicity of claims and passive recipients, do not permit this. Hence Socrates rejects poetry and rhetoric as the educational methods to acquire knowledge.

What does Socrates mean by "teach"? Let us call his conception of teaching "question and answer" or simply "dialectic."[3] In simplest outline Socratic dialectic is the following: First Socrates asks the answerer "What is φ?" where φ is some notion of importance to the answerer. Second Socrates seeks a clarification of the answer. Sometimes he will refute or satirize an answer to force an interlocutor to state another interpretation or clarify the original one. Third Socrates asks a number of simple questions which ideally have clear yes or no answers. These answers, when conjoined, either are inconsistent with the original account or they are not. In the former case the account is defeated, if it is less intuitively obvious than the intermediate answers. In the latter case one is justified in claiming to know that the account is true since it survives dialectical attack, but the attack must be of some duration and degree of severity. An answer, which defeats all presently known objections, and coheres with one's other beliefs, would count as knowledge. Hence Socratic dialectic produces a test for truth — a rational test — and the best humanly possible one. The test, of course, is only as good as the interlocutors' dialectical ability, and it is always possible that an account which survives Socratic criticism is false. Hence Socrates is always willing to reopen a position no matter how certain it may appear (cf. *Crito* 49d-e, *Gorgias* 508e-509a).[4]

Socratic dialectic, although it is best performed verbally, is still different in effect from the oral poetic and rhetorical education. It is rational and nonauthoritarian, while they are not. It seeks truth, while they demand conformity; it demands activity and thought from the learner, while they produce passivity. Socrates essentially connects dialectic with recollection in the *Meno*. Socrates denies that he teaches (82e, 84c-d) where by "teach" he means "give-over and state positions" like a rhetorician (84d). Learning is the recollection of beliefs already present somehow in the *psychē* (85b-d). Socrates' questions activate the answerer to recollect a response. The emphasis in Socrates' learning model is on the autonomous intellectual capacities of the answerer.[5]

Socrates calls recollection the "proper use of memory" (82e-83a). In nonmythological garb recollection simply is the ability to respond to questions. These responses require the activation of certain intellectual capacities. The answerer must interpret the question, see the connections it requires one to draw, and then answer it. But to activate these capacities may, itself, presuppose learning, and thus Socrates asks the slave boy whether he knows Greek.

Socrates and Meno also have different theories of practice. Meno, and his mentor Gorgias, rely on memory as the proper form of practice. Young people would memorize the poets and rhetoricians to recall their "wisdom." Ironically Socrates feigns a poor memory about what Gorgias says about virtue (71c) to entice Meno into dialectical discussion. For conventional education memory and recall are the major excellences. At 85c-d Socrates says:

> And at this moment these opinions have just been stirred up in him, like a dream; but if he were repeatedly asked these same questions in a variety of forms, you know he will have in the end as exact an understanding of them as anyone.

Socrates' notion of practice is simply endurance in dialectic. Practice is the constant effort to clarify and test one's beliefs; it is the asking and answering of questions. At some unspecifiable point in the dialectic process beliefs become claimable as knowledge (98a); that is, one is justified in claiming to know what he has clarified and defended.

Meno does not have any clear conception of nature, but Anytus does. Anytus comes into the conversation late in the dialogue, and he represents the conventional, conservative Athenian gentleman. He is also one of Socrates' three accusers. Anytus believes that excellence is a function of birth; one is either born a gentleman or one is not. Excellence comes from birth and mere maturation. Socrates says about this conception of nature (89b):

> No, for then, I presume, we should have had this result: if good men were so by nature, we surely should have had men able to discern who of the young were good by nature, and on their pointing them out we should have taken them over and kept them safe in the citadel, having set our mark on them far rather than on our gold treasure, in order that none might have tampered with them, and that when they come to be of age, they might be useful to their country.

Socrates rejects the above conception of nature. There is no natural goodness to spot at early age, nor does anyone achieve excellence and virtue without learning and practice. Socrates' point is that nature must be integrated with dialectical practice; that is, with learning and practice, and that none of these three components can stand as a complete education.

Socrates' conception of nature or what is innate is not easy to explicate. He claims that opinions and even knowledge are within a person at birth (85c-d). The *psychē* is immortal and has acquired these in a previous existence, or always had them (85e-86a). But neither opinion nor knowledge are consciously and explicitly innate because (1) learning (recollection) and practice are necessary for knowledge, and (2) one must be able to state and defend what one knows. Socrates, I believe, overstates the contribution of nature in his theory, to juxtapose his view of education with the conventional mode. In the conventional, rhetorical model opinions are put into blank tablets. Socrates' questions, on the other hand, stimulate the answerer to formulate a response for himself. With the slave boy Socrates first ascertains that the boy speaks Greek, and has not learned geometry (82b, 85e). The boy's speaking Greek symbolizes the trained intellectual capacities the learner must bring to a conversation. Socrates' questions activate these capacities. *"Educo"* means "lead out from within," and this is what Socrates does with the slave boy. Thus Socrates claims that the boy is responsible for his answers, and not Socrates. What is really innate for Socrates are a number of intellectual capacities, and not some mystifying notion of explicit innate knowledge.[6]

I will now summarize the above discussion. For Meno teaching is the giving over of information through speeches; for Socrates teaching is the dialectic art of asking questions. Meno believes, following Gorgias, that one ought to exercise one's memory by recalling the material given to one; Socrates believes that practice is the doing of dialectic. Anytus believes that we are by nature either gentlemen or not; Meno would agree with Anytus that by nature we either have the striking presence of a Gorgias or we do not. For Socrates what is innate is the ability to ask and answer questions, and even a slave can possess this ability.

Meno's Slave and Ideal Dialectic

Ironically this conversation with the least fortunate of humans—a slave—is a rare example of a successful, if incomplete, Socratic discussion. The slave first comes to see his own ignorance, and then what the correct answer is. The discussion with the slave boy is a paradigm of a good dialectical discussion. By contrasting this conversation with the larger one with Meno, we should be able to see why Socrates has such difficultly with Meno.

In the first half of the *Meno* Socrates refutes Meno's attempts to say what virtue is. In exasperation Meno compares Socrates with a stingray (80a-b).

. . . . I consider that both in your appearance and in other respects
you are extremely like the flat torpedo sea-fish; for it benumbs
anyone who approaches and touches it, . . . I feel my soul and
my tongue quite benumbed, and I am at a loss what answer to
give you. And yet on countless occasions I have made abundant
speeches on virtue . . . but now I cannot say one word as to what
it is.

Meno only admits that he cannot say what virtue is; he continues to
believe that he knows what it is. The irony is that Socrates' method
presupposes that one knows something only if one can state and defend it. Meno has not achieved an awareness of his ignorance.

Socrates ironically accepts the torpedo fish simile, but only if the
torpedo can itself be torpid (80c-d). Socrates claims that he is paralyzed and unable to say what virtue is. But just after this admission
he offers to help Meno inquire after virtue. Meno's surprise at this offer is justified since if Socrates is really paralyzed, then he should not
be able to help. Meno states a vague query, and Socrates makes it into
a paradox that is usually called "Meno's paradox." Socrates says (80e):
". . . a man cannot inquire either about what he knows or about what
he does not know. For he cannot inquire about what he knows, because
he knows it, and in that case is in no need of inquiry; nor again can
he inquire about what he does not know, since he does not know about
what he is to inquire." Meno's paradox makes two assumptions: (1)
that knowledge is an all or nothing matter; that is, either it exists as
a complete whole, or it is entirely absent, and (2) knowledge is the
only epistemic state used in inquiry. Socrates attacks both of these
assumptions by his theory of recollection. Recollection posits a movement from opinion to knowledge by way of practice and learning.

Socrates introduces recollection in an odd way. He hears about
recollection and the immortality of the *psychē* from certain priests and
priestesses who give a reasoned account of their ministry, as well as
from Pindar and other poets of heavenly gifts (81b). Since the *psychē*
is immortal, it has previously beheld all things, and has acquired
knowledge of everything, so that it can now recollect what was previously
learned (81c). We can only speculate about why Socrates attributes
the origin of this theory to other people. Perhaps the primary reason
is a debt to the Pythagoreans who believe in psychic transmigration.
Socrates is also modest by attributing his insight to others, and those

whom he picks may symbolize the inspired nature of discovery. Socrates, moreover, gives a certain legitimacy to recollection by attributing it to divinely inspired people.

At 81d Socrates says that there is no reason why having recollected one thing we cannot recollect everything else, since "all nature is akin." "All nature is akin" is a fascinating but puzzling phrase, and we can only speculate about what it means.[7] Socratic dialectic employs a coherence test for truth; it sees whether or not one's beliefs harmonize with each other. Beliefs form a system, and each belief has certain implications within the system. Socrates may believe that if we recollect one true belief then we can recollect other beliefs which it implies. Truth, however, is the correspondence between beliefs and reality, and Socrates probably believes that true beliefs somehow mirror reality. Hence nature and beliefs would hang together in roughly the same ways. Nature is akin, then, because its components are interrelated just as are our true beliefs about it.

To illustrate recollection Socrates then asks the slave boy about a mathematical problem which they are diagramming in the dust. First the slave thinks he knows the correct answer to the problem, and has no desire for further inquiry, although his answer is false. After more questions the slave comes to see that he is wrong. Socrates says, "Previously he thought that he knew, and confidently answered as though he knew, and was aware of no difficulty; whereas now he feels the difficulty he is in, and besides not knowing does not think he knows" (84a-b). The slave boy admits his ignorance; Meno, on the other hand, only admits that he does not know how to say what he thinks. *Elenchus* (refutation), the first phase of Socratic education, is successful with the slave. Successful *elenchus* destroys the old false or unjustified beliefs, and the confidence which goes with them. When the confidence is shattered a desire to inquire further should emerge. Indeed the slave boy now desires to reattack the mathematical problem.

The second phase of dialectic is *psychagogia* (*psychē*-leading). Socrates' questions guide the slave boy to the correct answer, and the answer is the boy's not Socrates'. This phase of dialectic with the boy is successful, and he comes to see for himself what is the correct answer to the geometrical problem. Dialectic, then, has both a negative, refutative phase, and a positive, truth seeking phase. The former unclogs the pores and makes possible the acquisition of knowledge, while the latter guides the *psychē* to it.

But Socrates does not guide the slave boy all the way to knowledge; more practice is required for that. His questions have only awakened a true opinion which is present in the boy, and this opinion has been stirred in him like a dream (85c). If the boy were to go over the problem from a variety of perspectives and defeat objections to his answer, then he would have as exact a knowledge of it as anyone (85c-d). The difference between knowledge and opinion is that the former is tied down by reasons, while the latter is not (98a). In the *Meno*, however, knowledge and opinion can be about the very same objects, unlike the *Republic* where knowledge is only of the Forms while opinion is only about phenomena. The *Meno*, unlike the *Republic*, is not focused on the theory of Forms; the *Meno* is about education and excellence of character.[8] Metaphysically the *Meno* has only a single world which we can cognize in different ways.

Socrates emphatically claims that he does not teach the slave boy (84c-d, 85d). In one sense this claim is true, and in another it is misleading. Socrates does not impart or give over opinions by rhetorical persuasion. Hence he does not teach in the traditional sense. But it is misleading for Socrates to claim (85d): "Without anyone having taught him, and only through questions put to him, he will understand, recovering the knowledge out of himself." It is not as if knowledge were completely there, and simply emerged under questioning. Knowledge itself emerges in the question and answer process. Socrates, in the recollection passage, downplays the contribution of questioning to emphasize what is brought to the discussion by the learner, and to contrast his procedure with conventional teaching where the student is passive.

The discussion with the slave boy is a microcosm of the whole *Meno*. The first half of the dialogue primarily is elenctic, and in the second half Socrates guides Meno to conclusions. But the discussion with the slave ends in correct geometrical answers, while the *Meno* concludes, as I will show, in paradox and perplexity. Why are the two different? Meno's slave is superior to Meno intellectually. Meno is utterly dogmatic; he only admits that he cannot say what virtue is, not that he does not know what virtue is. Meno is also arrogant and stupid. He asks Socrates to teach him what recollection is just after Socrates states that he does not teach (81e), and he forces Socrates to address the question of how virtue is acquired (86c), even though Socrates illustrates that this cannot be done until they know what virtue is (71a-b).

The sad truth is that Meno is not affected by Socratic dialectic, and he continues with his customary positions. Socrates is thus forced to modify the second phase of dialectic; there is no use in giving answers to someone who does not have the spirit of inquiry. Socrates most wants to elicit in Meno the desire for dialectic and truth; if Socrates were to guide him to an answer, then Meno would simply uncritically accept that answer. Socrates, in the second half of the *Meno*, takes Meno's own beliefs and shows that they lead to counterintuitive consequences. Socrates' procedure is *ad hominem* because it aims at destroying Meno's incoherent belief structure by working within the structure. For example, Socrates shows that virtue, on Meno's conception, cannot be taught. But Meno attempts to teach virtue with his many fine speeches. The second half must be aporetic, and not positive, because Meno dogmatically clings to received senses of "teaching" and "virtue."

Ad Hominem Dialectic With Meno

Socrates labors under handicaps with Meno that he does not have with the slave. Meno thinks himself an expert on virtue, and he has given many speeches about it; thus his ego is involved in the discussion. Hence Socrates must entice Meno to answer by ironic modesty-virtue has fled from Athens, and Socrates cannot remember what Gorgias says it is (70e-71d). The slave boy is not an expert at geometry; hence he does not resist Socrates' questions, and Socrates has no need for irony. Meno is the main reason why Socrates' discussion with him fails, but their subject matter is also much more serious and difficult than geometry.

Since Meno is too impatient to learn what virtue is, but immediately wants to know how it is acquired, Socrates agrees to investigate this subject, but on a hypothesis. The hypothesis is that if virtue is knowledge, then it is teachable (87b-c). I will first outline the remarkable argument of the second half of the dialogue, and then I will analyze it in detail.

(1) Major hypothesis: If virtue is knowledge, then it is teachable.
(2) Subargument in support of the antecedent:
    (2a) Virtue is essentially beneficial (87d).
    (2b) Neither the goods of the body nor those of the *psychē*

are beneficial unless guided by knowledge of good and evil (87df.).

∴ (2c) Virtue is the knowledge of good and evil (88e-89a).

(3) Argument against the consequent:

    (3a) If virtue is teachable, then there must be teachers and learners of it (89d).

    (3b) Neither Athenian gentlemen, nor sophists, nor poets teach virtue (89eff.).

∴ (3c) There are no teachers of virtue (96b).

∴ (3d) Virtue is not teachable (93c).

∴ (3e) Virtue is not knowledge (98e).

(4) The politicians are virtuous by opinion, not knowledge (99c), and opinion comes by divine fate (99e).

As one can see from the outline, this is an unusual set of arguments. First I will discuss (2), and then I will focus on (3) and (4).

What, if anything, about the arguments does Socrates accept? Socrates accepts all of (2). In other early dialogues he gains assent to (2a) about some virtue, and uses this premise to regulate the dialectic (cf. *Laches* 192cff.). (2b) is also agreed upon in other early dialogues (cf. *Laches* 196e-197b, *Charmides* 173eff.). There is, however, disagreement about how to interpret (2c). Is virtue identical with some form of wisdom, essentially some form of wisdom, or is wisdom a sufficient condition for virtue? Elsewhere I argue for the identity interpretation — virtue is the knowledge of good and evil — and so I will not present the lengthy considerations here.[9] What is important for our purposes is that on any of the above interpretations virtue is the sort of thing which is teachable. Socrates' position can be stated as follows: all men most desire what is really beneficial (77c-78b), and knowledge of this good is what makes them hit the right mark. This knowledge is, then, human virtue.

But does not Socrates go on to reject the conclusion at (2c)? I do not think so. The arguments in (3) are unsound against the conclusion at (2c), and they are unsound in such a way as to indicate that Socrates knows they are unsound. In (2) the virtue at issue is Socratic virtue, the sort of virtue Socrates displays in the *Crito*, when through dialectic he discerns that he ought to stay and drink the hemlock. Such virtue is teachable by a teacher like Socrates. In the *Gorgias* (521d-e) Socrates says that he is the only one in Athens who practices the true political art of attempting to make the citizens better. But (3) only denies that virtue is teachable in the conventional senses of "virtue" and "teach." For first Socrates only rejects Athenian gentlemen, sophists, and poets as teachers of virtue, but this is clearly an incomplete sample: there is Socrates himself. Second the type of teaching at issue gives over and imparts its "wisdom" by rhetorical means (93b-d). In (3) Socrates constantly emphasizes the "imparting" and "giving over" nature of the teaching at issue. Hence the only sort of "virtue" which has no teachers, and is not teachable, is conventional, demotic virtue. Socrates does sample all of the apparent teachers of this virtue. Therefore (2c) can still be Socrates' real conclusion.

(3) and (4) are, I believe, *ad hominem* arguments against Meno and Anytus.[10] The claims in (3) and (4) are true only when interpreted as about received virtue and teaching. Meno and Anytus dogmatically continue to hold the untested and confused tenants of popular virtue. Socrates tries to attack this dogmatism with the *aporia* that conventional virtue cannot be transmitted. Hence it cannot be a binding force in the state, and, at best, conventionally good men are good by chance or luck. These conclusions should be sufficiently paradoxical to make Meno and Anytus reconsider their concepts of virtue and teaching.

Socrates uses the self-proclaimed good Athenian gentleman, Anytus, to reject the pretensions of those sophists who purport to teach virtue. Anytus considers the sophists corruptors of the youth, since their teachings undermine the old virtues, but Anytus, himself, has never conversed with a sophist (92b-c). Socrates points to dissension within the sophistic ranks; Protagoras claims to teach virtue, but Gorgias does not, and Meno sides with Gorgias (95b-c). Evidently Meno held the incoherent view that virtue is teachable — by his own speeches — and is not teachable — on the authority of Gorgias. If Meno accepts the view that received virtue cannot be taught by its purported teachers, then not only will he obtain a true belief, but also he will be motivated to stop speaking about virtue. Socrates believes that the sophists cannot teach real virtue, because their speeches only produce mere belief by persuasion. But they are also unable to create received virtue, for their speeches go hand in hand with the actual decline of this virtue in Athens. Socrates also quotes Theognis (95b-96a) to show that the poets contradict themselves about whether virtue is teachable. Poets, who are replete with contradictions, cannot teach anything.

Anytus, the gentleman, claims that virtue is transmitted from one generation of gentlemen to another. Any good gentleman can impart virtue. Socrates shows that the most renowned politicians in Athens—Pericles, Aristeides, and Themistocles—tried to teach their children excellence and failed. Their sons are not even good at politics. Anytus, the gentleman, becomes angry with Socrates, and leaves the discussion threatening him. Anytus, who is later one of Socrates' three accusers, displays his own lack of any sort of virtue though his father was a good Athenian citizen. Gentlemen fail to transmit virtue to their children although they desire to do so.

Socrates produces the paradox that conventional virtue cannot be taught. Conventional virtue is the knack or whim of saying and doing what is pleasing to the many as Socrates emphasizes in the *Gorgias*. It is the knack of the successful rhetorician, but it cannot be transmitted because what is pleasing and gratifying to the multitude may constantly change for any or no reason. Hence people like Pericles gain renown partly because of luck.

What are we to make of (4) where Socrates says that correct action can also come through true opinion? Since virtue is not knowledge, the good politicians must be good by true opinion. Commentators tend to applaud Plato's discovery of the difference between true opinion and knowledge in these closing pages. But Socrates' point is not this discovery, although it may occur, nor is it to claim that anyone is really virtuous by true opinion. Socrates is ironically explaining why some politicians are thought good (99e-100a); those who grasp power in the state and keep it at best do so by true opinion. How do they achieve such opinion? By divine dispensation or luck! Such men are lucky at appealing to the people; they are in the right place at the right time. Socrates distinguishes knowledge from opinion in that the former is tied down in the *psychē* by reasons, while the latter is not (98a). Since opinion is not tied down, it can come and go by just about any means—hearsay, whim, persuasion, reading bird entrails, and the like. Real virtue cannot be based on such irrationality.

Conclusion

The *Meno* ends with Socrates comparing the really virtuous man with the man of mere opinion: the latter is a flitting shade or shadow of the former (99e-100a). Only the former can teach virtue, not the latter (99e-100a). The *Meno* concludes with a contrast between the real thing and its counterfeit copy.

I will now summarize the educations of the different interlocutors. Anytus is, so the many think, of good birth and breeding. He has received a standard education for a self-styled gentleman, and he has had none of the sophistic frills. He is also an intellectual failure, and a man of deep prejudices. Meno has received the new sophistical education. This education leaves him with an incoherent belief structure reminiscent of some of Gorgias' problems in the *Gorgias*. Meno learns rhetoric in order to transmit virtue, but his teacher Gorgias does not think that virtue can be transmitted. Meno's sophistic education does not give him the means to detect false beliefs. Finally Socrates is self-educated in dialectic, and this is what he does.

Does Socrates successfully educate Meno? Given Meno's character and educational condition, Socrates chooses a good means to attempt to educate Meno. Meno must suffer *elenchus* and he must be lead to see the inadequacy of his beliefs. Hence Socrates uses *elenchus* and *psychagogia*. But do the paradoxes at the end of the *Meno* perplex Meno? We do not know, but it seems doubtful. And if Socrates' best effort fails with Meno, then Plato may want us to see that dialectic is not sufficient for education. Meno does not have the range of character flaws of a Callicles, but he does have one, one big one. Meno is established in his belief structure. Hence the *Meno*, by displaying what may be Socrates' failure, points us to the need for the basic education of the *Republic*. Education must begin with the young, and it must create the proper beliefs and habits.

10. Models of Excellence and Education in the *Protagoras*

The conclusion of the *Protagoras* appears to be inconsistent with the beginning of the dialogue. Socrates argues, at the end of the *Protagoras* that since the virtues are some form of knowledge, they probably are teachable; Protagoras attempts to keep the virtues apart from knowledge, so that they are not likely to be teachable. Early in the dialogue, however, Socrates states that virtue is not teachable, while Protagoras maintains that it is. How are we to explain this apparent reversal of positions?

Socrates and Protagoras

Socrates and Protagoras are juxtaposed in the dialogue, and the contrast is important because these men represent different educational practices and modes of life.[1] Moreover, both men compete to educate Hippocrates.[2]

The opening paragraph hints at Socrates' care for the young. His pursuit of Alcibiades is not to seduce the beautiful young man; rather it is an attempt to make him virtuous. Mention of Alcibiades' outer beauty reminds us of Socrates' outer ugliness and inner beauty, and part of this inner beauty is his care for the *psychai* of young men. We see this care in the scene with Hippocrates. Hippocrates comes to Socrates at a very early hour of the morning, and he wants Socrates to introduce him to Protagoras. Socrates shows gentle good humor towards the earnest young man even with the early interruption of his sleep. He uses the occasion to question Hippocrates about how to care for his *psychē*, and they reach some agreement before they seek admission to see Protagoras (311b).[3]

Socrates will not give a speech, and he will not make a display (318a), even though a large crowd of sophists and young men is present. The sophists, whenever possible, give a speech and make a display; they compete for the best exhibition, and the greatest applause. The sophists tune themselves only to the crowd; Socrates is interested only in the person whom he questions.[4] He engages relentlessly in question and answer, and if the conversation is not conducted in this way, he has business elsewhere. When Socrates interprets a poem, it is only to show that such interpretations are not of any great importance compared with dialectical conversation (347c-e).

Socrates remains perplexed to the end even though he argues that some virtues are knowledge. He concludes that since they have not discovered the nature of virtue, they cannot tell whether or not it is teachable. Even though, as I will argue, Socrates believes that virtue is knowledge, he disclaims that he knows what virtue is.[5] Socrates always is non-dogmatic; he will not close an inquiry by a claim to knowledge. His educational posture is aporetic; only claims to ignorance motivate more discussion. Moreover, Socrates does not know that virtue is knowledge if by "know" we mean a type of certainty which precludes further investigation. No matter what the previous arguments show, Socrates believes that the issue should never be closed.[6]

Protagoras is a foreigner; Socrates is not (cf. 309c). Protagoras takes fees; Socrates does not (cf. 310d). Protagoras claims to transmit doctrines which are taken into the *psyche*; Socrates does not do this (cf. 314b).[7] There are other contrasts between them. Protagoras enters the dialogue with a speech (316c-317c), and whenever he does not have to answer one of Socrates' questions, he gives a rhetorical exhibition (328d, 334a-c). Protagoras aims at the crowd, and he wants to surpass the other sophists who compete for the favors of the young men.

Protagoras asserts that he is an educator and a sophist (317b). Socrates denies that he is a sophist (314d). Protagoras is confident about his educational powers; he says (318a-b):

> Young man, you will gain this by coming to my classes, that on the day when you join them you will go home a better man, and on the day after it will be the same; every day you will constantly improve more and more.

Socrates makes no similar claim. Protagoras is, with the help of Socrates, a braggart. Socrates attributes to Protagoras an unsurpassed skill either in lengthy speech or in short answers. Protagoras cannot quite deny the compliment (cf. 335a where he says that he would not be superior if he were to argue as his opponents want), and thus Socrates forces him to compete and to answer his questions.[8] For Socrates admits that he has no skill at rhetoric.

Protagoras fails to maintain his position in dialectical discussion, and he becomes thoroughly provoked and harassed (333e). When given the opportunity to ask questions, he gives a speech (339a). He becomes reluctant to answer, and at the end he refuses to answer, and falls silent. Protagoras is not skilled at dialectic, and he does not like it. He is, however, a rhetorician, and the values of rhetoric are engrained deeply in him. Socrates is not able to convert him from these values. Thus we have a sharp contrast between the dialectician Socrates and the rhetorician Protagoras. From Socrates' perspective Protagoras cannot be a knowledgeable person because he does not state, clarify, and defend his beliefs from dialectical attack.[9]

Even though Socrates and Protagoras are opposites, Socrates treats Protagoras more like Gorgias than Polus or Callicles in the *Gorgias*. Protagoras does not like dialectic, but he answers honestly, and he admits when he loses. Moreover, Protagoras agrees at least verbally with many of Socrates' beliefs, for example, that knowledge is most powerful, and that not all pleasure is good.[10] Socrates insists on finishing the argument, and he compels Protagoras to answer, but he does not engage in dialectical browbeating or in ironical harassment as he does with Callicles and Polus. Protagoras is a man with demotic virtue or basic justice, and he knows when he is shamed and beaten. Protagoras has a number of defects which cluster around his self-image as a rhetorician, and the defects make Protagoras unsuitable as a teacher. But even in defeat Protagoras is magnanimous; he praises Socrates as an exception to his age who will be renowned for his wisdom (361e). Plato's picture of Protagoras is complex; he is not a good educator — he could produce unintentionally a Cleon — but his personal qualities are not tyrannical. Protagoras keeps his eye on how best to lead his life (cf. 351d), but in the absence of knowledge, the results are mixed and unpredictable.[11]

Before Socrates and Hippocrates arrive at Callias' house, they discuss the nature of sophistry since Hippocrates wants to learn from Protagoras. But does this mean that Hippocrates wants to be a sophist?

He blushes at the suggestion, which shows that there is something un-savory about sophistry (312a). Protagoras is a foreigner, and he attracts the most noble young men away from their traditional teachers. Soph-istry is uncivic.[12] Hippocrates ventures that sophists know wise matters (312c), specifically they know how to make one a clever speaker (312d), and this does describe what Protagoras purports to do. Protagoras claims that he is better than other men because he inculcates maximal demotic virtue. Such virtue involves rhetoric, and Hippocrates senses this.[13]

Socrates does not leave the power of sophistry unchallenged. He concludes that the sophists are merchants in provisions for the *psychē* (313d-e). But some sophists may be ignorant about which provisions are good for the *psychē* (313d-e). Socrates does not condemn Protagoras for this failure; we are left to infer Protagoras' ignorance for ourselves. Ignorance about these provisions, however, is tragic; for the provisions are beliefs, and once unjustified or false beliefs enter the *psychē* they are very hard to expel.

Socrates begins to develop the psychology behind his critique of sophistry. The greatest concern is care for the *psychē*.[14] The *psychē* is of greater concern than the body because the good or ill condition of all our affairs depends on the *psychē* (313e). The *psychē* is the source of motion or, as we now say, action, and the beliefs in the *psychē* motivate how the person acts, and either benefit or injure a person (314b). Thus Socrates, uses the instrumental dative for how the con-ditions of the *psychē* affect us (cf.332a-e).[15] For example, by justice we are just, and by ignorance we are cowardly. Justice and ignorance, as motive forces in the *psychē*, move us to act in their respective ways— justly or ignorantly (viciously).[16] Socrates believes that all men must desire their own well-being, and that how we act is a function of what we believe about our own well-being. Knowledge or ignorance deter-mines how we will act. We cannot expel so easily the provisions of the *psychē* as those of the body; thus we must exercise great care in what we take into the *psychē*.

Socrates and Protagoras agree on the power of knowledge (352c-d):

> . . . do you [Protagoras] consider that knowledge is something noble and able to govern man, and that whoever learns what is good and bad will never be swayed by anything to act otherwise than as knowledge bids, and that intelligence is a sufficient suc-cour for mankind?

My view, Socrates, he replied, is precisely, that which you express, and what is more, it would be a disgrace for me above all men to assert that wisdom and knowledge were aught but the highest of human things.

They also agree that the deprivation of knowledge is the most real ill (345b). But we cannot infer that both men have the same conception of knowledge because, they would bring it about in the *psychē* by dramatically different ways—for Socrates by dialectic and for Protagoras by rhetoric—and dialectical knowledge, but not rhetorical "knowledge," must be tied down in the *psychē* by reasons.

Protagoras' Great Speech

Socrates, on behalf of Hippocrates, asks Protagoras what it is he professes to teach. Protagoras says that he teaches good judgment both in ordering one's own household and in the affairs of the city. Moreover, he teaches how to have the greatest influence on public affairs (318e). Because of these claims the best young men in Athens, including Alcibiades and the sons of Pericles, have come to see Protagoras. Protagoras professes to teach excellence in public affairs, the sort of excellence possessed by a Pericles. Pericles had good judgment about how to conduct the war, or so the many thought when he convinced them of his views.

Socrates replies that what Protagoras professes to teach is not teachable, and he cites two pieces of evidence for this reply. First while only expert craftsmen are allowed to advise the state about their respective crafts, everyone advises the state on nontechnical matters which require good judgment (319d). The city allows everyone to display their capacity for the civic art, since anyone may have the capacity for it, and there do not appear to be teachers or learners of it. Second illustrious fathers do not transmit their excellence to their children even though they certainly would if they could (319e). Pericles, for example, trained his boys in some arts, but he gave them no teachers for *politikē technē*. But if there were such teachers he would have employed them. But there are not.

Socrates asserts that *aretē* is not teachable. But what sort of *aretē* is this? Socrates is not talking about minimal civic decency, nor about that virtue which comes through dialectic. He is attacking the virtue

Protagoras professes to teach. This virtue involves the ability to persuade and to lead men.[17] The virtue at issue, then, is high demotic virtue, the virtue of a Pericles. But if this virtue is not teachable, how does it come to mankind? The conclusion of the *Meno* provides an answer to this question. High *politikē technē* comes, in part, by divine dispensation or luck. Pericles and other leaders are lucky. They have the beliefs and charisma which fit the situations they stumble into, but they do not defend their beliefs through dialectic, and they do not base their charisma on self-knowledge. Protagoras cannot teach luck even if he can transmit rhetorical skill. For he cannot insure that a student will use this skill with any probability of success. Hence Socrates denies that high demotic virtue is teachable.

Protagoras attempts to show that *politikē technē* is teachable. First he tells a story about how Zeus gave civic virtue to all in order that men can live in communities (322c-d). Some civic virtue is necessary for a community, and since communities exist, so does this virtue. Protagoras' point is that at least most citizens must have this virtue. Second Protagoras argues that while it is quite true that Pericles' sons are not virtuous like their father, so too the sons of other accomplished artists frequently are not as skilled as their fathers. Nevertheless, with training Pericles' sons acquire some virtue, and the sons of other artisans acquire some competence in their respective crafts (327c-d). Most citizens transmit this virtue to the next generation.

What sort of virtue is Protagoras talking about, and how is it taught? Protagoras is talking about minimal demotic virtue. It is the sort of virtue which is required to live in a community; to live in a community one must keep hands off the person and possessions of other community members, and subscribe to the *nomoi* of the city.[18] This virtue is like the minimal competence that an untalented son of a flute player can achieve with practice and instruction. But Protagoras has not refuted Socrates' claim that virtue is not teachable. Socrates denies that high demotic virtue is teachable, while Protagoras only shows that minimal demotic virtue is teachable. Hence Protagoras' reply is an *ignoratio*.

How is minimal demotic virtue taught? Protagoras believes that education is the giving over or impressing of virtue on others (324d, 325d). Virtue is like a commodity which can be procured (324d), and handed over. Protagoras has several methods for transmitting virtue. Punishment (325b-c), admonishment (325c, 326a), and threats (325d) are useful. The young should memorize the poets' praises and eulogies of good men, so that they may imitate such men (326a). The young should develop harmony and rhythm through music, so that gracefulness permeates their lives (326a-b). Finally the young should learn the laws, and treat them as patterns for organizing their lives (326d). Protagoras' speech is a splendid account of how to train the young.[19]

What is remarkable about Protagoras' speech is that it does not explain how he teaches virtue. Protagoras claims that he excels others because he is better able to make men virtuous (328a-b). He must produce high demotic virtue which includes the ability to persuade others. But the training techniques Protagoras describes are not the techniques he uses, whatever they may be. Thus Protagoras does not show that his teaching is effective even by his own tests for effectiveness.

Protagoras' training techniques are very like those Plato discusses in books II and III of the *Republic*. The imitation of good poetry and the inculcation of proper rhythm and harmony through music are common themes in both places. Protagoras' views on training are not mentioned again in the *Protagoras*. What happens to them? My answer to this is speculative, and the evidence only permits speculation. Protagoras does not show that he can teach high demotic virtue. But Socrates does not (1) convert Protagoras to the life of dialectical inquiry. (2) make Protagoras aware of his own ignorance, and (3) draw knowledge out of Protagoras. Dialectic alone is not sufficient to accomplish (1), (2), and (3) at least with Protagoras, and with most other interlocutors in the early dialogues. Protagoras continues as a rhetorician who is attuned to the applause of the crowd. Thus both educators fail with their respective tools—rhetoric and dialectic.

Why does Socrates fail? The answer seems to be that most persons with whom he speaks are so badly trained already that he cannot educate them. His interlocutors already have values which are not compatible with the philosophical life. The only way to remedy this is to pay more attention to early education. This is precisely what Plato does in the *Republic*. The *Republic* trains all of its citizens in music and gymnastics, and a select few go on to dialectic. The early education produces the correct beliefs and values. The *Protagoras*, like the *Gorgias*, may contain significant clues about educational developments in the dialogues. The *Gorgias* forges a notion of true rhetoric, and the *Protagoras* has the first major statement about early training. But in the *Gorgias* Socrates explicitly describes and uses true rhetoric, while in the *Protagoras* early training is "hidden" in Protagoras' speech. Thus we do not know whether Plato thought Protagoras' speech to be an important contribution to educational theory.

Prodicus, Hippias, and Poetry

Plato displays to us several specific models of education: that of Prodicus, that of Hippias, and that of literary, especially poetic, interpretation. Prodicus and Hippias speak when the conversation between Socrates and Protagoras breaks down. They purportedly attempt to restart the conversation, but in fact they give their own idiosyncratic displays. Prodicus makes a series of clever distinctions and ends with: ". . . for he is comforted who learns something and gets a share of good sense in his mind alone, whereas he is pleased who eats something or has some other pleasant sensation only in his body" (337c). These distinctions are irrelevant to the purpose at hand. Prodicus, a sophist, purports to educate others. But Prodicus shows that he puts his skill to no purpose beyond its own display. Care with words is important if it has some connection with care for the *psychē*. But Prodicus makes no such connection. Prodicus' display is greeted with much applause (337c).[20]

Hippias begins by making a distinction between law and nature and he says that "law, despot of mankind, often constrains us against nature" (337c-d). He recommends that Socrates should not require extreme brevity in speech, and that Protagoras should not use extreme length in speech. He further recommends that they appoint an arbitrator who will watch the length of the speeches (337c-338a). Hippias shows that he understands nothing about dialectic; dialectic cannot be done with speeches no matter how short they are. Hippias also contradicts himself; the sophistic distinction between law and nature, with praise for nature over law, is inconsistent with the recommendation of an arbitrator. An arbitrator would authoritatively constrain Protagoras and Socrates against their desires. Since Hippias contradicts himself, he is not knowledgeable about which of his wares is beneficial for the *psychē*. Hippias, receives great applause for his exhibition (338a), but the massive amount of information, contained in Hippias' copious memory, does not make him wise.[21]

Prodicus, Hippias, and later Protagoras receive applause for their

displays even when in the case of Protagoras the display is a misinter-
pretation of a poem by Simonides (339d-e). The large crowd of potential
pupils and fellow sophists provides a background against which we
can see the values of the speakers. All of the sophists give displays for
the crowd. Their main purpose is to win favor with the crowd. Only
Socrates makes no display and gathers no applause; his main purpose
is to educate the interlocutor with whom he speaks.[22]

Socrates prevails on Protagoras to carry on the discussion by letting
him first do the questioning. Protagoras' first "question" is a speech,
and in this speech Protagoras says that the greatest part of a man's education is to interpret poems and to see what is well and what is poorly
composed in them (338e-339a). Protagoras apparently means that this
is the highest educational achievement. What happens next is baffling
unless one keeps in mind Socrates' position on the value of literary
interpretation — it is akin to what market folk do at wine parties. Protagoras accuses Simonides of contradiction; Socrates defends him against
the charge; Socrates and Prodicus playfully misinterpret some words;
and Socrates interprets Simonides' poem, but prefaces his interpretation with a fantastic story about Spartan wisdom (342a-343c).

Socrates likens arguing about poetry to the wine-parties of common market folk (347c). The participants in these parties do not converse with each other, but rather hire an extraneous voice to entertain
them, e.g. a flute. Socrates then says (347e-348a):

> . . . we are generally told by some that the poet thought so and
> so, and by others, something different, and they go on arguing
> about a matter which they are powerless to determine. No, this
> sort of meeting is avoided by men of culture, who prefer to con-
> verse directly with each other, and to use their own way of speech
> in putting one another by turns to the test.

If the poet is not present, then we cannot be sure what he meant. Contradictory interpretations of the poets' words are possible from those
words alone. Even fantastic interpretations are consistent with his words.
Hence we see what Socrates previously illustrated by his playful interpretation. More important, literary interpretation does not commit one
to the truth of what one studies. Literary interpretation may have no
effect on what we believe, and how we believe it. This activity, then, has
little to do with care for the *psyche*. Hence Socrates rejects it in favor
of direct conversation which puts "one another by turns to the test."[23]

Socrates' Attempts To Educate Protagoras

I will not analyze the arguments of the dialogue in detail since this has been done very well by others.[24] Rather I will sketch Socrates' educational strategies.

Socrates asks Protagoras whether "justice," "temperance," "holiness," and the like are all names for one and the same thing, or whether virtue is a single thing, and these are parts of it (329c-d). Protagoras chooses the latter, and he also asserts that the parts of virtue are unlike one another like the parts of the face (329d-e). Moreover, he claims that the virtues are not coinstantiated; many men are just but not brave, temperate but not wise, and the like (329e-330a). Socrates will attack all three of Protagoras claims: that the virtues are distinct, unlike, and not coinstantiated.

Both *elenchus* and *psychagogia* are frequently at work concurrently in the *Protagoras*. Socrates does not transmit his views to Protagoras; rather he implies them by how he refutes Protagoras. Each successive refutation increasingly depends upon the identification of a virtue with knowledge, and each refutation reveals more about what this knowledge is; at first it is simply knowledge, but at the end it is the knowledge of good and evil. Thus Socratic dialectic slowly and indirectly shows us the nature of virtue. But Socrates does not transmit or impress his beliefs like the sophists; rather he leads one to them by indirect means which force one to think about them for oneself. *Elenchus* should make possible the entertaining of new beliefs, and *psychagogia* leads one to the beliefs to entertain.

I will illustrate the above claims by a brief look at the arguments. The argument at 330b-331d is a preliminary skirmish. Protagoras denies that the virtues are like one another, and Socrates attempts to show that justice and holiness are alike because each is just and holy.[25] Protagoras concedes that justice and holiness have some resemblance, but then anything has some resemblance to any other thing (331d). We only learn from this argument that two virtues are alike in two respects. The next argument (332a-333b) identifies temperance with wisdom and intemperance with folly. Socrates argues that it is by wisdom that we act temperately, and that it is by folly that we act intemperately. Hence temperance is wisdom. We do not learn from this argument what sort of wisdom is at issue.

The third argument (349d-351b) purports to show that courage is wisdom, and there is the suggestion that the wisdom at issue makes courage good (349e). Protagoras rejects this argument, and Socrates attempts to convince Protagoras by an appeal to premises that the many would accept.[26] Those who believe that pleasure is good and pain bad must also admit that what they call "being overcome by pleasure" really is acting out of ignorance; i.e., a failure to discern what on the whole, and in the long run, produces more pleasure than pain. So too the courageous go to meet those things which are really honorable, good, and pleasant, while the cowards go to meet those which are not (360a). Courage is, then, the knowledge of what is worth daring, and cowardice is ignorance about such matters. We now learn that a virtue is a certain sort of knowledge—a knowledge about what is on the whole good and bad.

Socrates' arguments both refute Protagoras' positions, and progressively imply an answer to the question "What is virtue?" We are invited to infer that since each virtue is intrinsically good, and only the knowledge of good and evil is intrinsically good, that each virtue is this knowledge. But what effects do these arguments have on Protagoras? He becomes more reluctant to answer with each successive argument. At 352c-d Protagoras admits that nothing is better and more powerful than knowledge, but he does not connect these admissions with the nature of virtue. Protagoras is so involved in the agonistic nature of the contest, and how he appears to the crowds, that Socrates neither engenders in him beneficial ignorance nor leads him to the correct position. The latter particularly is disheartening because the *psychagogia* is more explicit in the *Protagoras* than in most other early dialogues. In the end all that Protagoras does is congratulate the victor; he is a good sport (361d-e).

Conclusion

Socrates and Protagoras "switch" positions in this dialogue because they do not have the same conceptions of virtue and teaching. Socrates begins by denying that high demotic virtue can be taught, and Protagoras asserts that low demotic virtue can be taught. Socrates ends by suggesting that every real virtue is the knowledge of good and evil which can be taught, and Protagoras resists both of these suggestions. The peculiar switch in positions, itself, stimulates us to see what underlies the switch, and when we do this we discover different conceptions of virtue and teaching.

Protagoras does not show that what he professes to teach — which must be high demotic virtue — is teachable. Socrates shows that he does not educate Protagoras. Where, then, are we to look for successful education? The training methods Protagoras recommends are ignored, but they recur in the *Republic* as the bases for education. Perhaps Plato is beginning to think about how to prepare people for dialectical education when he writes the *Protagoras*.

11. The Failure of Socratic Education in the *Hippias Major*

The *Hippias Major*[1] is a scathing indictment of polymathic learning, embodied in Hippias, which is one of the new educational trends in Athens. Hippias is one of the most unsavory characters in the early dialogues, and his intellectual defects are so serious that it is difficult to see how, if at all, Socrates can educate him.[2] What sort of tactics might he use to improve a person like Hippias? Moreover, the overt topic of the *Hippias Major* is the beautiful or noble, but Socrates rejects all six definitions of this notion. Can we from the dramatic features of the dialogue, and from how Socrates rejects the definitions of the beautiful learn anything about the nature of the beautiful?[3]

Hippias, Socrates and the Mystery Tormentor

Hippias, a wise and noble sophist, comes to Athens to give a well-composed speech about what pursuits are noble and beneficial for young men to pursue.[4] Thus the topic of the dialogue will be the beautiful.[5] Hippias spends most of his time in Sparta, not Athens (281a-b). Socrates' queries about why Hippias is now visiting Athens are heavily ironical. Hippias, as we will see, is a polymath—a "knower" of many things. But Hippias does not desire to test his wisdom in Athens, the seat of learning, but prefers Sparta.[6] Hippias' "wisdom" has not yet seen a sophisticated, urbane test.

Socrates, in the *Hippias Major* more than in any other early dialogue, engages in constant sarcasm and irony. At the very beginning he praises Hippias for earning money, conferring benefit on the young, and making public speeches (281b-c). The wise men of old, Socrates says, did not have such versatility, and Hippias modestly explains that they could not compass by their wisdom both public and private matters (281c-d). But Hippias also surpasses the contemporary sophists like Protagoras and Prodicus because he sometimes earns more money than them. Hippias' desire to overreach all others shows his lack of moderation and self-control.[7]

Hippias fancies himself a rhetorician. He thinks himself to speak well in public, and he plans to give to fine rhetorical *display* to the young men in school (386b-c).[8] Hippias believes that teaching is pouring fine words upon the passive minds of his listeners.[9] At the end of the dialogue he reveals his attitude to Socratic dialectic: it cuts reality into little bits and pieces, but a real man gives great, continuous speeches about the whole of reality (301b, 304a-b). A great man gives great speeches. One theme of the *Hippias Major* is the clash between dialectic and rhetoric; Hippias manifests the rhetorical character, and Socrates the dialectical.[10]

Socrates questions Hippias about his travels to Sparta. The Spartans do not want to learn from him about the stars and phenomena of the heavens, nor about geometry, nor the processes of thought, nor about letters and harmonies (285c-d). Rather Hippias repeats the genealogies of heroes and men, the foundations of cities, and about antiquity in general (285d). Socrates asks whether this historical work strains Hippias' memory, and Hippias brags that he can remember fifty names on hearing them once (285e).[11] Hippias puts great stock in his ability to memorize much trivia. Hippias is a polymath, a man of great versatility. But as Socrates illustrates about the very same Hippias in the *Hippias Minor*, versatility on the one hand and superficiality and confusion on the other often go hand in hand. We will see that Hippias is, indeed, very superficial and confused.

Socrates presses Hippias about why the Spartans do not, by law, permit foreigners to teach their children. He makes Hippias concede the following claims (283cf.): (1) Hippias is able to teach virtue, (2) The Spartans desire to have their children taught it, (3) Sparta is well governed, (4) A well governed state would create virtue, (5) Spartan law prohibits foreigners from teaching virtue to their children, and (6) The Spartans have enough money to pay Hippias for instruction. The real Hippias believes that a true law must be for what is naturally best, and Socrates forces the dramatic Hippias to this same assent. They then agree that Sparta cannot be well governed because it has a bad law which prohibits Hippias from teaching there. But one might as well argue that Sparta, a well-governed state, correctly prohibits sophists like Hippias from corrupting its youth. If Socrates were not speaking with Hippias, and hence needed his minimal good will for the continuance of the discussion, this would be the correct conclusion. Socrates is ironical in this exchange with Hippias.

Hippias operates at only the level of superficial appearance and public opinion. He literally sees everything on the surface. Hippias supports his first account of the beautiful with the observation that no one would deny what he says (288a). Hippias' second answer is that gilded gold is what makes all beautiful things beautiful (289e), and his third answer is an attempt to say, "what will never appear ugly anywhere to anybody" (291d). A leitmotif of the *Hippias Major* is that Hippias' mind goes no deeper than the cosmetic interpretation of *cosmos*. Hippias' view of *cosmos* is one of surface adornment. He continually chooses the level of mere appearance, and interprets *cosmos* in its most debased sense (239d-e).

Throughout the *Hippias Major* there are references to Hippias' intellectual qualities. He operates only at the level of eristic, and has no conception of a search for truth. Hippias also is intellectually unable to do dialectic. I will list some of the passages pertaining to Hippias' intellectual traits:

(1) At 285b Hippias agrees with Socrates because the argument is in Hippias' favor!
(2) At 289e Hippias is very pleased with his answer because it will throw their opponent into confusion.
(3) At 292b Hippias thinks so because Socrates thinks so.
(4) At 294a Socrates asks Hippias whether the beautiful makes things seem, or be, beautiful. Hippias answers "Yes," being unable to see that there are two distinct questions.
(5) At 294c-d Hippias twice contradicts himself in adjacent answers.
(6) At 289b Socrates offers a persuasive counterexample to an account. Hippias responds that perhaps the objection will skip past the man whom both he and Socrates are trying to confute.
(7) At 287d-e Hippias is unable to distinguish "What is the beautiful?" and "What is beautiful?" In fact Hippias never grasps this distinction.
(8) Socrates makes explicit evaluations of Hippias at 288d, 292d, and 296a. The mystery tormentor (to be discussed below) seeks truth,

Hippias does not; Hippias does not listen and has no brain; Hippias does not understand the value of wisdom.

Socrates constantly shows that Hippias is as superficial intellectually as are his accounts of the beautiful. Hippias' entire aim is eristic rhetoric — to defeat in the eyes of the many an antagonist by any means possible.

Hippias' ignorance is only matched by his confidence and insolence. He is of the firm opinion that the wisdom Socrates seeks is of no great value (286e, 287b). Since Hippias is such a polymath, no single part of the broad learning is worth much. Hippias is always confident that he knows the correct answer — even after six refutations — and he is quite sure that he can teach Socrates what it is (287b, 295a, 297e). After all knowledge of the beautiful is not hard to find (295a). Socrates, by contrast, ends the dialogue with the proverb that "Beautiful things are difficult."

The *Hippias Major* gives us a thorough description of Hippias. He values most money and fame before the many. His means to these ends are his polymathic "wisdom," especially the ability to make speeches. Hippias' speeches are pure eristic, and they aim only to flatter their listeners. Hippias is also dogmatic and uneducatable. He says the same things at the end of the dialogue as at the beginning. Public speeches, he says, are beautiful and noble, not the dialectic which cuts reality into bits and pieces. Hippias is never stung by Socrates' *elenchus* (refutation), which is one reason why Socrates is so uniformly vitriolic about him. Vastness of "knowledge," intellectual confusion, and dogmatism are all magnified in Hippias.[12]

Socrates and Hippias cannot really communicate with each other. They lack sufficient shared beliefs and attitudes. But Hippias is not like Callicles in the *Gorgias*. Callicles and Socrates disagree fundamentally, but Hippias is so intellectually pliable that he agrees with just about anything Socrates says.[13] Socrates, then, hardly can refute Hippias. In this context we may expect more than mere straight-forward argumentation from Socrates.

One theme of the dialogue is who will appear ridiculous: Hippias or the mystery tormentor? The latter, Hippias claims, will appear ludicrous before the many; Hippias, Socrates shows, is ridiculous in argument. Some of Socrates' argumentative moves, I will show, make Hippias absurd, and Socrates intends just this.

The *Hippias Major* employs an unusual dramatic technique. At 286c Socrates introduces a man (I will call him the "mystery tormentor") who asks Socrates all sorts of questions about the beautiful. This man constantly torments Socrates with questions. Socrates requests from Hippias that he, Socrates, be permitted to take the role of this man, and ask Hippias the very questions which the tormentor asked him. With Hippias' instruction perhaps Socrates can escape from the tormentor. But slowly the tormentor is shown to be Socrates himself. Some commentators argue that the introduction of the tormentor is unworthy of Plato's great dramatic art. I disagree.[14]

The tormentor is an effective device which has several functions. I will list these functions with evidence for them:

(1) The tormentor says to Socrates what Socrates would like to say to Hippias. At 290a,d the tormentor insults Socrates, and at 291e he will beat Socrates with a stick for his stupid answer. The tormentor tells Socrates at 292c-d that Socrates is brainless and does not listen. Obviously Socrates could not say these things directly to Hippias and continue a conversation with him.

(2) Socrates can contrast Hippias with the vile tormentor without directly insulting Hippias. The tormentor, however, has Socrates' qualities. He is an "insolent questioner" who insists that one first says what the beautiful is before judging beautiful pursuits (286c-d); he constantly objects to what people say (287a-b); he is vulgarly only after truth and not public approval (288d); and he does not accept anything easily (289e, 290e).

(3) By putting the tormentor's and not his own questions to Hippias, Socrates is able to keep Hippias in the discussion.[15] At 291a Hippias states that he would not talk with a fellow who asks such questions; he will, however, talk with Socrates since they are in league together against this man.

(4) The tormentor gives Socrates a new weapon in his ironic arsenal. Socrates pretends ignorance before the tormentor's questions, and he asks Hippias for help in answering the man (286d). Socrates' feigned alliance with Hippias permits, as one might expect, numerous ironic variations. Hippias never seems to see that Socrates is his real opponent.

(5) The mask is slowly lifted from the tormentor, and he is revealed to be Socrates.[16] But even when the unmasking is explicit, Hippias does not see it. Hippias' ignorance is further displayed by his in-

ability to see who Socrates really is. At 290d-e Socrates tells Hippias that he would not know the tormentor even if he knew his name. But the reader sees who he is: Socrates will imitate that man in making objections, but Socrates, himself, is quite experienced at objection making; Socrates will not let an objection slip past the man before whom he is most reluctant to talk nonsense, not just the tormentor, but namely himself (298b-c); the tormentor is a close relative of Socrates, and even lives in the same house. (304d-e); finally the tormentor is starkly declared to be "Socrates, Son of Sophroniscus" (298c), but Hippias does not hear or understand or both. The tormentor is Socrates, and to the extent that Socrates accurately can project himself onto another, he displays self-knowledge.

There does not appear to be anything Socrates can do to educate Hippias. Hippias' character is such that Socratic refutation is unlikely with him. Hippias always believes that while he cannot say to Socrates what the beautiful is, if he goes away and thinks about it for a while, he will discover it (295a). Hippias is not like Callicles of the *Gorgias* with whom Socrates also cannot do dialectic. Callicles lacks knowledge, good will, and frankness, but he is not superficial intellectually. Behind Callicles' viciousness is a keen intellect. But Hippias is superficial, and no amount of training is able to alter this defect.

Hippias' Three Accounts of the Beautiful

Before Hippias attempts to say what the beautiful is Socrates gives him some hints about what a successful answer must be like. Just as all just men are just by justice, and wise men wise by wisdom, so too all beautiful things are beautiful by the beautiful (287c-d). The instrumental dative "by which" indicates that, in some sense, the beautiful is responsible for the beauty of all other things. Socrates does not explain in what way the beautiful makes other things beautiful, but it would instantiate one or more of Aristotle's four causes.[17] For Aristotle's four causes, or answers to "Why?" questions, accurately delineate the broad use of the Greek word for "cause." We also learn that the beautiful is responsible for the beauty of *all* other beautiful things. An answer which explains only the beauty of some beautiful things is not correct. Hippias admits that justice, wisdom, and the beautiful are *something* since they have their respective functions (287c). "Something" is a neutral term, and it does not carry any particular ontological import.[18] It need not, for example, refer to a transcendent Form. The beautiful could be some characteristic in things.

Socrates asks Hippias for the beautiful itself, not for a beautiful thing. "Itself" is an intensive word which simply adds emphasis; it too has no special ontological import.[19] Hippias is not able to distinguish the beautiful and a beautiful thing, nor does he ever see this distinction. He answers that a beautiful maiden is beautiful, and he confidently says that no one would disagree with this answer (287e-288a). Hippias thinks that he has captured what everyone thinks is beautiful. If the tormentor attempts to refute this answer, then he will appear ridiculous. Socrates sarcastically asks whether if a beautiful maiden is beautiful, then there is something by which all these things would be beautiful (288a)? His point is that a maiden is not the sort of thing by the addition of which other things are beautiful.

Hippias concedes that some mares and pots are also beautiful (288c-d). He next conveniently says that a pot is not beautiful in comparison with a maiden (288e), and this permits Socrates to point out that a maiden is ugly if compared with a god (289b). Since the maiden is beautiful and ugly, it cannot be that by which all other things are beautiful (289c).

By this account Hippias displays both his superficial grasp of beauty and his ineptness at dialectic. He does not see that there must be something about the maiden which makes her beautiful. Socrates, moreover, presupposes that only what is beautiful in all comparisons can be that by which other things are beautiful. Socrates, as we will see, uses similar presuppositions in the other refutations.

Hippias' second account is that the beautiful is gold. Socrates suggests this answer to him by how he phrases his request for an answer. Socrates says (289d):

> Do you think that the beautiful itself, by the addition of which all other things are adorned (*kosmētai*) and made to appear beautiful, when its form (*eidos*) is added to something — do you think that is a maiden or a mare or a lyre?

"*Kosmētai*" reminds Hippias of the process of gilding, and hence he chooses gold as his answer. "*Kosmētai*" has an interesting range of senses: it can mean anything from internal structure and harmony to superficial cosmetics. Socrates seeks the former, but Hippias only recognizes the latter. *"Eidos"* has a parallel range of senses: its meanings range from internal structure and nature to external manifestation.[20] The vagueness of Socrates' question permits Hippias the latitude to display his proclivities. He chooses a superficial, cosmetic entity, gold, as his answer.

Hippias admits that ivory and stone are also beautiful in the appropriate aesthetic contexts (290b-c). He also concedes that a wooden ladle is more excellent than a golden one for ladling hot soup (290d-291b). Hence wood is more beautiful than gold in the appropriate utilitarian contexts. Socrates concludes that gold is no more beautiful than ivory, stone, and wood (291c), and hence it cannot be the beautiful. What is in one context beautiful and in another not beautiful cannot be that by which all beautiful things are beautiful. The beautiful is, presumably, beautiful in all contexts.

Hippias introduces his third account by saying (291d):

> . . . for you seem to me to be seeking a reply that the beautiful is something of such a sort that it will never appear ugly anywhere to anybody.

John Malcolm believes that this passage sets the stage for the middle-period transcendent Forms.[21] But Hippias is simply after what all people think is beautiful; he wants to present an account which no one will disagree with. Hippias' third account is that "it is most beautiful to be rich and healthy, and honored by the Greeks, to reach old age, and after providing a beautiful funeral for his deceased parents, to be beautifully and splendidly buried by his own offspring" (291d-e). Socrates reminds Hippias that he asked for "the beautiful itself by which everything to which it is added has the quality of being beautiful, both stone and stick and man and God and every act and every acquisition of knowledge" (292c-d). Hippias insists that his answer is beautiful to all and will seem so; Socrates asks whether it will be so, "For the beautiful is always beautiful, is it not?" (292e) That by which all beautiful things are beautiful is itself always beautiful.

Socrates asks whether it is beautiful for the gods to be buried by their offspring, and Hippias allows that neither for the gods nor for the heroes who are children of the gods is it noble. Socrates concludes that the same thing has happened in this case as in the previous two: the events Hippias designates are beautiful for some and not beautiful for others" (293c).

Hippias gives these accounts without much prompting from Socrates. Each account displays Hippias' desire to find something which will seem beautiful to everyone. Hippias, the giver of beautiful speeches, is concerned only with what the many think. Socrates directly refutes the accounts, but Hippias is not stung by defeat, and he continues in his dogmatic wisdom.

What do we learn from these refutations? Socrates shows that a particular, a mass object (gold), and a set of events are not the beautiful. We can generalize Socrates' arguments to all things in these three groups. No particular, for example, is beautiful or noble in every comparison, nor is any set of events excellent for everyone. Hence the beautiful is not a particular, a mass object, or a set of events.

The beautiful is always beautiful, and the meaning of "always" is explained in the accounts. The beautiful is beautiful in every comparison, in every context, and for each thing which possesses it. Socrates does not say or imply that the beautiful always exists like a middle period Form. The most we may infer is that when the beautiful is added to something, then it is beautiful. To be always beautiful does not imply that something always exists; only that if it exists, then it is beautiful.

Socrates often repeats that the beautiful is that *by which all other* things are beautiful. Moreover, the beautiful is always beautiful. Is there a link between these two claims? Elsewhere I argue that Plato assumes the principle that a cause must have what it produces in something else—hereafter called the "causal principle" or "CP" for short.[22] By "cause" I mean any one of Aristotle's four causes; hence formal and final causes employ the CP as much as efficient causes. Since the beautiful is that by which all other things are beautiful, given the CP, the beautiful must itself be beautiful. Since whenever the beautiful is present to something it makes it beautiful, the beautiful must always be beautiful. We do not, however, have any strong evidence at this point about what the beautiful is, but we do know three types of things that it is not. Hence Socrates' refutations of Hippias are also psychagogic—they lead the reader if not Hippias to a deeper understanding of what the beautiful must be like.

Socrates' Three Accounts of the Beautiful

The tormentor, out of pity for the inexperience and lack of training of an answerer, sometimes suggests replies to him. Since the former accounts are too silly and easy to refute, the tormentor asks whether the beautiful is the appropriate (293d-e). Each of Socrates' three accounts, we may surmise, will be closer to the mark.[23] Socrates will no longer primarily refute Hippias; rather he will also try to get us, if not Hippias, to see certain answers. Socrates engages in *psychagogia* (*psychē*-leading); he tries by indirection to get one to see for himself what the answer is. Socrates will reject each of his own accounts, but, as I will show, each of these rejections tells us more about Hippias than about the accounts themselves.

Socrates first offers that the beautiful is the appropriate (293e). This account is most appropriate because earlier in the dialogue Socrates and Hippias agree that when appropriate something is beautiful or useful (290d). Thus the appropriate has both an aesthetic and an utilitarian function.

Hippias is asked whether the appropriate makes things be or appear beautiful, and he chooses the latter (294a). When Hippias mentions as paradigm examples of the appropriate, clothes and shoes that fit (294a), we see that he has much too superficial a notion of "fitness." Beautiful clothes do not make a beautiful person. But Socrates does not directly attack Hippias' crude claim; rather, he says that if the appropriate makes someone appear more beautiful than he is, then it would be a deceit in respect to the beautiful (294a). What is logically remarkable about Socrates' rejection of this account is that he completely ignores the aesthetic and utilitarian notions of the appropriate mentioned earlier in the dialogue; he simply does not attempt to invest the appropriate with any more meaning than Hippias gives it.

Plato has a limited objective in the first account. He tries to get us to see that the appropriate is not the beautiful because it makes things only appear but not be beautiful, while the beautiful makes them be but not appear so. Earlier in the dialogue Socrates shifted — to the discomfort of both Hippias and the reader — between be and appear. At 289d he asks for "that by which all other things are adorned and appear beautiful"; yet, at 292d, he wants to know "what it is that when added to something, makes that thing be beautiful." The first account teaches us, even if not Hippias, that Socrates is not interested in what people think is beautiful or what appears beautiful; rather, he is after what makes things be beautiful.

Moreover, the fate of the appropriate is not settled when Socrates rejects Hippias' interpretation of it. For the next two accounts are an aesthetic and an utilitarian, and so the first account reduces to the next two. Furthermore, we should note that when Socrates thinks of the appropriate as something other than a deceit in respect to the beautiful, he considers it a fitness or harmony of the elements in a thing (Pheidias' statue) or situation (a figwood spoon for eating soup), that produces aesthetic pleasure or utility.

The second account is that the beautiful is the useful (295c). A group of objects is given for which this account is most appropriate: eyes, the whole body, all the animals, all utensils, land vehicles, freight ships, ships of war, all instruments in music and the other arts, and even customs and pursuits (295c-d). Each of these is beautiful in the respect or way in which it is useful. Moreover, when Socrates states his third account, that the beautiful is the pleasant to hearing and sight, he gives a different group of objects for which that account is most appropriate. We would classify these under the fine arts, although Socrates does not distinguish the mechanical and the fine arts by denying excllence and beauty to the former. One reason for this is that *kalos* has a much broader meaning than the English word "beautiful."[24] It can mean "beautiful," "noble," "honorable," "fine," "fair," and "good," to give only a few examples. Likewise, *aischros* the opposite of *kalos* has as many contrary meanings. Thus when Socrates says at 292d, "Everything to which the beautiful is added is made beautiful, a stone, wood, man, god, every action, and learning," we see that *kalos* is much broader in meaning than our notion of aesthetic beauty. The beautiful is more akin to a thing's excellence (*aretē*), and different types of things can have different types of excellence. We should not be surprised, then, to see Socrates reject the second and third accounts because each is too narrow; each account focuses upon one type of excellence, and does not state the nature of the beautiful that is common to all excellence.

Socrates quickly amends the second account: only what is useful for something good is beautiful. On this view the beautiful is the cause (296e) or the father (297b) of the good, and since a cause is different from its effect, the beautiful is different from the good. So far everything is in order, but then Socrates makes the startling inference that since the beautiful and the good are different, "the beautiful (*to kalon*), is not good (*agathon*), and the good (*to agathon*) is not beautiful (*kalon*)" (297c). This conclusion is unacceptable, and they abandon the whole account.

The distinction between the beautiful and one of its effects, bene-fit, is correct, and we see Socrates reassert it in the *Gorgias* (474d-e). But what are we to make of the final and fatal inference? I believe that it is an intentional fallacy meant to stun Hippias and leave him in a state of bewilderment.[25] Only then would Hippias begin to in-vestigate, for himself, the real nature of beauty. Socrates knows that "the beautiful is the useful for something good" only states a mark of the beautiful and not its nature, and if he were to leave Hippias with this account, Hippias would simply incorporate it into the "beau-tiful" speech, the one he is to give to school-children, about what pur-suits are noble and beautiful. Moreover, Hippias has not the slightest idea what real benefit is; for him power in political affairs is most beautiful (295e-296a). Thus Socrates overturns everything in the vain hope that Hippias will postpone his speech until he discovers for himself the real nature of the beautiful. For Hippias really is a corruptor of the youth.

There are, moreover, other motives for the intentional fallacy. Does Socrates really believe that Hippias can be brought around to admit ignorance about the beautiful, much less to seek for it? Socrates' constant sarcasm and irony about Hippias, as well as Hippias' dogmatic belief that the beautiful is not hard to find, suggest a negative answer. Why, then, does Socrates use such a fallacy? Certainly he does not want to leave Hippias with any misunderstood information about the beautiful. Second Plato wants to stimulate the reader to spot the fallacy. Third Socrates desires to reveal Hippias' polymathic confusion, Hip-pias is the fox who "knows" many things, but not the one big one; Socrates is the hedgehog who knows one thing, one big thing—how to do dialectic. For without the ability to engage in dialectic, there is no way to discover and justify what one ought to believe.

One might object to my argument that 297c is not an intentional fallacy, but simply the denial of the identity:[26] "The beautiful is not the good, and the good is not the beautiful." But there are serious objections to this interpretation: (1) While it does not produce a *nonse-quitur*, it does make the conclusion a mere restatement of the premise from which it is derived: "The beautiful and the good are not iden-tical, therefore, they are not identical." But Socrates clearly indicates that two different assertions are at issue. (2) Nowhere in the *Hippias Major* is it agreed that the beautiful is the good, so a denial of the identity would not be sufficient to reject the account that the beautiful produces good. (3) The denial of an identity would not have the same shocking result—emphasized by the exclamation "My God" four times—as the predication translation. (4) The same argument recurs at 303e-304a, where it is used to reject the account that the beautiful is beneficial pleasure, but here "then neither would the good be beautiful nor the beautiful good" is clearly a purported consequence of "if each is different from the other." (5) Only if the consequence is read as a predication is it sufficient to require that the account be abandoned; for to say that the beautiful is not a good thing is, indeed, shocking. I conclude that the consequence is the denial of a predication.

But does Socrates intentionally produce the fallacy at 297c? Does he have enough of an intuitive grasp of the difference between a predication and an identity to see that it is fallacious to infer that "the beautiful is not good" from "the beautiful is not the good?" G.M.A. Grube denies that he does:[27]

> The *Hippias Major* was written at an early stage in Plato's life before the use of the predicate, i.e. the difference between: "Beauty is good," and "Beauty is the good," was clearly understood. The question of the copula is dealt with in the *Sophist* after which the *Hippias Major* could not have been written.

Grube claims that in the early dialogues Plato confuses identity and predicative assertions. But there is no compelling evidence for this claim. Even if Plato does not distinguish such assertions until the *Sophist*, he might use the distinction correctly in earlier dialogues.

What should we conclude about the second account? First all notions of benefit and utility must instance what is virtuous. Something cannot be really beneficial unless it is morally virtuous. Second the beautiful is something about an object which makes it beautiful. The beautiful is not benefit, but what it is about an object which makes it produce benefit. Benefit is an effect or test for the presence of beauty, but it is not its nature.[28] Finally, Hippias is unable to understand the point Socrates hints at.

Hippias is confident—even after five refutations—that he will find the beautiful, but Socrates is so eager to know the answer that he makes his own suggestion (297e): the beautiful is what is pleasant to hearing and sight (298a). Socrates focuses this account on aesthetic objects: "Beautiful persons, all decorations, paintings, and works of sculpture which are beautiful delight us when we see them; beautiful sounds, music in general, speeches, and stories accomplish the same thing" (298a). Socrates narrows his account to a subset of beautiful things, and he explicitly recognizes this when he asks whether customs and laws are beautiful because they are pleasant to hearing and sight. Hippias hopes that this objection will slip past the tormentor (298b). This account, just as the previous one, gives us a subset of the effects of the beautiful, and not its nature.

"What is pleasant" in Greek is an ambiguous phrase which either refers to the objects which produce pleasure or to the pleasures that are produced. Since the beautiful makes things beautiful, we could expect Socrates to investigate what it is about these things which makes them beautiful. But in a few lines he shifts the question from a focus on the particulars to the pleasures they produce (cf. 300a). What is common to the pleasures is then thought to be the beautiful.

Socrates leads Hippias in a lengthy discussion of what is common to both pleasures collectively and individually. That they are each and both pleasures will not do because there are some pleasures which are not beautiful. That they are pleasures through hearing and sight is wrong because this is common to both, but not to each. That they are pleasures through hearing belongs to one, but not both; the same objection applies to pleasures through sight. The purpose of this lengthy discussion appears to be the embarrassment of Hippias who during the discussion makes numerous bad answer and logical fallacies.

Socrates concludes that it seems to him necessary that the pleasures are beautiful because they are the most harmless and best of pleasures (303e). This conclusion leads to the very same sophistry with which Socrates rejects the previous account: ". . . the beneficial is that which creates the good, and that which creates and that which is created were just now seen to be different, and our argument has come around to the earlier one. . . . For neither could the good be beautiful nor the beautiful good, if each of them is different from the other" (303e-304a). Hippias sees nothing wrong with this conclusion, and he begins to denounce Socrates' style of conversation as mere scrapings and shavings of discourse which tears reality to pieces. Beautiful speeches, Hippias thinks, are great and continuous, and they are about the whole of reality. The irony here is obvious. Hippias, who has no logical skill at all and cannot spot even the grossest of fallacies, likes great, rhetorical speeches. Great, rhetorical speeches are condemned by the attitudes and deficiencies of the man who practices them.

Why does Socrates reject his third account with the same sophism as the second? Pleasures through hearing and sight are effects of the beautiful just as benefit is. The beautiful makes things beautiful so that they can produce these effects. To twist a classic phrase from the *Euthyphro*, "Beautiful things are not beautiful because they produce aesthetic pleasure and/or benefit, but they produce aesthetic pleasure and/or benefit because they are beautiful." Hence aesthetic pleasure and benefit are effects of the beautiful and not its nature; but Socrates will not "teach" Hippias by telling him this, and Hippias does not have the wit to see it for himself. Socrates attempts to penetrate Hippias' dogmatism, but his armor is too thick. All Socrates has left is sarcasm and irony. The *Hippias Major* closes with Hippias praising the beauty of great, continuous speeches, and castigating the dialectical chopping of Socrates' discussion.

The Nature of the Beautiful

Before we turn to the *Gorgias* to see what the beautiful is, I will briefly describe R. Hoerber's two important insights about the literary structure of the *Hippias Major*.[29] Hoerber argues that Plato writes the dialogue using two major construction devices: triads and intertwining. The dialogue is permeated with triads both in its major structural features—Hippias' three accounts and Socrates' three accounts—and in its minor features—Hippias outdoes three contemporary sophists. Hoerber lists numerous such triads, but we need not detail them here. The presence of so many triads must be intentional, and the question is why Plato composes the dialogue in triads. Hoerber argues that the triads hint at the three aspects of the beautiful: moral, aesthetic, and utilitarian. Hoerber's point is very close to correct, but the three aspects are effects of the beautiful. As effects of the beautiful they can be tests for it, but they are not its nature. "Intertwining" refers to the tendency Plato has to mention something—a topic, person, or the like—drop it, and then reintroduce it. The *Hippias Major* interlocks things like this: a, b, a; b, c, b, and so on. Hoerber speculates that intertwining invites us to unify the three aspects of the beautiful, but he does not show how this is to be done. I agree that we are to unify the effects of the beautiful, but we are to do this by finding their common cause.

Let us turn to the *Gorgias* to find this cause. At *Gorgias* 474d-e Socrates says:

> All fair things, like bodies and colors and figures and sounds and observances — is it looking at nothing that you call these fair in each case? Thus in the first place, when you say that fair bodies are fair, it must be either in view of their use for some particular purpose that each may serve, or in respect of some pleasure arising when, in the act of beholding them, they cause delight to the beholder.

Socrates offers aesthetic pleasure and utility as two tests for beauty; they are effects of the beautiful, and do not give its nature. In the *Euthyphro* Socrates asks a famous question that displays this distinction (10a): "Is the holy holy because the gods love it, or do they love it because it is holy?" Euthyphro has not said what the holy is, rather he gives an effect of it: "Euthyphro, when I asked you to say what the holy is, you did not want to reveal its nature to me, but rather gave some characteristic of it, something which happens to the holy, that it is loved by all the gods" (11a-b). Socrates does not deny that effects can mark out — put a boundary around — objects (see *Euthyphro* 9c), but he does deny that they give the nature of these objects. On the correct account of divinity, if something is pious then it is loved by the Gods, and if something is god-loved then it is pious; if something is beautiful then it either produces benefit or aesthetic pleasure, and if it produces benefit or aesthetic pleasure, then it is beautiful. Thus god-loved can be a test for pious objects, and benefit or aesthetic pleasure can be a test for beautiful things; but neither of them gives the nature of the pious or the beautiful respectively. Socrates at *Gorgias* 474d-e only wants to mark out the group of fair things in order to refute Polus; thus he uses aesthetic pleasure and benefit as effects of beautiful things.

But what is the nature of the beautiful? At *Gorgias* 503e ff. Socrates gives a lengthy analysis of artistic production:

> 503e He [the true rhetorician] is just like other craftsman, who having his own particular work in view, selects the things he applies to that work of his, not at random, but with the purpose of giving a certain form to whatever he is working upon. You have only to look, for example, at the painters, the builders, the shipwrights, or any of the other

craftsmen, whichever you like, to see how each of them arranges everything according to a certain order, and forces
one part

504a to fit and agree with another, until he has combined the
whole into a regular and well-ordered production; . . .
Then if regularity and order are found in a house, it will
be a good one, and if irregularity, a bad one. . . . For it
seems

504c to me that any regularity of the body is called healthiness,

504d and this leads to health being produced in it, and general
bodily excellence . . . . And the regular and orderly states
of the soul are called lawfulness and law, whereby men are
similarly made law-abiding and orderly; and these states
are justice and temperance. . . .

506d And is that thing pleasant by whose advent we are pleased,

506e and that thing good by whose presence we are good? . . .
But further, both we and everything else that is good, are
good by the advent of some virtue? . . . Then the virtue
of each thing is a matter of regular and orderly arrangement? . . . Hence it is a certain order proper to each exis-
tent thing that by its advent in each makes it good?

Similar statements occur in the late *Philebus* (26a-b), where measure
is responsible for all the beautiful things. Moreover, those commentators who believe that the *Hippias Major* is genuine also tend to think
that it is close in date of composition to the *Gorgias*. E. R. Dodds,
for example, places the *Gorgias* just after the *Hippias Major*, and claims
that the *Gorgias* presupposes the discussion of beauty in the *Hippias
Major*.[30]

The account of production at 503e ff. applies to all craftsmen:
painters, philosophers, and even boat builders. We may describe the
stages of *technē* as follows: (1) The true rhetorician, when constructing a speech, looks at (503e, 504d, e) what he wants to produce in
the *psychai* of his listeners, that is, justice and temperance. The other
craftsmen also look at their tasks (503e). These tasks are not simply
the replication of already existing houses, ships, or the like, but rather
the "ideal designs" for such things. (2) Then the craftsman gives a certain
form to the matter; he forces one part to fit and agree with another
until the whole is a regular and well-ordered production. The form
of an object emerges from within it as it is being produced, and it

is present to it when it is finished. Moreover, an object is a noble production, if the craftsman is successful in embodying the form well.

But where in all this talk about craft production is the beautiful? The *Gorgias* quotations give a clear account of it. The beautiful is added by the right use of craft, or in the case of natural objects, by the unhampered operations of nature. When a craftsman forces one part to fit and agree with another, until he combines the whole into a regular and ordered thing, then it is well made, good, and excellent (504a). The beautiful is an object's excellence (506d), and the excellence is its proper order (506e). Therefore, the beautiful is order or harmony. The beautiful is being added to something as it is being well made, and it is present to it when it is well made. The beautiful is not a particular; rather it is the harmony of a particular's elements; nor should the beautiful be identified with the material of art; rather it is the way in which the material is arranged. The *Gorgias* quotations, allowing for minor variations in language — "good" at 506e is nearly synonymous with "beautiful" — are a direct answer to the question at *Hippias Major* 292d: "What is the beautiful, itself, that when added to something, it belongs to that to be beautiful?"

The beautiful is not the type form of a product, although it is an *eidos* (see *Hippias Major* 289d). When the type form or nature of an object is placed into that from which it is made, then a certain type of object results (see *Cratylus* 389b-c). But the beautiful is present only when an object is well made, and its nature excellent. A poorly made shuttle still has the form of shuttle, but does not have the beautiful.

Particulars are not beautiful *simpliciter*, but neither do they have order *simpliciter*. Order is something relative to an end. A shuttle designed for the weaving of wool cloth may be unsuitable for silk cloth. From Socrates' second account we see that there is a general limitation on our judgment: no object suited for a bad end is noble no matter how well suited for the end. Also objects may possess different degrees of order, and hence one woman may be more beautiful than another. A pot, finally, is less beautiful than a woman because it is suited for a less important end.

How does the identification of the beautiful with order unify Socrates' three accounts? We need only discuss the last two since the appropriate reduces to them. The harmonious constitution of a particular both makes it useful (in some respect), and/or produces pleasure through sight or hearing. Thus we can say what is common to pleasures through hearing and sight: they are both produced by the same cause. The Doric rhythm produces pleasure; a strident sound does not. Likewise, a speech whose elements are well organized is pleasant to hear (cf. *Phaedrus* 264c), one that is disorganized is not. A well-proportioned statue is pleasant to sight; a poorly figured one is not.

Conclusion

Hippias is as bombastic, dogmatic, and hence uneducatable as any interlocutor in the early dialogues. Socrates responds to Hippias' character with constant irony and sarcasm. He frequently makes the wise and beautiful sophist look ridiculous. Hippias claims that the mystery tormentor will appear absurd, but it is Hippias who is so. Hippias is ridiculous where it counts, in dialectic. Socrates uses his standard educational techniques—dialectical refutation and *psychē*-leading. But unlike some early dialogues, e.g. *Laches* and *Charmides*, there is no ambiguity about whether Socrates has any effect on Hippias; he does not. Hence the *Hippias Major* is, from the perspective of Socratic teaching, a failure. It is almost as if Socrates is going through the motions since he certainly realizes that he cannot have any influence on Hippias.

But let us shift our perspective to the author of the dialogue, Plato. He certainly intends to instruct the listeners and readers of the dialogue. First the arguments, themselves, lead us to see, when we think about them, the nature of the beautiful; moreover, the triadic and interlocking structures of the dialogue facilitate our insight. But Plato also teaches us somethings about education, and about Socrates. While Socrates is a great educator, he is not successful in treating some types of natures. Hippias does not have the ability to do dialectic, and none of Socrates' techniques improve him. Hence Socrates fails in his educational mission.

The *Hippias Major* is considered by many commentators to be a late early dialogue; it may well stand on the threshold of the *Republic*. If so, it would provide Plato with ample reason to delineate a class of people—the appetitive class—whose erotic natures are more turned towards money and other such things than the use of reason. Appetitive natures require a different type of education than dialectic. The basic education in music and gymnastics of the *Republic* is Plato's answer to this problem.

12. The Serious Man in the *Euthydemus*

The *Euthydemus* depicts a contest for the *psychē* of the young man Cleinias.[1] There are three competitors in the contest: (1) the eristic brothers Euthydemus and Dionysodorus who recently just learn how speedily to teach human excellence, (2) Ctesippus who is Cleinias' lover, and who speedily learns eristic debate from the brothers, and (3) Socrates, who being concerned seriously about the welfare of Cleinias, tries to lead him by *elenchus* and *psychagogia* to a desire for wisdom. While the focus of the dialogue is on the *psychē* of Cleinias, the topic of the *Euthydemus* is education.[2] All three of the above competitors, in one way or another, represent educational alternatives which fight for possession of Cleinias' *psychē*.

The theme of education appears in the distinctions between eristic and philosophy, eristic clown and true philosopher, and trivial play and education. Some sophists give speeches, but others practice eristic debate which imitates the procedures of dialectic. The *Gorgias* is concerned with the former kind of sophist, and the *Euthydemus* with the latter. Sophists practice eristic for fees or to entertain; philosophers do dialectic with the serious intent of educating. The *Euthydemus* shows us that eristic and philosophy superficially can look alike.[3] Euthydemus and Dionysodorus practice a type of eristic which resembles Socratic *elenchus*. This eristic takes the form of question and answer, and the questioner attempts to refute the interlocutor's answers. An ignorant bystander might confuse what the brothers do with philosophical dialectic. An unnamed writer of speeches at the end of the *Euthydemus* makes just this confusion.[4] One of Socrates' purposes in the *Euthydemus* is to show Crito the distinction between eristic and dialectic. Crito then can distinguish true from false philosophy, and thus pick a good educator for his son. Plato, the author of the dialogue, has the same purpose for his audience. Crito, hopefully, will see that philosophy attempts to generate beneficial confusion, and the admission of self-ignorance which makes possible the acquisition of knowledge. Sophists, on the other hand, score points in eristic matches; they seek a fall in the *agon* (contest), and use confusion as a means to this fall. Euthydemus and Dionysodorus act like a pair of prize fighters who batter and confuse Cleinias with an unrelenting series of blows. The crucial difference between dialectic and eristic is not method, but intent. The former aims at the good of its subject, but the latter does not. The former is serious and honest, the latter is not. Eristic can be simple comedy, but the laughter stops when it is confused with education. For the goal of human life is *aretē* (excellence), and dialectic attempts to produce this goal, but eristic simply leads to abuse, anger, or laughter.[5]

Socrates speaks with Crito and an unnamed writer of speeches at the beginning and end of the dialogue. Crito and the writer symbolize, among other things, those who are not clear about the difference between philosphy and eristic. Crito is a close associate of Socrates; he offers to guarantee payment of a fine at his trial, talks with him about escape in the *Crito*, and receives Socrates' last request in the *Phaedo*. Crito is certain that eristic is not philosophy, and that the juggling brothers do not practice philosophy (305a-b). But while Crito knows that Socrates is somehow different from the ordinary run of men, he does not recognize him as the true practitioner of philosophy (306d-307a). The unnamed writer of speeches thinks that eristic is philosophy which is why philosophy is of little or no value (304e-305a). Nevertheless, he senses that Socrates is different from the brothers, but he thinks that the brothers are the consumate philosophers (305a). The *Euthydemus*, as I will show, reveals that Socrates is the true philosopher. He is the only participant who really cares to make Cleinias better. At the end of the dialogue Socrates exhorts Crito to search for a real philosopher, and not to be discouraged, for the duffers and charlatans are numerous in every field (307a). It is important that Crito makes this search, for he has a son who needs education. Therefore Socrates attempts to educate both Cleinias and Crito. Socrates provides both of them with a paradigm of the serious philosophical inquirer.

Background Description

The *Euthydemus* is divided into seven sections, and I will discuss each of them seriatim. Socrates directly talks with Crito at the beginning and end of the dialogue, and reports on the events of yesterday's conversation with the brothers. Socrates' direct conversations with Crito permit him to develop the physical setting, characters of the speakers, and other background material. Socrates' report of yesterday's conversation has the effect of focusing the dialogue on him. Socrates is always center stage no matter who speaks. He emerges as the hero of the dialogue both from the sharp contrast between him and the comic brothers, and from how the dialogue is narrated.[6]

We can schematize the reported conversations as follows (S = Socrates asks questions, D&E = Dionysodorus and Euthydemus ask questions): D&E, S, D&E, S, D&E. The seating arrangement reflects the order of the conversations. Socrates and Cleinias are in the center, and the sophists flank them on either side. The participants have eyes only for the beautiful Cleinias, but Socrates is also center stage. There are precisely two sophists, one flanking Socrates on either side. The symbolism here is very significant. The duality of sophists represents the multiple, unconnected refutations they launch; their positions permit them to throw the argument back and forth, and to attack from the rear and flanks.[7] The sophists desire nothing but victory and fame, but they will not honestly meet an opponent face to face to get it. There is only a single philosopher in the dialogue, Socrates, and his singleness reflects the unity and coherence of his discourse. The Socratic sections form a unified whole which is constituted from an ordered sequence of questions. Moreover, Socrates keeps to his purpose which is to exhort Cleinias to seek wisdom.

Crito asks Socrates who he was talking with yesterday in the Lyceum. The crowd standing and sitting around Socrates was so large that Crito could not hear anything distinctly (271a). The crowd is composed primarily of the students of Euthydemus and Dionysodorus, and the lovers of Cleinias. A crowd is essential to the eristic enterprise; the brothers give a display and exhibition; they play to the crowd with their comic, eristic moves. Socrates frequently urges the brothers to give, or describes them as giving, displays and exhibitions (274b,d, 275a, 278c-d). Eristic is a spectacle designed to garner praise, money, and laughter; in contrast dialectic is a personal conversation between two people who earnestly search for truth.

Crito describes young Cleinias as "having come on finely" (271b), and Socrates agrees on this point. Cleinas is going to be the object of attention for he is young and beautiful and full of potential—he is related to Alcibiades.[8] All of the other participants desire in one way or another to possess either Cleinias' body or his *psychē*. Cleinias is pursued eagerly; we learn this from the amusing scene of his entry where he is followed by a line of lovers who are strung out behind him (273a-b). But Cleinias' great potential could work for good or for evil. Socrates observes that Cleinias is related to the Alcibiades (275a-b), and Alcibiades had immense potential which turned out bad. Cleinias' enormous potential is as yet undirected, and thus Socrates expresses a serious concern for Cleinias' future. Those clustered around Cleinias, who compete for his attention (274c), are a representative sample of the types of influences he will meet. Some will benefit him and some will not. Cleinias' *psychē* hangs in the balance between eristic, false love, and philosophy. The brothers represent the first, Ctesippus the second, and Socrates the third.

The sophists receive ample and scathing description in the introduction. Crito observers that they are fresh additions to the local sophistic sect, and Socrates relates how they were born at Chios, went as colonists to Thurii, were exiled from there, and have spent many years wondering about Greece (271b-c). The sophists are men without a city, and this is important for understanding Socrates' attitude about sophists, especially those who travel from city to city.[9] The *polis* is where men become civilized, and learn to speak and reason. The *polis* is the *sine qua non* of the civilized, rational life because it educates its citizens, and provides them with a community (cf. *Crito* 50d-e). For this reason Socrates seldom leaves his city; the rivers and the trees do not teach him anything (cf. *Phaedrus* 230d). To be without a *polis*, or to be exiled from one, is to miss these civilizing arts. Of course the brothers have acquired speech, but they do not know how to use it. The brothers lack the seriousness or earnestness to be citizens of a *polis*; real citizens properly educate the young. Socrates, throughout the dialogue, exhorts them to be serious, to give up their play, and to exhibit their real art. Of course the brothers have no such real art.

Socrates sarcastically says that the sophists know all things (271c). They are also willing to impart their massive wisdom for a fee (272c). We have met with polymathic knowledge before in the early dialogues. Hippias, in the *Hippias Major*, is a polymath. Hippias is also shallow and easily refuted. For Socrates broad "wisdom" is shallow "wisdom." Whenever we meet a polymath, in a Socratic dialogue, we know we are in the presence of a charlatan. Hippias is going to talk to schoolboys about the beautiful, but he does not know what the beautiful is. The brothers are equally unreflective and unconcerned about the effects of their activities on Cleinias. Moreover, the brothers teach their wisdom for a fee. The taking of fees symbolizes the misplaced object of art. An art is for the benefit of its subject, a knack is not (cf. *Gorgias* 464b-465a). A real educator is concerned with the benefit of the learner, not his fee. Euthydemus and Dionysodorus only care for fame, applause, and a high fee. Hence they do not practice the real educational art.

Euthydemus and Dionysodorus are remarkable in many ways. Until recently they only taught fighting in arms and wrote speeches for the courts (272a, 273c), but now they proclaim that they teach virtue (273e). The brothers speedily have acquired the ability to teach virtue, and, as we will see, they will transmit it to Ctesippus in less than an afternoon! The brothers, moreover, rapidly acquired their ability even though they are far advanced in age (272b-c). They assure everyone that they can transmit — hand over — virtue to someone else in an excellent and speedy manner (273e). Socrates describes the brothers' "teaching" as transmission, or giving over; he describes Gorgian rhetoric with the same terms. There is a sharp contrast on the one hand between eristic/rhetoric, and on the other philosophical dialectic. Dialectic should activate the intellectual capacities and stimulate further inquiry; the forms of sophistry transmit their techniques and information by the imposition of material on passive recipients.

The speed with which Euthydemus and Dionysodorus transmit their "excellence" falsifies their claim to teach excellence at all. They transmit fads, and eristic is "in" at the moment. For philosophers like Plato and Aristotle the acquisition of virtue requires much time, effort, and practice. Socrates, moreover, believes that virtue is acquired through dialectic; one is virtuous when one can state, clarify, and defend one's accounts, and this takes considerable time, effort and practice. For Aristotle the virtues are habits which are produced by doing right actions; moreover, the virtues involve practical wisdom, and only those with sufficient experience and judgment can be practically wise. Aristotle even denies that young men have these prerequisites (*N.E.* 1142a10-20). Euthydemus and Dionysodorus believe in the speedy transmission of virtue, but real philosophers do not. The brothers' opinions are dramatically at odds with the best opinions on the subject. Socrates ironically notes that the brothers must have picked-up their art by luck (273e).

Socrates describes their knack as "a faculty they have acquired for wielding words as weapons and confuting any agument as readily if it be true as if it be false" (272a-b). The brothers are not serious. They use words to refute whether they attack true or false beliefs. They aim at victory and laughter but not at truth. Euthydemus and Dionysodorus show that they are not even serious debaters; they do not care if they appear to make fair refutations. As we will see, they often require Cleinias to answer even when he does not understand the question. Socrates will point out many other unfair tricks they use. The brothers, in the end, degenerate into comics, and hence they are parodies of the whole clan of eristic sophists. To do question and answer to win or to clown is to be equally unserious about the most important human matters; it is not to be serious when one ought to be.

Socrates ironically relates how his divine sign kept him in the gymnasium so that he could meet the wise brothers (272e). Socrates opposes their low comedy with his own subtle humor. The *daimon* does not prevent Socrates from going to his trial and death, but it does prevent him from missing a futile discussion with the brothers. Socrates with mock piety invokes the Muses to help him recall yesterday's extraordinary conversation (275c-d). To recall such enormous knowledge requires more than human aid.[10]

First Eristic Conversation

Socrates exhorts the brothers to give a display and exhibition of the skill which they claim to transmit (274d, 275a). The sophists are very eager to improve Cleinias (274b), provided only that he answers their questions (275c). Socratic dialectic also starts by procuring the service of an answerer. Dialectic and Eristic, then, in this respect resemble one another.

Socrates asks the sophists whether their art convinces men that virtue is teachable, and that they teach it (274e). The sophists answer affirmatively, and Socrates ironically says that they are the best persons now on earth to exhort Cleinias to pursue virtue and knowledge (274e-275a). The question about whether virtue is teachable never receives an explicit hearing in the *Euthydemus*. But the conversations, themselves, will show who is and who is not a real teacher of virtue.

Euthydemus starts to question Cleinias: which sort of men are

the learners, the wise or the foolish? Socrates urges the embarrassed
Cleinias to answer, for Euthydemus is doing him "the greatest service
in the world" (275d-e). Dionysodorus whispers to Socrates that however the boy answers he will be refuted (275e). We immediately see
the agonistic and trifling features of eristic. The point is not truth,
but to confound the young man however he answers. The sophists
want to confuse Cleinias, but it is not the beneficial confusion which
leads to an admission of self-ignorance. Eristic confusions cause distrust
of if not hate for philosophy. Cleinias first replies that it is the wise
who learn. Euthydemus refutes this by forcing him to admit that we
learn what we do not know already. Hence it is the foolish who learn.
The followers of Euthydemus and Dionysodorus raise a cheer and a
laugh "like a chorus at the signal of a director" (276b-c). Dionysodorus
catches the ball, and before Cleinias can catch his breath, Dionysodorus compels him to admit that it is the wise who learn not the foolish. Only the wise have the capacity to learn. Again there is laughter
and applause.

Euthydemus, striking in upon Cleinias' dismay and confusion,
asks him whether we learn what we know or what we do not know.
Dionysodorus again whispers to Socrates that the boy will fall however he answers. First Cleinias says that we learn what we do not know,
but Euthydemus forces him to admit that he knows his letters, and
teachers dictate letters, and hence he learns what he knows. Dionysodorus then forces him to admit that we learn what we do not know
because we learn knowledge which we do not yet possess.[11]

The implicit conclusion of these paradoxes is that we cannot learn
at all. The disjunctions are meant to be exhaustive, and if neither the
wise nor the foolish learn, or if we do not learn either what we know
or do not know, then no one learns, and hence there is no learning.
This conclusion is ironical since the sophists purport to teach excellence.
Later Socrates will explicitly show that many of the sophists' paradoxes
are self-refuting: in the present case they negate the brothers' stated
purpose for their activity which is to exhort Cleinias to seek virtue.
The brothers do not engage in a harmless sport, for the result of their
play could be the corruption of Cleinias.

Eristic moves, we learn, are planned and set. Socrates has heard
them before from many other people. Furthermore, they do not take
into account the educational condition of the learner; the learner is
simply the butt of the refutation and laughter. Socratic dialectic, on

the other hand, is to some extent improvised (cf. 278d-e). A good dialectician asks his questions in a proper logical order, but he must also respond to the answers and confusions of the learner. The argument must stop and start when there is good reason to do so. Eristic, however, does not stop to clarify confusion or make distinctions. The brothers treat the teaching of *aretē* as if it were warfare: they take out their stock weapons and shoot them at their opponents.

The brothers' extensive use of destructive dilemmas recalls the Eleatic methods of argumentation. Zeno and Parmenides, among others, use the destructive dilemma as an effective weapon, and they use this weapon to support some very counterintuitive conclusions — the denial of change, diversity, and so on. As we know, many other eristic arguments in the dialogue also have a clear Eleatic heritage. But Socrates is not parodying the Eleatics. Any new weapon, logical or military, has a good or a bad use. Eleatic modes of argument, when seriously practiced for the sake of truth, are paradigms of rationality. Socrates pays proper respect to the Eleatics, and takes them quite seriously, in dialogues like the *Parmenides*.[12] But in the *Euthydemus* we see the most sophisticated philosophical weapons put to a bad use.

We clearly see the intent of the two brothers in this opening battle. They are only interested in the *agon*; the boy must fall however he answers. They hit him from the sides and back, and spin him around, as they throw the ball back and forth. They confuse, befuddle, and whip the young man, never thinking of his benefit or welfare. The students of the two brothers are well pleased with the exhibition.

First Socratic Conversation

Socrates interrupts Euthydemus, and as any humane teacher would, gives the boy a rest before he caves in (277c-d). Socrates also tries to harmonize and reconcile the different participants in the discussion. He tells Cleinias that the two brothers are only sporting with him; they initiate him into the first stage of their great wisdom: the proper use of words (277e). Cleinias must first master the art of Prodicus; for example, Socrates explains, "learning" is used both of someone who actualizes the capacity to acquire knowledge and of someone who exercises the knowledge which he possesses. But, Socrates goes on to say, such distinctions are only the play of wise men, they are not wisdom itself. The brothers are hiding their wisdom, but they will undoubtedly get down to their serious work.

Socrates then improvises a paradigm example of a protreptic argument. What is remarkable about Socrates' discussion with Cleinias is the extent to which it smoothly achieves its desired effect. Socrates leads Cleinias to see that wisdom is the most important human possession. By the end of the first Socratic discussion Cleinias desires to acquire that knowledge which will make him do well and be happy.[13]

Socrates leads Cleinias by *psychagogia* and this sharpens the contrast between him and the sophists. Euthydemus and Dionysodorus employ sharp, disjointed refutations, while Socrates soothingly leads Cleinias to the truth. Socrates is gentle and kind to Cleinias, while the sophists simply use him for their jokes.

Why is positive Socratic dialectic successful with Cleinias? We see in many other early dialogues that Socratic *elenchus* is anything but benign, and usually it is unsuccessful. Callicles, Polus, and Thrasymachus, for example, never admit their ignorance. Socrates' only other successful discussions are with the slave boy in the *Meno* and Lysis in the *Lysis*.

Cleinias is very like the slave boy, and they both are well suited for positive *psychagogia*. Socrates first mentions that Cleinias is "young and good hearted" (279d). Cleinias has what Aristotle calls "natural virtue" (*N.E.* 1144b15-20); he has naturally correct habits and postures, but he does not yet possess wisdom. Socrates is very concerned for how Cleinias will turn out precisely because of his excellent natural endowment. Socrates already had seen what can happen to such great potential in the case of Alcibiades, which is why he mentions the kinship between Cleinias and Alcibiades. Socrates emphasizes that Cleinias is no vain pretender to knowledge (283c-d). Since Cleinas is not filled with the false pretense to knowledge, Socrates does not need to practice *elenchus* on him; Cleinias does not have false beliefs which need to be purged before positive *psyche*-leading. Cleinias also agrees with certain important positions, for example, that virtue is teachable (282c). Socrates mentions in the *Meno* (86b-c) that holding the opposite belief makes one indolent. Cleinias is not intellectually lazy. Part of Cleinias' natural virtue is his good sense to recoil from sophistry. Cleinias, for the above reasons, is an excellent partner in a positive, dialectical discussion.

Cleinias through Socrates' questions comes to see that the search for wisdom is the most important activity in human life. Thus Socrates' protreptic questioning is successful. Socrates then connects true love with real dialectic. There is no disgrace, he tells Cleinias, if one submits to a lover to acquire wisdom (382b). Socrates' comment should shame Cleinias' lover Ctesippus who is quite unconcerned with wisdom. For Socrates true *eros* is philosophy.

Socrates has given the sophists an example of a real philosophical discussion. Ironically he now urges them to get serious, display their real art, and show whether one ought to acquire every sort of knowledge, or just one (282d-e).

Second Eristic Conversation

Two themes emerge at the beginning of the second eristic section. Socrates reaffirms that he is very earnest about wanting the boy to become wise. Socrates' earnestness is diametrically opposed to the low comedy of the brothers; their moves eventually will degenerate into slapstick. We also see Dionysodorus create and exploit confusion (283d). The sophists love confusion for its own sake.

We need not discuss the sophist's eristic moves at length since others amply have treated them. Dionysodorus strikes in and states that since they want Cleinias to become wise, they "want him to become what he is not, and to no longer be what he now is" (283d). He concludes that they must want their dear boy to be dead. Dionysodorus slides from "not be ignorant" to "not be anything at all." As with many jokes, this one manifests a serious underlying problem in language. The Greek verb "to be" has as its primary root meaning what Charles Kahn calls the "veridical meaning." "To be" primarily should be translated as "What is so," or "What is the case."[14] Our distinctions between predicative, identity, and existential uses of the verb are fused in the root meaning, and only emerge secondarily. It is, then, easy to construct counterintuitive philosophical positions and even jokes with the Greek verb "to be." Parmenides, for example, moves from "is different from" to "is not *simpliciter*," and ends up denying change and multiplicity.[15] Parmenides is a serious philosopher, but Dionysodorus is not. Plato, in the *Sophist*, begins to get clear about the different senses of "to be," and he recognizes a problem with the verb by constructing the eristic jokes in the *Euthydemus*.

Ctesippus begins to display his real character: that of an insolent person. He accuses Dionysodorus of falsely accusing him of wanting his beloved Cleinias dead (283d). Soon Ctesippus will learn the sophists' game, and then he will exchange abusive blows with them. Ctesippus will show that there is, indeed, a thin line between abuse and contradiction. Ctesippus also represents the bad lover; he hopes that Cleinias will admire his mimicry of the sophists, and he has some regretable success in fulfilling his hope.[16]

Euthydemus responds to Ctesippus' accusation by compelling him to admit that there is no false speaking. When one speaks, one speaks about something (284e). But if one speaks about something, then he speaks about a thing which is; for things that are not cannot be (284a-b). All that Ctesippus can say in reply to this is that "somehow or other he speaks what is, only not as it is" (284c). Dionysodorus catches on and admits that we speak of things as they are; we speak good of the good, and evil of the evil. Ctesippus, having mastered the sophists' wisdom, declares that we also speak frigid of the frigid, and lying of the lying. He adds that the brothers ought to watch out or they will be included among the frigid liars. The sophists' shafts are increasingly absurd, and Ctesippus is quickly learning their game. These are the dominating features of the remaining eristic discussion.

Dionysodorus' denial of false speaking and thinking is again rooted in a serious philosophical problem. Parmenides, better than any philosopher, states this problem: Thought and speech must be about being, for they find their expression in being (B8.34-36). The ancient Greeks do not have a concept of intentional inexistence where the object of thought need not exist in reality. Thus Socrates says in the *Cratylus* (420b-c) that a belief is like an arrow which is shot out into space. The arrow must land on something, and the belief must be about something, something which is, or else there is no belief at all. Ctesippus vaguely divines the solution to this problem which Plato exploits in the *Sophist:* false speaking is about something, but it is about something different from what is the case. Plato even in the *Sophist* preserves the assumption that thought and speech must be about something.[17]

Socrates sees that the participants are becoming savage with each other, and he ironically tries to soothe Ctesippus. The brothers, Socrates says, know how to destroy someone in his wickedness, so that they can later make him sensible (285a-c). Socrates, himself, amusingly conflates the sophists' refutations to his own use of *elenchus*; of course the sophists do not purge one of wickedness, nor do they intend to produce wisdom.

Dionysodorus pulls from his bag of tricks a stock sophistic argument against contradiction. Socrates says that he has heard that very argument before from Protagoras, and even earlier from others (286b-c). Socrates begins to apply the sophists' tricks to their own activities. If there is no contradiction, then there are no mistakes, and hence there are no ignorant men. Socrates asks Dionysodorus whether he really believes all these things or whether he says them just to say something startling (286d-e). Dionysodorus snaps back, "Refute me." Of course Socrates cannot refute him if he cannot be mistaken; hence Dionysodorus' command makes no sense. Dionysodorus glibly replies that only an old dotard would remember what was said earlier (287b); Socrates should only be concerned about the immediate statement.

Dionysodorus (and we may presume his brother too) displays both character and intellectual defects which would disqualify him as a proper opponent in a dialectical conversation. Dionysodorus is not frank; he does not say what he really believes (cf. *Gorgias* 487a). He does not really believe that there are no ignorant men. Dionysodorus does not care if his claims are consistent; Socrates is to answer each question in isolation from any other statement. Consistency, Socrates believes, is a prerequisite for any form of rational discussion. These contrasts help distinguish the philosopher from the eristic sophist, and philosophy from eristic.

Second Socratic Conversation

Ctesippus and the brothers are at each others' throats, and Socrates again intervenes. He urges the brothers to become serious since they all earnestly desire Cleinias' real benefit (288c-d). Socrates, then, gives a second example of a serious educational conversation; he begins where he previously left off, showing us that a good discussion is organized; its questions and answers should form a unified series.[18]

Socrates helps Cleinias to see that they seek the knowledge which makes the use of everything else beneficial. Speechwriting and generalship are not this knowledge, since neither knows the proper use of what it produces. This point reminds us that Euthydemus and Dionysodorus previously taught speechwriting and fighting. The brothers, and the unnamed speechwriter at the end of the dialogue, do not, then, possess the wisdom they seek. Without this wisdom they cannot produce real benefit.

Socrates and Cleinias next test the kingly art to see if it possesses the required knowledge. They agree that the kingly art makes men good, and that to make them good is to make them wise. But now they have *twisted around* and found themselves right back at the beginning of their search (291 b-c); for they still do not know what sort of wisdom they are after, except that it is the knowledge which good men possess. Their discussion ends in *aporia* (lack of passage), and Socrates calls upon the divine strangers to help them.

Aporia has a definite function in Socratic education. To successfully complete an argument would tend to stop further inquiry into a problem. *Aporia* particularly is appropriate here because the purpose of Socrates' discussion with Cleinias is to exhort the youth to seek wisdom. If the conversation were successful, then Cleinias might not be motiviated for further search. The strong circular imagery at 291b-c, however, hints at a passage through the *aporia*. The circular imagery invites us to reflect on what is now going on; Cleinias is to turn around upon what he is now doing—dialectic. A successful dialectical defense of one's beliefs is knowledge, and this is the knowledge which makes one prosper.[19]

Third Eristic Conversation

Socrates calls upon the sophists to reveal the sort of knowledge which they seek. But Euthydemus goes them one better and shows them that they already have it. His "argument" is that Socrates cannot at the same time be both knowing and not knowing (293d), and hence if he knows anything, then he knows everything. Ctesippus glories in driving the sophists to the wall "like boars driven up to face the spears" (294d) by asking them whether they know all sorts of absurd things. Does Euthydemus know how many teeth Dionysodorus has?

Euthydemus next purports to show that if Socrates knows something always by the same thing, then Socrates always knows what he knows. Socrates playfully qualifies his answers, but the sophist does not want such clarifications. Euthydemus is content with Socrates' obscure, unqualified answer, even if Socrates can give a better one (295c). Eristic does not require clear questions and answers, but dialectic does (cf. *Gorgias* 463d-e). Eristic is only a game, but dialectic requires consent and commitment.

Socrates continues to qualify his answers in order to avoid Euthydemus' verbal snares, but since Euthydemus knows so much more about debating than anyone else, Socrates agrees to stop the clarifications. The eristic refutations now come thick and fast, but rather than describe them seriatim, I will list what we learn from them.

(1) Socrates emphasizes *ad hominem* attacks on the sophists; either their claims have absurd consequences, or they are self-defeating (196e).

(2) The brothers become more shameless, and will say anything to avoid refutation (298b).

(3) The brothers become more excessive and intemperate in their use of sophistry.

(4) The eristic "arguments" no longer have any deeper meaning; they do not betray what in other mouths might be serious philosophical worries; rather they degenerate into mere plays on words. This signals the brothers' complete lack of seriousness. Finally Dionysodorus finds a really baffling answer: "Neither and both" (300cd)!

(5) Ctesippus shows that eristic can be mastered quickly, because he does it. Ctesippus' new skill delights Cleinias (300d) which both shows that Ctesippus is a false lover, and that false love is having some effect on Cleinias. At the end of the dialogue we really do not know which influence—philosophy or eristic—prevails on the boy's *psychē*.

(6) Dionysodorus displays an ignorance of Ionian religious practices (302b-d), which symbolizes the brothers' estrangement from the *polis*. They are also outside the serious religion, education, and culture of the *polis*.

(7) When the brothers finally crush Socrates and Ctesippus with their invincible words, the whole audience breaks into wild applause and clapping. Formerly only the sophists' students reacted so, but now everyone in the Lyceum does (303b). The brothers are successful in spreading the contagion of eristic.

(8) Socrates ironically praises the brothers for the following (303c-e): (a) so quickly acquiring such a great accomplishment, (b) caring

not at all for the opinion of the multitude, (c) stitching-up not only other men's mouths, but also their own, and (d) teaching their art in such a short time.[20]

Socrates is ironical in (8). He himself does not care for the opinion of the multitude, and neither do the brothers. But the brothers are comics, and they need not worry about the intellectual content of their juggleries. Socrates, as a serious philosopher, often finds his views at odds with those of the multitude. Socrates often is accused of stitching-up the mouths of men, like the brothers. Socrates also claims in the *Meno* his own paralysis due to the *aporia*. But Socrates attempts to get an interlocutor to admit that he cannot say what something is to engender a beneficial ignorance which might lead to a desire to acquire wisdom; the brothers simply leave one speechless. Socrates' paralysis, as in the *Meno*, incites others to speak, while the brothers do not even bother with the fact that their claims imply that they cannot do what they claim to do — speak truly and teach. Socrates' mock comparison between himself and the brothers highlights the differences between philosophy and eristic. Finally we should note that while eristic can be imitated at once, dialectic — to judge by the interlocutors in the early dialogues — takes a long time to learn.

Conclusion

After Socrates' narration of the conversation to Crito, Crito relates what an unnamed writer of speeches for the law courts said to him after the speech (304e-305a).[21] The speech writer believes that the brothers are at the head of the philosophical profession, and hence he also believes that philosophy is of little worth. Ironically, a man who is steeped in the knack of speech writing cannot distinguish philosophy and eristic. Eristic and rhetoric basically are the same, but in the eyes of this speech writer rhetoric is great because it is influential in the court and assembly, and eristic is worthless because it is practiced on inconsequential children. Socrates would reverse the order of priority.

The end of the dialogue brings us back to the main theme of the *Euthydemus*: education. Crito needs to find a teacher for his older son (306d-307a). When in Socrates' presence he is ashamed that he has not provided him with a good education. But Crito also is repulsed by the purported teachers of philosophy. Socrates reminds him that the pretenders in every area are numerous, and the real experts few; Crito must continue to search for a true philosophical teacher. But Socrates by his very ability to shame Crito for his inability to educate his son shows us that he is the real teacher and philosopher.[22]

I will close by listing some educational purposes of the *Euthydemus*: (1) Socrates attempts to save the noble soul of Cleinias; (2) He attempts to get Crito to see what true and false philosophy and philosophers are, and (3) He tries to show Cleinias that Ctesippus is a false lover. Plato in writing the dialogue means to show us: (4) the enticements of eristic, especially for the young, and (5) who the true and false lovers/educators of Cleinias are.

Notes

1. INTRODUCTION

1. G. Vlastos, "Introduction," in *Plato's Protagoras* trans. B. Jowett, revised by M. Ostwald (Indianapolis, 1956), xxxi-xxxvi.

2. G. Vlastos, "The Socratic *Elenchus*," in *Oxford Studies in Classical Philosophy* (Oxford, 1983), 27-74.

3. G. Vlastos, "The Paradox of Socrates," in *The Philosophy of Socrates*, ed. G. Vlastos (New York, 1971), 10-12.

4. R. E. Allen, *Plato's Euthyphro and the Earlier Theory of Forms* (New York, 1970), 6, 67.

5. Socrates states positions in the *Meno* 86b-c, *Gorgias* 508e-509a, and *Crito* 46b-c.

6. I do not have essays on some dialogues which have a high probability of being spurious, e.g. *Alabiades* I, and I do not have essays on some early dialogues which while interesting in themselves do not supplement my discussion of Socrates, e.g. *Menexenus, Hippias Minor*.

7. See W. D. Ross, *Plato's Theory of Ideas* (Oxford, 1953), ch. 1.

8. Vlastos, "The Paradox of Socrates," 2-3.

9. H. Teloh, *The Development of Plato's Metaphysics* (State College, Pa., 1981), ch. I.

10. I borrow this phrase from the title of Quine's book *The Web of Belief*.

11. T. Penner, "The Unity of Virtue," *Philosophical Review* 82 (1973): 41-49.

12. Ibid., 35-68.

13. P. Woodruff, "Socrates on the Parts of Virtue," *Canadian Journal of Philosophy*, Supplementary Volume II (1976): 101-116.

14. See *Phaedrus* 228 a-e for the sophistic use of memory.

15. Education is an art when it meets the requirements for an art as stated in the *Gorgias* (465 a). An art must analyze the nature of its subject in order that it act for the good of its subject, and that it know how to achieve this good.

16. R. G. Hoerber, "Plato's *Euthyphro*," *Phronesis* 3 (1958): 98-99, emphasizes these contrasts between Socrates and Euthyphro.

17. Vlastos, "The Paradox of Socrates," 10-12.

18. Teloh, *Plato's Metaphysics*, 22-29.

19. Penner, "The Unity of Virtue," 35-68.

211

20. R. Robinson, *Plato's Earlier Dialectic,* reprinted (Oxford, 1941).
21. Allen, *Plato's Euthyphro,* 6, 67.
22. See T. Penner, "Socrates on Virtue and Motivation," in *Exegesis and Argument,* ed. E.N. Lee, A.P.D. Mourelatos, and R. M. Rorty (Assen, 1973), 137.

2. IRONY AND CONFUSION IN THE *EUTHYPHRO*

1. I show that in many of the early dialogues the opening paragraphs set major themes which are illustrated later in those dialogues.
2. On the close association between a city and its civic religion see L. Versényi, *Holiness and Justice: An Interpretation of Plato's Euthyphro,* (Washington, D.C. 1982), 3-4.
3. Thus I disagree with Versényi, p. 100 when he claims that just about everything Euthyphro says is orthodox and traditional. Versényi goes on to point out, however, that tradition is inconsistent, at least the tradition Euthyphro respresents. On this issue see W. K. C. Guthrie, *A History of Greek Philosophy,* Vol. IV (Cambridge, 1975), 103, who denies that Euthyphro represents orthodoxy. Guthrie rightly emphasizes that Euthyphro is a radical conservative, p. 109.
4. Hoerber, "Plato's Euthyphro," 98-99, emphasizes these contrasts.
5. Socrates does not teach if by "teach" is meant the transmission or handing over of information.
6. Euthyphro purports to be godlike in that he is prosecuting his father on the model of what Zeus did to Cronos, and Cronos to Heaven. Socrates wants us to be godlike in that we care for our *psychai* and make them orderly like the *Cosmos.*
7. See Guthrie's excellent discussion of blood pollution, *Greek Philosophy,* p. 109.
8. See Hoerber, "Plato's Euthyphro," 95-97.
9. Constant attempts to disambiguate tangled situations often fail to recognize the pedagogical purpose of such descriptions.
10. *Elenchus* is always *ad hominem* in that it aims at the beliefs of an interlocutor. *Psychagogia,* however, is not *ad hominem* since it tries to guide the *psychē* to beliefs it does not yet possess. The positive search for truth would occur when a hypothesis tentatively put forth by both questioner and answerer is tested.
11. Vlastos, "The Paradox of Socrates," 10-11.
12. Guthrie, *Greek Philosophy,* 117-120.
13. Ibid., 118-119.
14. Allen, *Plato's Euthyphro,* 69ff.
15. Penner, "The Unity of Virtue," 35-68.
16. I defend this position at length in *The Development of Plato's Metaphysics,* Ch. 1.
17. This shift is found in many other early dialogues.

18. Allen, Plato's *Euthyphro* 6, 67, argues that no views are explicit or implied in the *Euthyphro*. Socrates offers dialectic, not doctrine. C.C.W. Taylor, "The End of the *Euthyphro*," *Phronesis* 27 (1982): 112-113, argues that the *Euthyphro* clearly hints that our service to the gods is to care for our *psychai* by acquiring a knowledge of good and evil. I agree with Taylor's arguments against the views of Allen as well as those of Versényi, *Holiness and Justice*, 11-16. But what most commentators miss is that *psychagogia* is an important aspect of Socratic dialectic and that *psyché*-leading is quite compatible with and in fact sometimes requires the aporetic endings of the dialogues.

19. The best discussion of the structure of this argument is found in S. Marc Cohen, "Socrates on the Definition of Piety: *Euthyphro* 10A-11B," in *The Philosophy of Socrates*, 158-176. Euthyphro's crucial assent, that piety is loved by the gods because it is pious, does not follow from the previous analogies because the argument is analogical, but even more important the analogies give no analogical support to persuading Euthyphro to change his position. Euthyphro is confused, and because of his confusion he changes his view.

20. *Gorgias* 503a-504e, 513d.

21. See the comments of Taylor on this passage, "The End of the *Euthyphro*," 112-117.

22. See Taylor's refutation of Vlastos' position that piety is a part of virtue, ibid., 116-117.

23. See Versényi, *Holiness and Justice*, 1, 3 on how piety becomes the whole of virtue.

3. CHARACTER AND EDUCATION IN THE *LACHES*

1. On the interplay between philosophical content and dramatic features see R. Hoerber, "Plato's *Laches*," *Classical Philosophy* 63 (1968): 97, 105; and M. J. O'Brien, "The Unity of the *Laches*," printed in *Essays in Ancient Greek Philosophy*, ed. J. P. Anton and G. L. Kustas (Albany, 1972), 307-08. Hoerber argues that the contrasts and doublets in the *Laches* are dramatic clues to its philosophical content, and O'Brien states that the dialogue is carefully guided by the author's hand; Nicias' definition displays Laches' defects and the converse, and Plato reveals these defects through a planned structure.

2. T. Buford, "Plato on the Educational Consultant: An Interpretation of the *Laches*," *Idealistic Studies*, 7 (1977), argues that the theme of the dialogue is the educational consultant, and not courage; he claims that only from this perspective can one see the dialogue as a real unity. Guthrie, *Greek Philosophy*, 130, warns that we should not magnify any single theme, since it would be at the illegitimate expense of other themes. I agree with Guthrie's view, although Buford provides a useful corrective to the prevailing view that courage is the theme of the dialogue.

3. Hoerber, "Plato's *Laches*," 103, makes the interesting suggestion that the characters in the *Laches* represent what later become the different levels on the divided line of the *Republic*. The fathers would be on the lowest level, the generals on the level of opinion, and Socrates higher yet.

4. Word and deed is a major theme in the *Laches*. See D. Devereux, "Courage and Wisdom in Plato's *Laches*," *Journal of the History of Philosophy* 15 (1977): 134; Hoerber, "Plato's *Laches*," 99-100; and O'Brien, "Unity of the *Laches*," 304.

5. See O'Brien, ibid., 309.

6. Guthrie, *Greek Philosophy*, IV, 126, is, I will show, wrong when he says that Nicias is thoughtful and cultured. Nicias always uses the position of others, and hence he is not thoughtful.

7. Laches will not endure in the discussion, and hence Guthrie, *Greek Philosophy*, IV, 130, is wrong when he says that Laches shows dogged persistence.

8. O'Brien, "Unity of the *Laches*," 311-12, correctly states that Socrates embodies in his life and his death both characteristics. Socrates also embodies both characteristics in the *Laches*.

9. See Teloh, *Plato's Metaphysics*, ch. 1. and P. Friedländer, *Plato*, II (New York, 1964), 43, who notes correctly that courage is in the *psychē*.

10. On the turn away from behavior and circumstances in defining courage, see G. Santas, "Socrates at Work on Virtue and Knowledge in the *Laches*," *Review of Metaphysics* 22 (1969): 441-42.

11. See Guthrie, *Greek Philosophy*, IV, 133-34, among others, who denies that there are transcendent Forms in the *Laches*. The virtues are states of the *psychē*.

12. See Penner, "The Unity of Virtue."

13. Socratic *elenchus* is *ad hominem* in that it attacks the core beliefs of an answerer.

14. Both Buford, "Plato on the Educational Consultant," 153ff., and Friedländer, *Plato*, II, 49, note that Socrates emerges as the educator.

15. Devereux, "Courage and Wisdom," 134, notes that Nicias is a caricature of the wise person.

16. On Laches as a man of deeds not words, and Nicias as a man of words not deeds see Devereux, "Courage and Wisdom," 134, Hoerber, "Plato's *Laches*," 100, and Buford, "Plato on the Educational Consultant," 158.

17. On the lives of these generals see Thucydides, especially books V and VII.

18. Santas, "Socrates at Work in the *Laches*," 441-42, states that Socrates so broadens the concept of courage that it would be hard to define it by its circumstances and behavior; Guthrie, *Greek Philosophy*, IV, 133-34, states that Socrates conflates courage and temperance at 191d.

19. See *Meno* 88c-89d, and *Charmides* 172c-d.

20. We see this shift in the *Euthyphro* and *Charmides*, among others.

21. On this as a major purpose of Socratic education see Vlastos, "Paradox of Socrates," 13-14.

22. See Friedländer, *Plato*, II, 42, 44; Devereux, "Courage and Wisdom," 136; Hoerber, "Plato's *Laches*," 101; O'Brien, "Unity of the *Laches*," 307. Santas, "Socrates at Work in the *Laches*," 444-45, argues that the examples in this passage leave out different circumstances and variables of courage such as the end of action, and the agent's appraisal of an action, but the examples, I show, manifest a common defect.

23. Friedländer, *Plato*, II, 46, states that Nicias is obscure and does not understand what he, himself, says.

24. The readers of the *Laches* are, of course, reminded of what happened to Nicias in the Sicillian expedition when he listened to a seer.

25. See Devereux, "Courage and Wisdom," 137-138, who, I believe, refutes Vlastos' position.

26. This is the position of Devereux, "Courage and Wisdom," 129-132, who argues that the *Laches* is a criticism of the earlier Socratic position that courage is knowledge; Hoerber, "Plato's *Laches*," 101, agrees with Devereux.

27. See Penner, "Unity of Virtue," Santas, "Socrates at Work in the *Laches*," 460, oddly claims that the *Laches* does not deal at all with the endurance aspect of courage.

28. See Teloh, *Plato's Metaphysics*, 64.

29. Vlastos, "Paradox of Socrates," 16-17.

30. I am indebted to J. Tlumak for this suggestion.

31. Hoerber, "Plato's *Laches*," 97-100.

4. NATURAL VIRTUE AND EDUCATION IN THE *CHARMIDES*

1. Gerasimos Santas, "Socrates at Work on Virtue and Knowledge in Plato's *Charmides*," in *Exegesis and Argument*, ed. E. N. Lee, A. P. D. Mourelatos, and R. Rorty (Assen, The Netherlands, 1973), 105, notes that moderation and harmony are missing as accounts of temperance because of the later, notorious careers of Critias and Charmides.

2. Friedländer, *Plato*, II, 68, states that Charmides possesses natural temperance, Socrates perfect temperance, and Critias neither. Socrates' perfect temperance consists in natural temperance and philosophic insight. Friedländer is, I believe, basically correct in his hierarchical ordering.

3. W. Thomas Schmid, "Socrates' Practice of *Elenchus*," *Ancient Philosophy* 1 (1981): 142, argues that Socrates and Critias fight for moral authority over Charmides. Their contest is to see who will teach Charmides.

4. But even this victory has a deep shadow over it. D. Hyland, *The Virtue of Philosophy* (Athens, Ohio, 1981), 147, notes that the last paragraphs of the dialogue prefigure the conspiracy of the tyrants to stop Socrates from his prattle.

5. Hyland, ibid., ix-x, forcefully argues that the drama and arguments of the dialogues must be integrated for an adequate understanding of the dialogues.

6. Guthrie, *Greek Philosophy*, IV, 173, argues that the *Charmides*,

like many other early dialogues, leads us to the knowledge of good and evil as the correct account of temperance, and that the aporetic ending of the dialogue does not hide totally this fact.

7. Friedländer, *Plato*, II 68-69 states that Socrates reveals the close connection between two, commonly thought to be contrasting, virtues—temperance and courage. Hyland, *Virtue of Philosophy*, 69, claims that temperance and courage, if not identical, are nevertheless very close, and that Socrates reveals this by his behavior.

8. Santas, "Socrates at Work in the *Charmides*," correctly states that Socrates' repeated claim that temperance is noble and good is the key premise for the whole search.

9. On this issue see ibid., 109-110.

10. And yet as Santas, "Socrates at Work in the *Charmides*," 106, points out, Charmides causes temptation which shows that his behavior is not unambiguous.

11. Critias' accounts of temperance are not his own. Rather he receives them from his sophistic instructors, and hence Critias is also like Nicias in the *Laches*. See Schmid, "Socrates' Practice of *Elenchus*," 144, and Santas, "Socrates at Work in the *Charmides*," 107-108. Santas also emphasizes that Critias views his conversation with Socrates as a contest, and that he changes definitions so as to be safe from refutation. Critias cannot learn from Socrates.

12. As Schmid, "Socrates' Practice of *Elenchus*," 145, points out, Socrates must refute a shameless person like Critias to show Charmides and us that he is not a wise authority.

13. See Hyland, *The Virtue of Philosophy*, 41-42.

14. Hyland, *The Virtue of Philosopy*, 55, 65-66, believes that we do not define the internal idea, but its icons, actions. But as I will show, Socrates does seek a definition of the psychic cause of our actions, and uses actions to help test the definition.

15. Santas, "Socrates at Work in the *Charmides*," 110, points out the shift in this definition from behavior to an internal cause of behavior.

16. Schmid, "Socrates' Practice of *Elenchus*," 144 notes that Plato ironically juxtaposes a quote from Homer with Charmides' Homeric/aristocratic value structure.

17. On the principle that a cause must have what it produces in something else, see Teloh, *Plato's Metaphysics*, Ch. 1.

18. Schmid, "Socrates' Practice of *Elenchus*," 142, emphasizes that Socratic philosophy is centered on the life one leads, and Charmides, unlike Critias, states his real life views.

19. The play on doing and making also indicates that Hippias is behind the scenes since he is temperate because he makes all his own clothes. Prodicus is also near with his verbal distinctions. Critias is trained by sophists. See Hyland, *The Virtue of Philosophy*, 73, 84; Friedländer, *Plato*, II, 67.

20. See Hyland, *The Virtue of Philosophy*, 76, 80.

21. Vlastos, "The Paradox of Socrates," 1-21.

22. Hyland, *The Virtue of Philosophy*, 52-54, 88-91, 98, and 116, argues the following: (1) Socrates' stance is always one of questioning, he does not prove assertions; (2) Our lack of knowledge is based on erotic incompleteness; (3) Temperance is doing dialectic; and (4) Temperance is not, then, knowledge. I disagree with some of what Hyland says. Temperance is knowledge, not dialectic even though any knowledge we obtain is open to revision. Dialectic is the means to obtain knowledge.

23. I disagree, then, with Chung-Hwan Chen, "On Plato's *Charmides* 165c4-175d5," *Apeiron* 12 (1978), 13-28, who claims that 165-175 is irrelevant to the search for temperance. As Guthrie, *Greek Philosophy*, IV, 164, says, Socrates is puzzled about the notion of self-knowledge, and he investigates alternatives to see what self-knowledge is. By elimination of possibilities Socrates leads us to the knowledge of good and evil which comes through the dialectical testing of one's beliefs.

24. Dreaming also suggests that what Socrates is about to say is inspired, but tentative. Dream material must also be tested dialectically.

25. Critias, we must remember, borrows his accounts from other sophists. He is like Nicias in the *Laches*, and Socrates cannot leave him with any other borrowings.

5. FRIENDSHIP AND EDUCATION IN THE *LYSIS*

1. See R. Hoerber, "Plato's *Lysis*," *Phronesis* 4 (1959): 15-28. On pp. 23-26 Hoerber emphatically states that the highest friendship is not based on utility, and that it is between good persons.

2. Wisdom and the knowledge of good and evil are necessary and sufficient for well-being or happiness, and so it might be better to say that the first friend is happiness. See Laszlo Versényi, "Plato's *Lysis*," *Phronesis* 21 (1976): 193-94.

3. Friedländer, *Plato* Vol. I (New York, 1964), 93, is the only commentator whom I have consulted who states correctly that love and education are the principle topics of the dialogue.

4. On the interconnection between drama and philosophy in the *Lysis* see Hoerber, "Plato's *Lysis*," 17-19.

5. Friedländer, *Plato*, I, 94-95, correctly observes that the *Lysis* is a rich source for different types of friendship.

6. L. Versényi, "Plato's *Lysis*," states that the *Lysis* is negative in method, but positive and substantive in doctrine. But it is hard to see how a negative method could have positive results. Versényi fails to see that part of Socrates' dialectical method is *psychē*-leading.

7. D. Hyland "*Eros, Epithumia*, and *Philia* in Plato," *Phronesis* 13 (1968): 32-46; Hoerber, "Plato's *Lysis*," 19.

8. See Versényi, "Plato's *Lysis*," 187, who says that the terms under scrutiny in the *Lysis* are used loosely, but with coordinate and overlapping

connotations as in ordinary language. G. Vlastos, "The Individual as Object of Love in Plato," in *Platonic Studies* (Princeton, 1973), 4, states that "love" is the only word broad enough to translate *philein*.

9. On different opinions about the chronology of the *Lysis*, see D. N. Norman, "Some Observations Concerning Plato's *Lysis*," in *Essays in Ancient Greek Philosophy*, ed. J. P. Anton and G. L. Kustas (Albany, 1971), 236-258. On p. 237 Norman states that he believes that the *Lysis* is an early dialogue. Also see Hoerber, "Plato's *Lysis*," 15-17; Guthrie, *Greek Philosophy*, IV 134-135. Both Hoerber and Guthrie believe that the *Lysis* is an early dialogue.

10. See Friedländer, *Plato*, I, 94, on natural friendship.

11. Friedländer, *Plato*, I, 95, correctly sees that this is why Socrates is eristic with Menexenus.

12. David Bolotin, *Plato's Dialogue on Friendship* (Ithaca, NY, 1979), 106-108, argues that Lysis is not quite as pure as he appears. His friendship with Menexenus is not innocent because Lysis betrays Menexenus, and conspires in secret with Socrates to have Menexenus refuted. I agree that the naturally good Lysis has the potential for corruption.

13. See Friedländer, *Plato*, I, 207-210, who gives an excellent analysis of Socrates' conversation with Lysis.

14. Bolotin, *Plato's Dialogue on Friendship*, 65-66, 85-86, develops the interesting thesis that Plato hints to us that Socrates undermines parental authority. In the beginning of the *Lysis* Lysis is a model child who is obedient to his parents, but at the end he and Socrates engage in a mini-rebellion against the family slaves who come to take Lysis home. Socrates undermines parents by pointing to the wise as one's true friends, and hence Socrates is subversive of parental authority. Oddly Bolotin pulls back from this thesis when he says that Socrates only tries to make children worthy in wisdom of their parents.

15. See ibid., 103.

16. Bolotin, *Plato's Dialogue on Friendship*, 66-67, notes that it is easier for Socrates to discuss his lack of real friends with the two boys than with his own associates.

17. Guthrie, *Greek Philosophy*, IV, 143-146, dislikes the *Lysis*. The *Lysis* is not a success; it is bumbling. Socrates indulges in word sophistries and fallacious arguments without a hint at their solution, and this is not a good thing to do with young boys. According to Guthrie, if Socrates wants to make the boys think, then he uses an outrageously brutal and sophisticated way to do it (144). Plato, Guthrie believes, upholds Socrates as the great language misuser (146).

18. Bolotin, *Plato's Dialogue on Friendship*, 122-23, 135, says that Socrates wants to show that the poetic tradition is inconsistent in order to show that it is not an adequate guide to wisdom.

19. As Bolotin, *Plato's Dialogue on Friendship*, 152-53, notes, the possession of evil renders its possessor bad when it blinds its possessor to its presence.

20. On the utilitarian nature of Socrates' conception of friendship in

the *Lysis* see Versényi, "Plato's *Lysis*," 188-190; Vlastos, "The Individual as Object of Love in Plato," 8-10; Guthrie, *Greek Philosophy*, IV, 144-45. Vlastos and Guthrie contrast the *Lysis* with Aristotle's position that the true lover loves his friend for his friend's sake.

21. Friedländer, *Plato*, I, and Guthrie, *A History of Greek Philosophy*, IV, 152.

22. Versényi, "Plato's *Lysis*," 193-94, correctly states that goods are as many as and relative to our deficiencies; moreover, the final good is well-being or happiness. Vlastos, "The Individual as Object of Love in Plato," 11, 35-37, agrees that happiness is the final good and not some transcendent form.

23. Friedländer, *Plato*, I, 99 states that dialectical education requires such an overturning.

24. See Vlastos, "The Paradox of Socrates," 1-21.

25. Thus Versényi, "Plato's *Lysis*," 191, states that love arises between those who are neither perfectly like nor perfectly unlike.

26. Bolotin, *Plato's Dialogue on Friendship*, 12, prefaces his book with the observation that possibly Socrates for educational reasons uses intentionally false assertions and unsound arguments.

27. Friedländer, *Plato*, I, 98.

6. FORCE AND PERSUASION IN *REPUBLIC* BOOK I

1. Those sorts of interpretations are common among recent analytic philosophers.

2. I am indebted to A. Sesonske, "Plato's Apology: *Republic* I," *Phronesis* 6 (1961): 29-36, in my analysis of the introductory paragraph.

3. The translations are based upon the Loeb texts of Plato.

4. Teloh, *Plato's Metaphysics*, 22-27.

5. Ibid., ch. 1.

6. See E. A. Havelock, *Preface to Plato* (Cambridge, 1963), 3-15, 20-31.

7. See Vlastos, "The Paradox of Socrates," 12-14.

8. On what I call the "bivalence principle" see Penner, "Socrates on Virtues and Motivation," 137-143.

9. See Teloh, *Plato's Metaphysics*, 42-46.

7. TO KEEP THE CONVERSATION GOING IN THE *APOLOGY* AND *CRITO*

1. R. E. Allen, *Socrates and Legal Obligation* (Minneapolis, 1980), 83, states that Socrates goes to his death out of a commitment to his argument. Allen adds that to focus on the man, but not his arguments, is to miss the essence of the man.

2. Another way to put this is that injustice always harms the *psyche*,

while a just act benefits it. Andrew Barker, "Why Did Socrates Refuse to Escape," *Phronesis* 12 (1977): 25, states correctly that a person is harmed or made unjust only if their human excellence is harmed. This human excellence, I would add, is the rational ability to give and receive accounts.

3. See M. I. Finley, *Aspects of Antiquity* (New York, 1969), 58-73.

4. Allen, *Socrates and Legal Obligation*, 28-30 emphasizes that both laws and facts are introduced as evidence.

5. See N. Smith and T. Brickhouse, "Socrates' Proposed Penalty in Plato's *Apology*," *Archiv Für Geschichte Der Philosophie* 64, (1982): 1-18.

6. Allen, *Socrates and Legal Obligation*, 25, goes so far as to claim that the entire trial has a circus like atmosphere.

7. Allen, *Socrates and Legal Obligation*, 10-12, states that while the *Apology* is a parody of standard rhetorical techniques, it is also an example of true rhetoric as defined in the *Gorgias*. True rhetoric benefits the listeners' *psychai*, and only the truth can do this.

8. Finley, *Aspects of Antiquity*, 58-73; and Allen, *Socrates and Legal Obligation*, 28, 30.

9. R.E. Allen, *Socrates and Legal Obligation*, 29-30.

10. R.E. Allen, *Socrates and Legal Obligation*, 29-30, notes that what is at issue is not what Socrates did, but the sort of man he is.

11. R.E. Allen, *Socrates and Legal Obligation*, 33-35; Vlastos, "The Paradox of Socrates," 2-4.

12. Guthrie, *Greek Philosophy*, IV, 78, also believes that Plato writes what he remembers that Socrates said even if the details are not accurate entirely.

13. For similar reasons Allen, *Socrates and Legal Obligation*, 17-18, believes that corrupting the youth and not impiety is the heart of the charge against Socrates. Although everyone has the obligation to practice dialectic, we see from other early dialogues that not everyone can practice it because of a prior bad education.

14. Hence there is a close connection between the two charges against Socrates.

15. Allen, *Socrates and Legal Obligation*, 6-9, argues that Socrates' rhetorical parody of rhetoric aims not at acquital but truth, and in the process Socrates is defiant and unfriendly to the jury.

16. Allen, *Socrates and Legal Obligation*, 5ff; K. Seeskin "Is the *Apology* of Socrates a Parody," *Philosophy and Literature* 6 (1982): 94-99, argues that the *Apology* is a parody of courtroom speeches, and that in particular it is modeled on Gorgias' *Apology of Palamedes*. Even Socrates' disclaimer that he can give a good speech fits the Gorgian model. Seeskin persuasively argues that Socrates' performance is very professional in that it employs all the tricks of the trade.

17. T. G. West, *Plato's Apology of Socrates*, (Ithaca, 1979).

18. R.E. Allen holds this new in *Plato's Euthyphro and the Earlier Theory of Forms* (New York, 1971), 4-5.

19. Vlastos, "The Paradox of Socrates," 10-11, emphasizes the revisable nature of Socrates' conception of knowledge.

20. See my chapter on *Euthyphro*.

21. A. D. Woozley, *Law and Obedience: The Arguments of Plato's Crito* (Chapel Hill, 1979), 46, argues that there is a conditional court release and not a court order.

22. See Smith and Brickhouse, "Socrates' Proposed Penalty in Plato's *Apology*," 1-18.

23. Both Woozley, *Law and Obedience*, 19-20, and Allen, *Socrates and Legal Obligation*, 84-85, make the useful distinction between actual harm and injury or treating badly where no actual harm may occur. Many passages in the *Apology* and *Crito* should be read in the second way.

24. See Woozley, *Law and Obedience*, 50-52, who emphasizes that Socrates especially upholds procedures because he acts in an official capacity.

25. N. Smith and T. Brickhouse, in an as yet unpublished essay.

26. G. Young, "Socrates and Obedience," *Phronesis* 19 (1974): 1-29, presupposes throughout his essay that the *Apology* and *Crito* are inconsistent. Young is but one of many commentators who hold this position.

27. Allen, *Socrates and Legal Obligation*, 86, 110, is one of the few commentators to state correctly Socrates' position on civil disobedience. One must either obey the law or suffer the penalty for disobedience, and disobedience is required if the law commands one to do an injustice.

28. Woozley, *Law and Obedience*, 4, emphasizes that the *Crito* is a positive non-aporetic dialogue where Socrates gives a sophisticated analysis of a moral position.

29. Woozley, *Law and Obedience*, 8-9, notes that since Socrates acts on a higher legal authority he does not commit suicide.

30. Young, "Socrates and Obedience," argues that Socrates must fit his *logoi* to the *psychai* of his interlocutors. Crito cannot be persuaded by real Socratic views, and so Socrates has the personified laws state an extreme position which Crito can understood and respond to with empathy.

31. Woozley, *Law and Obedience*, 6ff., has an excellent discussion of Crito's arguments.

32. This is Socrates' answer to Woozley who believes that Socrates should pay more attention to public opinion. See *Law and Obedience*, 13-14.

33. Ibid., 8.

34. Ibid., 10-11.

35. This line is cited frequently as a serious objection to Young's thesis that the laws do not represent Socrates' position.

36. Barker, "Why Did Socrates Refuse to Escape," 24-25, argues that whether or not an action is wrong depends upon the intention or character from which the agent acts, and whether the action effects a person's excellence. Both Allen and Woozley distinguish acting badly from actual harm which I capture with the phrase "attempt to harm."

37. Allen, *Socrates and Legal Obligation*, 72-76 concurs with my in-

terpretation. Woozley, *Law and Obedience*, 56-57, believes that the passage only says that one must do what he has agreed to do provided that what he has agreed to do is just. I do not find Woozley's interpretation to be persuasive especially given the context of 49e. Socrates has just finished saying that the principle premise for his whole argument is that one ought not do an injustice. For the correct interpretation see Francis C. Wade, S.J., "In Defense of Socrates," *Review of Metaphysics* 25 (1971): 311-25.

38. Woozley, *Law and Obedience*, 58, does not seem to understand this when he says that perhaps Socrates harms himself.

39. See Allen, *Socrates and Legal Obligation*, 84.

40. Woozley, *Law and Obedience*, 76-110, has an excellent discussion of the difference between tacit, implied, and explicit agreement.

41. Woozley, *Law and Obedience*, 19-20; Allen, *Socrates and Legal Obligation*, 76-77.

42. J. Dybikowski, "Socrates, Obedience, and the Law: Plato's *Crito*," *Dialogue* 13 (1974): 524, argues that it is hard to determine the consequences of Socrates' act but that he would not influence others. I am not so sure of this, since Socrates is a teacher and an example to others.

8. SOCRATIC EDUCATION OF THE *PSYCHĒ* IN THE *GORGIAS*

1. See Adele Spitzer, "The Self-Reference of the *Gorgias*," *Philosophy and Rhetoric* 8 (1975): 1-22, reprinted in *Plato: True and Sophistic Rhetoric*, ed. Keith Erickson (Amsterdam, 1979), 129-151. Spitzer argues that Gorgias represents the aesthetic aspect of rhetoric, Polus the power aspect, and Callicles the political. See pp. 133-35. Spitzer's essay is the essay most relevant and helpful to the themes in this paper.

2. Spitzer, "The Self-Reference of the *Gorgias*," 132, also argues that the *Gorgias* is self-referential in that it illustrates different types of rhetoric and their defects.

3. More moderate views are held by Dodds and Friedländer. Dodds claims that Socrates uncharacteristically uses rhetoric in the *Gorgias*, and Friedländer states that Socrates usurps the sophistic form of long speech. E. R. Dodds, *Plato's Gorgias* (Oxford, 1959), 17; Friedländer, *Plato*, II, 252.

4. R. W. Hall argues that the craft analogy of the *Gorgias*, where the craftsman/statesman imposes form on matter, is incompatible with the notion of a moral citizenry. A person does not become moral by the passive reception of another's actions. R. W. Hall, "Techne and Morality in the *Gorgias*," in *Essays in Ancient Greek Philosophy*, 202-219. See pp. 202-3, 209-10. I will argue that rhetorical education is only a preliminary stage to dialectical education, and hence it is open for Socrates to claim that someone whose desires are controlled through rhetorical persuasion and nothing more, is not fully virtuous. The *Gorgias* would then anticipate the later position found in the *Republic* where there are two ways to be just—through knowledge or true opinion, and where the former is preferable.

5. In most other early dialogues professional teachers and sophists also give displays. Protagoras and Hippias are excellent examples. The intended audience for such displays would be the potential and actual students and fellow teachers who are listening.

6. Protagoras, for example, gives a sophisticated display while Euthydemus plays the fool.

7. W. Jaeger notes correctly that there is an irreconcilable spiritual enmity between Socrates and Callicles. This enmity makes it impossible for either one to convert the other. See W. Jaeger, *Paideia: The Ideals of Greek Culture*, trans. G. Highet (New York, 1943), II, 141.

8. Dodds appropriately recalls *Phaedrus* 261a ff. where Socrates develops the notion of an art of *psyche*-leading, and one condition of this art is that it must take into account the type and condition of *psyche* which is addressed. Dodds, *Plato*, 10.

9. Commentators often worry about how question and answer, since it primarily is refutative, can produce knowledge. I believe that the answer is that if a hypothesis survives a sufficient amount of testing, then one can claim to know it, but not to know it in a sense which implies that one's knowledge is irrevisable.

10. I will later argue that Socrates attempts to do this with Callicles.

11. Spitzer, "The Self-Reference of the *Gorgias*," 147-151, and Friedländer, *Plato*, II, 268, 272, recognize that the *Gorgias* develops notions of true rhetoric and the true rhetorician. Spitzer has an excellent discussion of the characteristics of a true rhetorician.

12. I am indebted to a lecture by Jon Moline on the rules for dialectic in the *Gorgias*.

13. Hence Socrates discusses courage with Laches and Nicias, and piety with Euthyphro; but no special topic with Enthydemus and Dionysodorus because they do not have any serious beliefs.

14. Dialectic is not *ad hominem* in the abusive or circumstantial senses, but in that it aims at the beliefs of an interlocutor.

15. Laches and Euthyphro display the same defect when they leave the conversation.

16. Dodds, *Plato*, 14 misses the irony in Socrates' praise of Callicles. Because of character defects Callicles will not be a good test for Socrates' *psyche*.

17. Jaeger, *Paideia*, 129 states that Plato displays degenerate types stage by stage in the *Gorgias*. Gorgias has a "half ashamed love of power," while Polus displays "cynical amoralism." Hence Polus is harder to shame than Gorgias.

18. Thus I disagree with Hall, "Techne and Morality," 206-7 who claims that Socrates' values are conventional. Jaeger, *Paidia*, 132, 134, correctly notes that Socrates transvaluates values, he turns them upside down, and Callicles, just as he enters the conversation, states just this.

19. Thus dialectic tests not just one's beliefs, but also the way one lives.

20. Commentators such as Allen, *Plato's Euthyphro and the Earlier*

Theory of Forms, and Robinson, *Plato's Earlier Dialectic* (Oxford, 1941), ignore *psyche*-leading as a component of dialectic. Allen for that reason concludes that there is neither explicit nor implicit content to the early dialogues. But Socrates does hold beliefs, even some well tested beliefs (cf. *Gorgias* 508e-509a), and he sometimes directly, but usually indirectly, communicates them to an interlocutor. The *Gorgias* has more direct communication than earlier dialogues because it develops a notion of true rhetoric.

21. Friedländer, *Plato*, II, 272, notes that Socrates is not dogmatic, but is always willing to revise his views. Also see Vlastos, "The Paradox of Socrates."

22. Spitzer "The Self-Reference of the *Gorgias*," 136, notes that Gorgias has an overwhelming concern with appearances.

23. Friedländer, *Plato*, II, 244, claims that each successive interlocutor morally is removed further from Socrates, and Dodds *Plato*, 4-5, 15, notices that each successive interlocutor is the intellectual heir of his predecessors.

24. Friedländer, *Plato*, II, 251, states that Gorgias is trapped in inconsistency because he in part adheres to traditional morality.

25. Dodds *Plato*, 11, emphasizes that Polus is also a professional teacher of rhetoric.

26. See Spitzer, "The Self-Reference of the *Gorgias*," 137-39, who gives an excellent description of Polus.

27. The theme of the serious man is underplayed in the early dialogues even though it is a main theme of *Euthydemus*.

28. See Hall, "Techne and Morality," 212.

29. This chapter was read at the joint meeting of the Society for Ancient Greek Philosophy and the Society for the Study of Islamic Philosophy and Science, and at Hillsdale College in Michigan. I thank the participants in those conferences for their comments and especially Patricia Curd for her help.

9. EDUCATIONAL THEORY IN THE *MENO*

1. Hoerber, "Plato's *Meno*," *Phronesis* 5 (1960): 78-102, 83, notes the loose connection of the clauses, and what this implies.

2. The following essays, to some extent, discuss the different conceptions of teaching, nature, and practice in the *Meno*: D. Devereux, "Nature and Teaching in Plato's *Meno*," *Phronesis*, 23 (1978), 118-125; Hoerber, "Plato's *Meno*." I am especially indebted to the former essay.

3. See R. Robinson, *Plato's Ealier Dialectic* (Oxford, 1953), ch. 2.

4. On Socrates' nondogmatic stance where he is always willing to reopen a question, see Vlastos, "The Paradox of Socrates." 10-11.

5. On Socrates' attempting to get the answerer to discover knowledge for himself see ibid., 13-14.

6. On innateness claims in the doctrine of recollection, see J. Moravcsik, "Learning as Recollection," in *Plato I*, ed. G. Vlastos (Garden City, N.Y., 1971), pp. 53-69.

7. On the "kinship of all nature" see S. Tigner, "On the 'kinship' of 'all nature'. in Plato's *Meno,*" *Phronesis* 15 (1970): 1-5.

8. See Teloh, *Plato's Metaphysics*, ch. 1.

9. Ibid., 46-61.

10. Devereux, "Nature and Teaching in Plato's *Meno,*" 122-124, has noted the *ad hominem* nature of the arguments.

10. MODELS OF EXCELLENCE AND EDUCATION IN THE *PROTAGORAS*

1. Friedländer, *Plato*, II, 5, correctly sees that the theme of the *Protagoras* is education, and in particular the contrast between sophistic and Socratic education. A. E. Taylor, *Plato, The Man and his Work* (London, 1949), 237, notes that the *Protagoras* is the fullest and earliest exposition of the character and aims of sophistic "education in goodness."

2. See Friedländer, *Plato*, II, 5. Guthrie, *Greek Philosophy*, IV, 214-15, reminds us that the scene of the dialogue is before the war, the great intellectuals are at their best, and that the dialogue is most vivid in its presentation of the characters.

3. Friedländer, *Plato*, II, 7, notes that a proper Socratic discussion should have a completion. In contrast Protagoras seriously will desire to break off the discussion.

4. And yet Socrates' influence over the young men is in part due to his winning against the sophists. Care for the *psychē* is Socrates' ultimate aim, but the agonistic contest is sometimes a means to this end.

5. On the identity of the knowledge of good and evil with each virtue and virtue as a whole see Penner, "The Unity of Virtue," 35-38; Guthrie, *Greek Philosophy*, IV, 222, 228; and Taylor, *Plato*, 235. Taylor takes the main point of the dialogue to be that all of the virtues are knowledge. Friedländer, *Plato*, 19, and M. Gagarin, "The Purpose of Plato's *Protagoras,*" *Transactions and Proceedings of the American Philological Association* 100 (1969): 146-48, believe that Socrates attempts to show that the virtues are identical, but that this attempt is ironical and filled with intentionally fallacious arguments.

6. See Vlastos, "The Paradox of Socrates," 1-21.

7. Taylor, *Plato*, 246, amusingly notes that it will be hard for a foreigner to be the best teacher of the demotic *nomos*. In all the early dialogues the sophists transmit their products to passive students, and Plato, by his language, emphasizes this fact.

8. Gorgias in the *Gorgias* makes the same claim and gets into the same difficulties.

9. We must remember that for Socrates only dialectic can produce knowledge, and that speeches cannot. Friedländer, *Plato*, II, 22, states that the *Protagoras* is a struggle over the proper form of discourse.

10. Guthrie, *Greek Philosophy*, IV, 232-33, argues that Socrates is not hostile to Protagoras. Gagarin, "The Purpose of Plato's *Protagoras,*" 140, 153, notes that since Protagoras is likened to Orpheus, he, like Socrates, is not

among the (intellectually) dead, and that Protagoras, in his great speech, shows a genuine concern for *arete*. G. Vlastos, in the introduction to Plato's *Protagoras*, trans. B. Jowett, rev. M. Ostwald (Indianapolis, 1956), viii-ix, xxiv-xxv, argues that Protagoras has character, and he has moral inhibitions; he is not a huckster of ideas. Socrates, on the other hand, is not a wholly attractive figure; he is a jokster, and he is cruel to Protagoras. Vlastos correctly concludes that although Plato worships Socrates, he leaves no wrinkle out of his picture of him.

11. We must remember that Protagoras agrees with Socrates about the need to care for the *psyche* and about the value of knowledge.

12. The irony here is that he undermines the demotic *nomos* which he thinks is *arete*.

13. Maximal demotic virtue would make one famous in a state.

14. See Friedländer, *Plato*, II, 37.

15, See Teloh, *Plato's Metaphysics* ch. 1.

16. On psychic states as motive forces see Penner, "The Unity of Virtue," 35-40.

17. Most, if not all, commentators fail to sort out the different types of virtue at issue. Friedländer, *Plato*, 13, 16, correctly distinguishes technical knowledge from virtue, but he does not see that there are distinct types of virtue. He is, thus, perplexed that Socrates denies that virtue is teachable. Friedländer does not see that high demotic virtue cannot be taught, and that Socratic virtue is not any form of demotic virtue. Taylor, *Plato*, 262, recognizes that Socratic and demotic virtue are distinct, but he does not distinguish different types of demotic virtue. M. Gagarin, "The Purpose of Plato's *Protagoras*," 134, 144, argues that there is not so great a difference between Socrates and Protagoras. Gagarin concludes that Socrates, at the end of the dialogue, embraces Protagoras' views on virtue and the teaching of virtue. Gagarin also believes that Socrates would endorse the positions in Protagoras' great speech. Gagarin distinguishes *arete* and *techne*, but he does not see that Socrates and Protagoras have different conceptions of *arete*.

18. Of course minimal demotic virtue is more than just justice. Taylor, *Plato*, 244, connects minimal demotic virtue with the conventions and traditions of one's community; it is *nomos*. Morality is imbibing a sound moral tradition according to Taylor. Taylor does not, however, distinguish high and low demotic virtue.

19. Training is an inculcation of certain habits, beliefs, and the like, while education, for Socrates, is a leading out from within by means of questions.

20. Prodicus, unlike Protagoras, is not a serious sophist. He does not use his technology for any serious purpose.

21. Hippias symbolizes massive technology for its own sake, and why such technology is worthless.

22. Guthrie, *Greek Philosophy*, IV, 235, states that the gathering of sophists and potential students produces a competitive atmosphere which engenders niggling arguments, irrelevant digressions, and downright fallacies.

Socrates, I would add, probably cannot educate Protagoras in front of such a crowd because the competitive atmosphere is too intense. So why does Socrates enter into such a conversation?

23. Guthrie, *Greek Philosophy*, IV, 227, correctly says that Socrates treats Simonides with great levity because he sees no point in taking moral lessons from a poet. Gagarin, "The Purpose of Plato's *Protagoras*," 151-52, and Taylor, *Plato*, 251, 54, 56, concur with Guthrie. Taylor adds that Socrates shows that one can extract anything from a poet.

24. See Penner, "The Unity of Virtue," with whose position I agree as against Vlastos.

25. See D. Gallop, "Justice and Holiness in *Protagoras* 330-331," *Phronesis* 6 (1961): 86-93, who correctly argues that Socrates only attempts to show in this preliminary skirmish that justice and holiness are alike.

26. There is considerable debate about who, if anyone, are the hedonists in these passages. I do not intend to solve this problem, except to say that it is typical for Socrates to argue *ad hominem*, i.e. from the beliefs of others, to show them the consequences of their beliefs. In this case the consequence is the importance of knowledge. Gagarin, "The Purpose of Plato's *Protagoras*," 155-56, correctly states that the equation of pleasure and good is not important; what is important is the role of knowledge. Vlastos, *Introduction*, xl-xli, argues that Socrates does not equate good and pleasure, but rather he claims that what is in fact best is most pleasant. The standard view is held by, for example, Taylor, *Plato*, 259, who claims that hedonism is the view of the many.

11. THE FAILURE OF SOCRATIC EDUCATION IN THE *HIPPIAS MAJOR*

1. Some years ago Dorothy Tarrant and G. M. A. Grube debated the authenticity of the *Hippias Major*. Grube supports Plato's authorship of the dialogue, and most scholars believe that his arguments are successful. Although I believe that the *Hippias Major* is by Plato, it is not my concern to reopen the question of authenticity. See D. Tarrant, *The Hippias Major, Attributed to Plato* (Cambridge, 1928); G. M. A. Grube, "Plato's Theory of Beauty," *Monist* 37 (1927): 269 ff. Also see P. Woodruff, *Plato's Hippias Major* (Indianapolis, 1982), 93-103; Hoerber, "Plato's Greater Hippias," *Phronesis* 9 (1964): 143-44.

2. See Woodruff, *Plato's Hippias Major* 115, on the versatile and shallow nature of Hippias.

3. Some commentators believe that the *Hippias Major* hints at harmony and proportion as the essence of beauty. See Hoerber, "Plato's Greater Hippias," 155; R. L. Nettleship, *The Theory of Education in Plato's Republic* (Oxford, 1955), 70-74; Friedländer, *Plato*, II; and Dodds, *Plato's Gorgias*, 334-35. Dodds closely connects *Gorgias* 503e ff. with the *Hippias Major*. The *Gorgias* passage states that *cosmos* lies behind all excellence. Guthrie, *Greek Philosophy*, IV, 183, states that *cosmos* is absent wholly from the dialogue,

and Woodruff, *Plato's Hippias Major*, 181, says that no single theme unifies the *Hippias Major*. I will disagree with the last two commentators whom I do not think entertain the dramatic hints in the dialogue.

4. On character assessments of Hippias see Woodruff, *Plato's Hippias Major*, 115; and Guthrie, *Greek Philosophy*, IV, 176. Guthrie believes that Plato writes a little comedy about an insensitive and stupid man—Hippias.

5. The dialogue begins by connecting *cosmos* and beauty. Hippias' speech is beautiful because it is well composed, and Hippias is "beautiful" because his clothes are well composed.

6. In the *Laches* the teachers of fighting in heavy armor avoid Sparta like the plague. False experts will not dare to go where the real art is practiced.

7. Friedländer, *Plato*, II, 106, comments on Socrates' ironic portrait of modern sophists.

8. Giving a display is a common characteristic of sophists in the early dialogues.

9. The standard Gorgian model of learning is the speech which is given over to the passive listeners.

10. We see the same conflict in the *Gorgias* and *Euthydemus*, among other early dialogues.

11. We should contrast Hippias' art of memory with Socrates' denial that he has a good memory. Dialectic does not require us to memorize facts.

12. Woodruff, *Plato's Hippias Major*, 120, 127, claims that Hippias is harmless, and that Socrates' attacks on him are gratuitous and remarkably savage. Woodruff does note that Hippias is versatile and shallow. But Hippias is a teacher, and he is going to give a speech about beautiful pursuits before a classroom of young boys. Hippias is a corruptor of the youth just like Gorgias and Cephalus because they all are bad teachers even if they all have demotic virtue.

13. See Woodruff, *Plato's Hippias Major*, 169, who claims that Hippias generally practices a philosophy of agreement because he is a diplomat!

14. Woodruff, *Plato's Hippias Major*, 107-8; Hoerber, "Plato's Greater Hippias," 150-51; and Guthrie, *Greek Philosophy*, IV, 176, all praise the device of the mysterious stranger. Friedländer, *Plato*, II, 105, believes that the *Hippias Major* is a work of great dramatic vitality.

15. Guthrie, *Greek Philosophy*, IV, 176, notes that the mysterious stranger permits Socrates to question Hippias and still appear courteous.

16. Friedländer, *Plato*, II, 115, says that as the mysterious stranger is revealed to be Socrates, the true self of Socrates is also revealed in the stranger.

17. Woodruff, *Plato's Hippias Major*, 150, following Vlastos, insists that the beautiful is a logical not a real cause. I doubt that the early Plato had such a distinction. What sort of cause is the *cosmos* in something which makes it beautiful? We cannot place easily such a cause within our categories.

18. See Teloh, 79-80.

19. Ibid., 79ff.

20. See C. M. Gillespie, "The Use of Εἶδος and Ἰδέα in Hippocrates," *Classical Quarterly* 6 (1912): 179-203.

21. J. Malcolm, "On the Place of the *Hippias Major* in the Development of Plato's Thought," *Archiv für Geschichte der Philosophie* 50 (1968): 189-95.

22. Teloh, *Plato's Metaphysics*, ch. 1.

23. In dialogues like the *Laches* and *Euthyphro* there is also a transition from an interlocutor's attempts at definition to Socrates' suggestions, and I argue for these dialogues that Socrates' suggestions are closer to the correct answer.

24. See Woodruff, *Plato's Hippias Major*, 109-10; Hoerber, "Plato's Greater Hippias," 151-52; and Guthrie, *Greek Philosophy*, IV, 176-77.

25. I am not alone in the belief that this is an intentional fallacy. See Guthrie, *Greek Philosophy*, IV, 185-86, who says that Socrates uses a "barefaced sophism" on a "noble" sophist; and Hoerber, "Plato's Greater Hippias," 153-54, who believes that Socrates designs his fallacies to provide hints about the nature of beauty. Also see Teloh, *Plato's Metaphysics*, 72-74, for other arguments for this claim.

26. See Grube, "Plato's Theory of Beauty," 75-76.

27. Ibid.

28. Friedländer, *Plato,* II, 114, recognizes that the last two accounts give secondary characteristics, not the essence, of the beautiful.

29. Hoerber, "Plato's Greater Hippias," 145-49.

30. Dodds, *Plato's Gorgias*, 22, 244-45, believes that the *Gorgias* and *Hippias Major* are close in date of composition, and in their views about the beautiful.

12. THE SERIOUS MAN IN THE *EUTHYDEMUS*

1. R. K. Sprague, *Plato's Use of Fallacy* (London, 1962), xv, notes that the *Euthydemus* is one of the most important Socratic dialogues, and that it is all but neglected by commentators.

2. Friedländer, *Plato*, II, 180-181, is the only commentator I know of who emphasizes that the dialogue really is about the boy's *psyche*, and that in the *Euthydemus* Socrates manifests a personal concern for the young man's *psyche*. Friedländer, in part, sees the dialogue as a contest between opposing principles of education as represented in the different characters.

3. Friedländer, *Plato*, II, 181, states that eristic cannot be distinguished from dialectic by its external form alone. The sophistic brothers require one to answer just as Socrates does, and Socrates, so Friedländer claims, does not avoid conscious fallacies. Friedländer goes on to say that the difference between an eristic sophist and a philosopher is in their attitude and orientation.

4. Friedländer, *Plato*, II, 194, claims that the nameless bystander represents the many, and the opinion of the many that all philosophy is worthless.

5. Sprague, *Plato's Use of Fallacy*, 3, emphasizes the contrast between eristic and dialectic as it is illustrated in the alternating scenes of the dialogue.

Dialectic, she correctly claims, has a serious concern for the truth, but eristic does not. Guthrie, *Greek Philosophy*, IV, 275, states that Plato contrasts eristic and dialectic in order to show that Socrates does not corrupt the young. Guthrie, pp. 276-79, claims that Plato probably believes that Socrates was thought to be a sophist, and that Plato's chief concern is to defend Socrates against this charge.

6. Sprague, *Plato's Use of Fallacy*, xii, says that both Socrates and Ctesippus are heroes in the dialogue, but this cannot be correct, for Ctesippus frivolously imitates the eristic brothers. Friedländer, *Plato*, II, 180, correctly says that Ctesippus represents the false mode of love.

7. Friedländer, *Plato*, II 182, emphasizes how the brothers throw the argument back and forth. The brothers are not serious.

8. Friedländer, *Plato*, II, 180, notes that Cleinias is a cousin of Alcibiades, which indicates what a noble youth he is, and in turn Cleinias' nobility highlights his potential for either good or evil.

9. See ibid., 182.

10. Friedländer, *Plato*, II, 1979, argues that we have good reason to doubt that any such conversation really took place by how Socrates ironically relates why he stays to speak with the brothers. Socrates, Friedländer claims, interlocks play and seriousness in the *Euthydemus*.

11. Sprague, *Plato's Use of Fallacy*, xi, 5, states that Plato deliberately uses fallacies to set forth his principles not only in the *Euthydemus* but also in other dialogues where Socrates speaks. The present passages involve the fallacy of equivocation on "learn," and "know". Friedländer, *Plato*, II 187, claims that these passages ironically reveal a deeper true meaning, that of the theory of recollection. I do not know whether or not we should see recollection hinted at in these passages; they may simply illustrate the sophistic arguments which gave rise to that theory.

12. Guthrie, *Greek Philosophy*, IV, 277, traces most of the fallacies to Eleatic logic. Sprague, *Plato's Use of Fallacy*, also claims that Eleatic logic and metaphysics lie behind the arguments of the brothers. Sprague thinks that Plato banishes Eleatic logic as a nest of deliberate confusions, and hence that the *Parmenides* as well as the *Euthydemus* are not serious dialogues which reveal Plato's positions. The *Parmenides* is an eristic attack on the theory of Forms. See R. K. Sprague, "Parmenides' Sail and Dionysodorus' Ox," *Phronesis* 12 (1967): 91-98. But Plato often treats Eleatic arguments with great respect. See Teloh, *Plato's Metaphysics*, ch. 4.

13. Guthrie, *Greek Philosophy*, IV, 274, 280-81, claims that this is one of the earliest extant examples of a protreptic discourse. Socrates gently leads Cleinias, Guthrie claims, so that Cleinias will not loose heart in the *aporiai*. Guthrie correctly goes on to state that under Socrates' gentle prodding Cleinias makes genuine contributions to the conversation. Sprague, *Plato's Use of Fallacy*, 10, 21-22, accurately observes that Socrates does not in the transmission sense teach the boy, but rather exhorts the boy to make a choice. Socrates is successful in his exhortation since at 291b f. Cleinias emerges as an independent thinker. Friedländer, *Plato*, II, 186, goes so far

as to claim that Socrates lovingly leads the boy to wisdom. Socrates, as I explain elsewhere, is most successful with young boys who have not been ruined by a previous bad education.

14. C. Kahn, "The Greek Verb 'To Be' and the Concept of Being," *Foundation of Language* 2 (1966): 245-65.

15. See Sprague, *Plato's Use of Fallacy*, 12-13; Guthrie, *Greek Philosophy*, II, 277. Both Sprague and Guthrie emphasize that Plato knows how to disarm Eleatic sophistries which employ *einai*.

16. There is a tension in the *Euthydemus* about whether or not Socrates saves the boy's *psychē*. Cleinias makes philosophical progress, but he also comes under the entertaining influence of Ctesippus.

17. See Teloh, *Plato's Metaphysics*, ch. 5.

18. This is true for a protreptic discussion, but it is not true when *elenchus* is needed.

19. Sprague, *Plato's Use of Fallacy*, 9-11, correctly sees that the solution to the *aporia* is that only the knowledge of good and evil is good intrinsically, and that all other things are at best derivative goods depending upon whether they are used in accordance with the knowledge of good and evil.

20. Sprague, *Plato's Use of Fallacy*, 24-27; Friedländer, *Plato*, II, 192-93, believe that 300b-301e are clear references to the middle period theory of Forms, and that there is an eristic Eleatic attack on the Forms in these passages. Sprague goes on to say that Plato rejects self-predication in 301-02. For a denial that Forms are at issue in these passages, see Teloh, *Plato's Metaphysics*, chs. 1 and 2.

21. Guthrie, *A History of Greek Philosophy*, IV, 282-83, believes that the unnamed writer is an intentional allusion to Isocrates. Friedländer, *Plato*, II, 194, is noncommital on this issue, but correctly believes that the nameless one represents the ignorant misconceptions of the many.

22. Is it not strange that Crito, who is a close associate of Socrates, does not see this?

Bibliography

Allen, R.E. *Plato's Euthyphro and the Earlier Theory of Forms.* New York: 1970.

_____. *Socrates and Legal Obligation.* Minneapolis: 1980.

Barker, Andrew. "Why Did Socrates Refuse to Escape?" *Phronesis*, 12 (1977), pp. 13-28.

Bolotin, David. *Plato's Dialogue on Friendship.* Ithaca, NY: 1979.

Buford, T. "Plato on the Educational Consultant: An Interpretation of the *Laches.*" *Idealistic Studies*, 7 (1977), pp. 151-171.

Chen, Chung-Hwan. "On Plato's *Charmides* 165c-175d5." *Apeiron*, 12 (1978), pp. 13-28.

Cohen, S. Marc. "Socrates on the Definition of Piety: *Euthyphro* 10A-11B." *The Philosophy of Socrates*, ed. G. Vlastos, New York: 1971, pp. 158-176.

Devereux, D. "Courage and Wisdom in Plato's *Laches.*" *Journal of the History of Philosophy*, 15 (1977), pp. 129-141.

_____. "Nature and Teaching in Plato's *Meno.*" *Phronesis*, 23 (1978), pp. 118-125.

Dodds, E.R. *Plato's Gorgias.* Oxford: 1959.

Dybikowski, J. "Socrates, Obedience, and the Law: Plato's *Crito.*" *Dialogue*, 13 (1974), pp. 519-535.

Finley, M.I. *Aspects of Antiquity.* New York: 1969.

Friedländer, P. *Plato.* Vol. I, New York: 1964.

_____. *Plato.* Vol. II, New York: 1964.

Gagarin, M. "The Purpose of Plato's *Protagoras.*" *Transactions and Proceedings of the American Philological Association*, 100 (1969), pp. 133-164.

Gallop, D. "Justice and Holiness in *Protagoras* 330-331." *Phronesis*, 6 (1961), pp. 86-93.

Gillespie, C.M. "The Use of Εἶδος and Ἰδέα in Hippocrates." *Classical Quarterly* 6 (1912), pp. 179-203.

Grube, G.M.A. "Plato's Theory of Beauty." *Monist*, 37 (1927), pp. 269-288.

Guthrie, W.K.C. *A History of Greek Philosophy.* Vol. IV, Cambridge: 1975.

Hall, R.W. "Techne and Morality in the *Gorgias.*" *Essays in Ancient Greek Philosophy*, ed. J.P. Anton and G.L. Kustas, Albany: 1971, pp. 202-219.

Havelock, E.A. *Preface to Plato.* Cambridge: 1963.

Hoerber, R.G. "Plato's *Euthyphro*." *Phronesis*, 3 (1953), pp. 95-107.
_____. "Plato's *Greater Hippias*." *Phronesis*, 9 (1964), pp. 143-155.
_____. "Plato's *Laches*." *Classical Philosophy*, 63 (1968), pp. 95-105.
_____. "Plato's *Lysis*." *Phronesis*, 4 (1959), pp. 15-28.
_____. "Plato's *Meno*." *Phronesis*, 5 (1960), pp. 78-102.
Hyland, D. "*Eros, Epithumia, and Philia* in Plato." *Phronesis*, 13 (1968), pp. 32-46.
_____. *The Virtue of Philosophy*. Athens, Ohio: 1981.
Jaeger, W. *Paideia: The Ideals of Greek Culture*. Trans. G. Highet, New York: 1943.
Kahn, C. "The Greek Verb 'To Be' and the Concept of Being." *Foundations of Language*, 2 (1966), pp. 245-65.
Malcolm, J. "On the Place of the *Hippias Major* in the Development of Plato's Thought." *Archiv für Geschichte der Philosophie*, 50 (1968), pp. 189-95.
Moravcsik, J. "Learning as Recollection." *Plato I*, ed. G. Vlastos, Garden City: NY: 1971, pp. 53-69.
Nettleship, R.L. *The Theory of Education in Plato's Republic*. RPT. Oxford: 1955.
Norman, D.N. "Some Observations Concerning Plato's *Lysis*." *Essays in Ancient Greek Philosophy*, ed. J.P. Anton and G.L. Kustas, Albany: 1971, pp. 236-258.
O'Brien, M.J. "The Unity of the *Laches*." *Essays in Ancient Greek Philosophy*, ed. J.P. Anton and G.L. Kustas, Albany: 1972, pp. 303-315.
Penner, T. "Socrates on Virtue and Motivation." *Exegesis and Argument*, ed. E.N. Lee, A.P.D. Mourelatos, and R.M. Rorty, Assen, The Netherlands: 1973, pp. 133-151.
_____. "The Unity of Virtue." *Philosophical Review*, 82 (1973), pp. 35-68.
Robinson, R. *Plato's Earlier Dialectic*. Oxford: 1941.
Ross, W.D. *Plato's Theory of Ideas*. Oxford: 1953.
Santas, G. "Socrates at Work on Virtue and Knowledge in the *Laches*." *Review of Metaphysics*, 22 (1969), pp. 433-460.
_____. "Socrates at Work on Virtue and Knowledge in Plato's *Charmides*." In *Exegesis and Argument*, ed. E.N. Lee, A.P.D. Mourelatos, and R. Rorty, Assen, The Netherlands: 1973, pp. 105-132.
Schmid, W. Thomas. "Socrates' Practice of *Elenchus*." *Ancient Philosophy*, 1 (1981), pp. 141-147.
Seeskin, K. "Is the *Apology* of Socrates a Parody?" *Philosophy and Literature*, 6 (1982), pp. 94-99.
Sesonski, A. "Plato's Apology: *Republic* I." *Phronesis*, 6 (1961), pp. 29-36.
Smith, N. and Brickhouse, T. "Socrates' Proposed Penalty in Plato's *Apology*." *Archiv für Geschichte der Philosophie*, 64, (1982), pp. 1-18.
Spitzer, Adele. "The Self-Reference of the *Gorgias*." *Philosophy and Rhetoric*, 8 (1975), pp. 1-22; reprinted in *Plato: True and Sophistic Rhetoric*, ed. Keith Erickson, Amsterdam: 1979, pp. 129-151.

Sprague, R.K. "Parmenides' Sail and Dionysodorus' Ox." *Phronesis*, 12 (1967), pp. 91-98.
_____. *Plato's Use of Fallacy*. London: 1962.
Tarrant, D. *The Hippias Major, Attributed to Plato*. Cambridge: 1928.
Taylor, A.E. *Plato, The Man and his Work*. London: 1949.
Taylor, C.C.W. "The End of the *Euthyphro*." *Phronesis*, 27 (1982), pp. 109-118.
Teloh, H. *The Development of Plato's Metaphysics*. State College, PA: 1981.
Tigner, S. "On the 'kinship' of 'all nature' in Plato's *Meno*." *Phronesis*, 15 (1970), pp. 1-5.
Versényi, L. *Holiness and Justice: An Interpretation of Plato's Euthyphro*. Washington, D.C.: 1982.
_____. "Plato's *Lysis*." *Phronesis*, 21 (1976), pp. 185-198.
Vlastos, G. "The Individual as Object of Love in Plato." *Platonic Studies*, Princeton: 1973, pp. 3-42.
_____. "Introduction." *Plato's Protagoras*, trans. B. Jowett, revised by M. Ostwald (Indianapolis, 1956), pp. XXIV-LVI.
_____. "The Paradox of Socrates." *The Philosophy of Socrates*, ed. G. Vlastos, New York: 1971, pp. 1-2.
_____. "The Socratic *Elenchus*." *Oxford Studies in Classical Philosophy*, 1 (1983), pp. 27-74.
Wade, Francis C., S.J. "In Defense of Socrates." *Review of Metaphysics*, 25 (1971), pp. 311-25.
West, T.G. *Plato's Apology of Socrates*. Ithaca: 1979.
Woodruff, P. "Socrates on the Parts of Virtue." *Canadian Journal of Philosophy*, Supplementary Volume II, (1976), pp. 101-116.
Woozley, A.D. *Law and Obedience: The Arguments of Plato's Crito*. Chapel Hill: 1979.
Young, G. "Socrates and Obedience." *Phronesis*, 19 (1974), pp. 1-29.

Index

237

240 INDEX